STUDY GUIDE

BUSINESS

STUDY GUIDE

Douglas W. Copeland

Johnson County Community College

BUSINESS

sixth edition

Ricky W. Griffin

■

Ronald J. Ebert

Assistant Editor: Jennifer Surich
Production Editor: Carol Zaino
Manufacturer: Quebecor World Book Services

ISBN 0-13-091592-0

10 9 8 7 6 5 4 3 2

CONTENTS

PREFACE

From the beginning I have tried to create a *Study Guide* that I would want as a student. Therefore, this *Study Guide* is designed to serve two major goals. First, by complimenting the material presented in *Business*, Sixth Edition, I hope to increase your understanding and appreciation of business. If I am successful, you will be better equipped to respond intelligently to real-world business-related issues that you read and hear about every day. After all, many business affairs have far reaching implications for your personal life. Furthermore, a firm grasp of the material presented in the textbook is invaluable to those of you pursuing careers in business.

Second, and possibly of more immediate and practical concern to you, this *Study Guide* has been designed to prepare you for your examinations--to help you maximize your grade from this class given your limited studying time. I am confident that if you work through each chapter of the *Study Guide* in its entirety after you have studied the chapter in the textbook, you will enter your tests with confidence and will score accordingly. I hope you come to view this *Study Guide* as a close and helpful companion.

It should be kept in mind that this *Study Guide* is not a substitute for the textbook. Instead, it is a supplement. You should work through each chapter in the *Study Guide* only after you have studied the assigned chapter in the textbook.

The format of each chapter of this book has been designed to maximize your mastery of the material and therefore your ability to perform well on the exams. The order in which you tackle each of these sections is up to you. But you are strongly encouraged to work through *all* of the sections for each of the chapters you are assigned. This is because some sections focus more intently on some concepts introduced in the textbook than do other sections. The specific sections of each chapter are outlined below.

LEARNING OBJECTIVES
You should be able to accomplish these learning objectives after studying the chapter and working through the *Study Guide*.

TRUE-FALSE
These true-false questions will be very similar to the types of true-false questions found on your exams (if your professor gives these types of questions--ask your teacher whether or not that is the case). Even if your professor does not ask these types of questions on the exams, you are still strongly encouraged to work through this section anyway. To increase your learning, you are asked to correct any false statements by making them true statements. The answers for this section, as well as all others, are provided at the end of the chapter.

MULTIPLE CHOICE
These multiple-choice questions will be very similar to those you find on your exams—especially considering that most professors give multiple-choice type exams. Choose the one best answer from the options provided. You are strongly encouraged to correct the incorrect responses to make them correct. By doing so, you will come to recognize the subtle differences between potential answers. This is a skill required to be successful in performing well on multiple-choice type exams.

JEOPARDY
The "Jeopardy" games are intended to be a fun way to learn some of the key points and concepts introduced in the textbook. For added "fun," you are asked to provide the "question" to the answer provided within approximately 5 seconds. If you are unable to do so, you may want to review that concept or topic.

MATCH THE TERMS AND CONCEPTS TO THEIR DEFINITIONS
This section is important because many test questions will ask you to define a term or a concept. Moreover, learning the language of business is half the task to understanding business.

WORD SCRAMBLE
This has been added for the fun of it. Many people enjoy these.

LEARNING OBJECTIVES--POTENTIAL SHORT ANSWER OR ESSAY QUESTIONS
Many of you will have professors that will give you "Short Answer" and/or "Essay" type questions. If so, then this section will be particularly useful to you. However, even if you do not expect these types of questions on exams, you are still strongly encouraged to work through this section. It will help you accomplish the learning objectives of this chapter.

CRITICAL THINKING QUESTIONS
These questions are designed to elicit a higher level of thinking by requiring you to pull together various concepts introduced in the chapter.

BRAIN TEASER
This section consists of one question that is generally one step up in the level of difficulty from the "Critical Thinking Questions." Do not be distraught if you have some difficulty with this question. Remember, "no pain, no gain." You can always consult with your teacher if you are distressed. But, as always, an answer is provided at the end of the chapter.

ANSWERS
This final section of each chapter provides the answers to all of the exercises.

It should not take you too long to work through the material for each chapter in this *Study Guide*. Considering the payoffs, I strongly urge you to do so!

I hope you find this *Study Guide* useful and your course fulfilling.

People to Thank

I wish to thank Jennifer Surich, editor, for providing me the opportunity to write this book. A very special thanks also goes to Marcia Kruse for all her typing help. She was very professional and conscientious. Finally, my very deep thanks go to my wife, Mette.

Douglas W. Copeland
Johnson County Community College

To My Children...

Katrine, Nina, and Paul

Chapter 1

Understanding the U.S. Business System

LEARNING OBJECTIVES

After studying this chapter, you should be able to:

1. Define the nature of U.S. *business* and identify its main goals.
2. Describe the different types of global *economic systems* according to the means by which they control the *factors of production* through *input and output markets*.
3. Show how *demand* and *supply* affect resource distribution in the United States.
4. Identify the elements of *private enterprise* and explain the various *degrees of competition* in the U.S. economic system.
5. Explain the criteria for evaluating the success of an economic system in meeting its goals and show how the federal government attempts to manage the U.S. economy.
6. Discuss the current economic picture in the United States and summarize expert opinions about its future.

TRUE-FALSE

Indicate whether the statement is generally true or false by placing a "T" or "F" in the space provided. If it is a false statement, correct it so that it becomes a true statement.

_____ 1. A socialist economy is characterized by private ownership of production and encourages entrepreneurship by offering profits as an incentive.

_____ 2. A market economy is an economic system where individuals—producers and consumers—control production and allocation decisions through supply and demand.

_____ 3. The input market is a market in which firms supply goods and services in response to demand on the part of households.

_____ 4. Privatization has, in part, been occurring in many countries because of the difficulty many governments have had in efficiently running state-run enterprises.

_____ 5. The law of supply indicates that the quantity supplied rises as the price falls.

_____ 6. Whenever the current price is above the market or equilibrium price then a shortage exists.

_____ 7. Agriculture is a good example of pure competition in the U.S. economy.

_____ 8. A few dominant sellers characterize oligopolies, and entry of new competitors is difficult.

_____ 9. The basic goals of an economic system are stability, full employment, and growth.

_____ 10. One of the challenges facing businesses in the United States today is the need to ignore global economic trends and to focus instead on the needs of consumers at home.

_____ 11. Countries that encourage free trade, innovation, and open financial systems will prosper in the years ahead.

MULTIPLE CHOICE
Circle the one best answer for each of the following questions.

1. Which of the following are factors of production?
    a. Labor and entrepreneurs
    b. Capital and information resources
    c. Physical (natural) resources
    d. All of the above.

2. In a market economy,
    a. businesses are almost guaranteed to earn a profit.
    b. the way people spend their money largely determines which products will be produced and what those products will cost.
    c. business owners have little control over pricing, quality, and innovation.
    d. there is little economic freedom and choice.

3. Capitalism is characterized by
    a. economic freedom and competition.
    b. public ownership over all productive resources.
    c. public ownership and operation of key industries combined with private ownership and operation of less vital industries.
    d. government control over prices and what gets produced.

4. Which of the following is true concerning a market?
    a. Demand indicates that as the price goes up, sales increase.
    b. An equilibrium price exists when the quantity demanded equals the quantity supplied.
    c. Supply shows how much people will buy at various prices.
    d. If demand increases in a market, then the price of the product will likely fall.

5. Private enterprise found within market economies requires the presence of
    a. private property rights.
    b. freedom of choice.
    c. profits and competition.
    d. All of the above.

6. Pure competition is a situation in which
   a. there are so many buyers and sellers that no single buyer or seller has the ability to influence market price.
   b. many sellers differentiate their products from their competitors in at least some small way.
   c. the market is dominated by a few sellers.
   d. the market is dominated by a single seller.

7. Which of the following is true?
   a. Successful product differentiation allows monopolistically competitive firms some control over the prices they charge.
   b. A natural monopoly exists when one company can most efficiently supply all the needed goods and services.
   c. In an oligopoly, a change in the price by one firm can significantly affect the sales of other firms.
   d. All of the above.

8. Which of the following comes closest to being a monopoly?
   a. A local cable television provider.
   b. A local grocery store.
   c. An airline company like *United Airlines*.
   d. A farmer.

9. Pure competition is characterized by
   a. firms selling differentiated products.
   b. buyers and sellers unaware of the prices that others are paying and receiving in the marketplace.
   c. market prices set exclusively by supply and demand and accepted by both sellers and buyers.
   d. difficult entry and exit by firms.

10. Which of the following is true?
    a. One of the biggest threats to national economic stability is inflation.
    b. Real gross national product (real GNP) has been adjusted for unemployment.
    c. Gross *domestic* product includes foreign production by U.S. companies.
    d. Greater rates of economic growth typically result in lower rates of inflation.

11. Which of the following is *false*?
    a. A negative balance of trade (a trade deficit) means a country is exporting more than it is importing.
    b. A budget deficit means the government is spending more money than it has collected as taxes and this increases the country's national debt.
    c. Fiscal policy is the manipulation of government spending and taxes.
    d. Monetary policy is the manipulation of the nation's money supply to affect interest rates.

12. Which of the following is a major force driving the economy for the next decade?
    a. The information revolution will reduce productivity across all sectors of the economy.
    b. New technological breakthroughs in such areas as biotechnology will create entirely new industries.
    c. Nations will withdraw from participating in globalization reducing competition and the need for firms to innovate.
    d. All of the above.

13. Which of the following is true concerning the projected trends and patterns in economic indicators and competitive dynamics for at least the next decade?

a.   The economy will weaken significantly and grow much more slowly.
b.   Inflationary surges and large budget deficits will become less likely.
c.   Countries that discourage free trade, innovation, and open financial systems will prosper.
d.   All of the above.

14. Globalization implies
a.   opportunities as well as challenges and threats for businesses.
b.   a more integrated global economic system.
c.   a more competitive global marketplace in which only the most efficient firms will survive.
d.   All of the above.

JEOPARDY

You have 5 seconds to complete the question to each of the following answers.

	Economic Systems	**The Ways Companies Compete**	**Evaluating Economic Systems and Government Management**
$100	A nation's system for allocating its resources among its citizens. What is_____ _____?	Market or industry characterized by numerous small firms producing an identical product. What is_____ _____?	Every economic system's three broad economic goals. What is_____ _____?
$200	Economy in which individuals control production and allocation decisions through supply and demand. What is_____ _____?	The term for when a firm attempts to distinguish its good or service from other firms' good or services. What is_____ _____?	The total value of all the goods and services produced in an economic system within one year. What is_____ _____?
$300	Planned economic system in which the government owns and operates only selected major sources of production. What is_____ _____?	A market or industry dominated by a few producers with the power to influence the prices of their products. What is_____ _____?	When the government spends more than it collects as taxes; this adds to the national debt. What is_____ _____?
$400	Economic system featuring characteristics of both planned and market economies. What is_____ _____?	Industry in which one company can most efficiently supply all needed goods and services. What is_____ _____?	The government's manipulation of the nation's money supply to affect interest rates. What is_____ _____?
$500	Market economy that provides for private ownership of production and encourages entrepreneurship by offering profits as an incentive. What is_____ _____?	The most prevalent form of competition in real-world markets where firms try to differentiate their products from their rivals' products. What is_____ _____?	The government's manipulation of its spending and taxes. What is_____ _____?

MATCH THE TERMS AND CONCEPTS TO THEIR DEFINITIONS

a. business
b. profits
c. economic system
d. factors of production
e. labor (or human resources)
f. capital
g. physical resources
h. information resources
i. planned economy
j. market economy
k. market
l. input market
m. output market
n. capitalism
o. mixed market economy
p. privatization

q. socialism
r. demand
s. supply
t. law of demand
u. law of supply
v. demand & supply schedule
w. demand curve
x. supply curve
y. market price
z. surplus
aa. shortage
bb. private enterprise
cc. private property rights
dd. competition
ee. pure competition
ff. monopolistic competition
gg. oligopoly

hh. monopoly
ii. natural monopoly
jj. stability
kk. inflation
ll. depression
mm. unemployment
nn. knowledge workers
oo. growth
pp. gross national product (GNP)
qq. real gross national product
    (real GNP)
rr. gross domestic product (GDP)
ss. productivity
tt. budget deficit
uu. national debt
vv. monetary policies
ww. fiscal policies

_____ 1. Mechanism for exchange between buyers and sellers of a particular good or service.

_____ 2. The funds needed to create and operate a business enterprise.

_____ 3. The difference between a business' revenues and its expenses.

_____ 4. An organization that provides goods and services to earn profits.

_____ 5. A nation's system for allocating its resources among its citizens.

_____ 6. Economy that relies on a centralized government to control all or most factors of production and to make all or most production and allocation decisions.

_____ 7. Economy in which individuals control production and allocation decisions through supply and demand.

_____ 8. Tangible things organizations use in the conduct of their business.

_____ 9. Data and other information used by business.

_____ 10. The physical and mental capabilities of people as they contribute to economic production.

_____ 11. Resources used in the production of goods and services—natural resources, labor, capital, and entrepreneurs.

_____ 12. Market in which firms buy resources from supplier households.

_____ 13. Process of converting government enterprises into privately owned companies.

_____ 14. The willingness and ability of buyers to purchase a good or service.

_____ 15. The willingness and ability of producers to offer a good or service for sale.

_____ 16. Principle that buyers will purchase (demand) more of a product as its price drops and less and its price increases.

_____ 17. Principle that producers will offer (supply) more of a product for sale as its price rises and less and its price drops.

_____ 18. Assessment of the relationship between different levels of demand and supply at different price levels.

_____ 19. Graph showing how many units of a product will be supplied (offered for sale) at different prices.

_____ 20. Graph showing how many units of a product will be demanded (bought) at different prices.

_____ 21. Planned economic system in which the government owns and operates only selected major sources of production.

_____ 22. Economic system featuring characteristics of both planned and market economies.

_____ 23. Market in which firms supply goods and services in response to demand on the part of households.

_____ 24. Market economy that provides for private ownership and encourages entrepreneurship by offering profits as an incentive.

_____ 25. Industry in which one company can most efficiently supply all needed goods and services.

_____ 26. Market or industry characterized by numerous buyers and relatively numerous sellers trying to differentiate their products from those of competitors.

_____ 27. Market or industry characterized by numerous small firms producing identical products.

_____ 28. Market or industry characterized by a handful of (generally large) sellers with the power to influence the prices of their products.

_____ 29. Market or industry in which there is only one producer, which can therefore set the prices of its products.

_____ 30. Vying among businesses for the same resources or customers.

_____ 31. Situation in which quantity supplied exceeds quantity demanded.

_____ 32. Situation in which quantity demanded exceeds quantity supplied.

_____ 33. Profit-maximizing price at which the quantity of goods demanded and the quantity of goods supplied are equal.

_____ 34. Economic system that allows individuals to pursue their own interests without undue governmental restriction.

_____ 35. The right to buy, own, use, and sell almost any form of property.

_____ 36. Particularly severe and long-lasting recession.

_____ 37. Level of joblessness among people actively seeking work.

_____ 38. Phenomenon of widespread price increases throughout an economic system.

_____ 39. Condition in which the balance between the money available in an economy and the goods produced in it are growing at about the same rate.

_____ 40. Increase in the amount of goods and services produced by a nation's resources.

_____ 41. Skilled employees in high-tech industries.

_____ 42. The value of all goods and services produced in a year by a nation's economy through domestic factors of production.

_____ 43. The value of all goods and services produced by an economic system in a year regardless of where the factors of production are located.

_____ 44. Gross national product adjusted for inflation and changes in the value of a country's currency.

_____ 45. Government economic policies that determine the size of a nation's money supply.

_____ 46. Government economic policies that determine how the government collects and spends its revenues.

_____ 47. Total amount that a nation owes its creditors.

_____ 48. Situation in which a government body spends more money than it takes in.

_____ 49. Measure of economic growth that compares how much a system produces with the resources needed to produce it.

WORD SCRAMBLE

1. _____
   sibnuses

2. _____
   namded

3. _____
   plysup

LEARNING OBJECTIVES--POTENTIAL SHORT ANSWER OR ESSAY QUESTIONS

Learning Objective #1: "Define the nature of U.S. *business* and identify its main goals."

Learning Objective #2: "Describe the different types of global *economic systems* according to the means by which they control the *factors of production* through *input* and *output markets*."

Learning Objective #3: "Show how *demand* and *supply* affect resource distribution in the United States."

Learning Objective #4: "Identify the elements of *private enterprise* and explain the various *degrees of competition* in the U.S. economic system."

Learning Objective #5: "**Explain the criteria for evaluating the success of an economic system in meeting its goals and show how the federal government attempts to manage the U.S. economy.**"

Learning Objective #6: "**Discuss the current economic picture in the United States and summarize expert opinions about its future.**"

CRITICAL THINKING QUESTIONS

1. Why isn't the United States economy described as a *pure* market economy?

2. Which type of market environment do most businesses operate within: pure competition, monopolistic competition, oligopoly, or monopoly? How do you know?

BRAIN TEASER

1. Using demand and supply concepts, explain how a market would respond to an increase in demand.

ANSWERS

True-False--*Answers*

1. False: A *capitalist* economy is characterized by private ownership of production and encourages entrepreneurship by offering profits as an incentive.
2. True
3. False The *output* market is a market in which firms supply goods and services in response to demand on the part of households.
4. True
5. False The law of supply indicates that the quantity supplied rises as the price *rises*.
6. False: Whenever the current price is above the market or equilibrium price then a *surplus* exists.
7. True
8. True
9. True
10. False: One of the challenges facing businesses in the United States today is the need to *become more aware of* global economic trends and *to focus even more on innovation and cost cutting*.
11. True

Multiple Choice--*Answers*

1. d	5. d	9. c	13. b
2. b	6. a	10. a	14. d
3. a	7. d	11. a	
4. b	8. a	12. b	

Jeopardy--*Answers*

	Economic Systems	The Ways Companies Compete	Evaluating Economic Systems and Government Management
$100	an economic system	pure competition	stability, full employment, and growth
$200	a market economy	product differentiation	gross national product (GNP)
$300	socialism	an oligopoly	a budget deficit
$400	a mixed market economy	a natural monopoly	monetary policy
$500	capitalism	monopolistic competition	fiscal policy

Match the Terms and Concepts to Their Definitions--*Answers*

1. k	8. g	15. s	22. o	29. hh	36. ll	43. pp
2. f	9. h	16. t	23. m	20. dd	37. mm	44. qq
3. b	10. e	17. u	24. n	31. z	38. kk	45. vv
4. a	11. d	18. v	25. ii	32. aa	39. jj	46. ww
5. c	12. l	19. x	26. ff	33. y	40. oo	47. uu
6. i	13. p	20. w	27. ee	34. bb	41. nn	48. tt
7. j	14. r	21. q	28. gg	35. cc	42. rr	49. ss

Word Scramble--*Answers*

1. business   2. demand   3. supply
Learning Objectives--Potential Short Answer or Essay Questions--*Answers*

Learning Objective #1:
  Businesses are organizations that produce or sell good or services to make a profit. *Profits* are the difference between a business' revenues and expenses. The prospect of earning profits encourages individuals and organizations to open and to expand businesses. The benefits of business activities also extend to wages paid to workers and to taxes that support government functions.

Learning Objective #2:
  An *economic system* is a nation's system for allocating its resources among its citizens. Economic systems differ in terms of who owns or controls the five basic *factors of production*: labor, capital, entrepreneurs, physical resources, and information resources. In *planned economies*, the government controls all or most factors. In *market economies,* which are based on the principles of *capitalism,* individuals and businesses control the factors of production and exchange them through *input* and *output markets*. Most countries today have *mixed market economies* that are dominated by one of these systems but include elements of the other. The process of *privatization* is an important means by which many of the world's planned economies are moving toward mixed economic systems.

Learning Objective #3:
  The U.S. economy is strongly influenced by markets, demand, and supply. *Demand* is the willingness and ability of buyers to purchase a good or service. *Supply* is the willingness and ability of producers to offer goods and services for sale. Demand and supply work together to set a *market* or *equilibrium price*—the price at which the quantity of goods demanded and the quantity of goods supplied are equal.

Learning Objective #4:
  The U.S. economy is founded on the principles of *private enterprise: private property rights, freedom of choice, profits,* and *competition.* Degrees of competition vary because not all industries are equally competitive. Under conditions of *pure competition,* numerous small firms compete in a market governed entirely by demand and supply. An *oligopoly* involves a handful of sellers only. A *monopoly* involves only one seller.

Learning Objective #5:
  The basic goals of an economic system are *stability, full employment,* and *growth.* Measures of how well an economy has accomplished these goals include *gross national product, gross domestic product, productivity, balance of trade,* and *national debt.* The U.S. government uses *fiscal policies* to manage the effects of its spending and revenue collection and *monetary policies* to control the size of the nation's money supply.

Learning Objective #6:
  The United States is riding the crest of a long-term economic boom. Growth has been strong, and unemployment and inflation remain low. Experts believe that these trends will continue for at least another few years. Particularly important areas of the economy will include information technology, other forms of technological innovation, and globalization.

Critical Thinking Questions--*Answers*

1. The United States economy is not a *pure* market economy because it combines the elements of a market economy (private ownership of resources; economic activity coordinated through a system of markets and prices) with some government involvement designed to promote the general welfare. All governments have become involved in their market economies to correct for the shortcomings associated with an unbridled market economy (by, for example, enforcing laws and regulations, fostering competition, contributing to economic stability, and spending for the public good).

2. Most companies operate within a monopolistically competitive market environment because most firms compete by differentiating (distinguishing) their product from their rivals' products in some way or another (in terms of quality, service, packaging, hours of operation, etc.).

Brain Teaser--*Answer*

1. An increase in demand means buyers are willing and able to purchase more at any price (this is reflected graphically as a rightward shift of the demand curve). This creates a temporary shortage at the original market or equilibrium price (shown graphically as the extent to which the new demand curve lies beyond the supply curve). Buyers will then competitively bid up the price (or sellers realize they can charge a higher price). Over time, as the price rises, the quantity demanded falls, and the quantity supplied rises. As a consequence, the shortage gets smaller. The price continues to rise until the quantity demanded once again equals the quantity supplied. At this point, the new market equilibrium price will be established. Graphically, an increase in demand (an outward or rightward shift of the demand curve) will result in a new point of intersection with the supply curve where the equilibrium price and the amount bought and sold are both greater than before.

Chapter 2

Conducting Business in the United States

LEARNING OBJECTIVES

After studying this chapter, you should be able to:

1. Trace the history of business in the United States.
2. Identify the *major forms of business ownership*.
3. Explain *sole proprietorships* and *partnerships* and discuss the advantages and disadvantages of each.
4. Describe *corporations*, discuss their advantages and disadvantages, and identify different kinds of corporations.
5. Describe the basic issues involved in creating and managing a corporation.
6. Identify recent trends and issues in corporate ownership.
7. Discuss *mergers, acquisitions, divestitures*, and *spin-offs*.

TRUE-FALSE

Indicate whether the statement is generally true or false by placing a "T" or "F" in the space provided. If it is a false statement, correct it so that it becomes a true statement.

_____ 1. The Sherman Antitrust Act of 1890 and the Clayton Act of 1914 were passed in response to price fixing and other forms of market manipulation that became common business practices during the later 1800s and the beginning of the twentieth century.

_____ 2. During the production era of the early 1900s, scientific management focused largely on manufacturing efficiency by adopting fixed workstations, increasing task specialization, and moving the work to the worker.

_____ 3. Today, business, government, and labor are often referred to by economists and politicians as the three *countervailing powers* in society.

_____ 4. A major disadvantage of corporations is unlimited liability.

_____ 5. Corporations have the disadvantage of having their income taxed twice.

_____ 6. A general partnership is owned by at least one general partner who runs the business and limited partners who are passive investors generally liable for no more than the amount of their investment.

_____ 7. In a general partnership, partners are legally responsible for paying off the debts of the group.

_____ 8. Partnerships are superior to sole proprietorships in that partnerships offer a diversity of skills that can lead to innovation and greater chances at success.

_____ 9. Publicly traded corporations withhold their stock from public sale.

_____ 10. Corporations have the power to raise large sums of capital, they offer the shareholders protection from liability, and they have an unlimited life span.

_____ 11. No other form of business can match the success of the partnership in bringing together money, resources, and talent; in accumulating assets; and in creating wealth.

_____ 12. The three major groups that govern a corporation are the shareholders, the board of directors, and the officers of the corporation.

_____ 13. Common stock guarantees holders fixed dividends while preferred stock usually pays dividends only if the corporation makes a profit.

_____ 14. In a strategic alliance, two or more firms collaborate on a project for mutual gain; when the partners share ownership in what is essentially a new enterprise, it is called a joint venture.

_____ 15. An initial public offering is an arrangement in which a corporation holds its own stock in trust for its employees, who gradually receive ownership of the stock and control its voting rights.

_____ 16. In recent years, institutional investors have purchased more and more stock and they have exerted more influence over the management of corporations.

_____ 17. An acquisition occurs when two firms combine to create a new company; a merger occurs when one firm buys another outright.

_____ 18. A horizontal merger combines two companies where one is a supplier to, or a customer of, the other.

MULTIPLE CHOICE

Circle the one best answer for each of the following questions.

1. Which of the following is *false* concerning the history of business in the United States?
   a. The rise of the factory system during the *Industrial Revolution* brought with it *mass production* and *specialization of labor*.
   b. During the *entrepreneurial era* in the nineteenth century, huge corporations—and monopolies—emerged.
   c. During the *production era* of the early twentieth century, companies grew by emphasizing output and production.
   d. During the *global era* of the 1950s and 1960s, businesses began focusing on sales staff, advertising, and the need to produce what consumers wanted.

2. The growing use of the Internet will likely
   a. reduce trade in all sectors of the economy, especially services.
   b. serve to level the playing field, at least to some extent, between larger and smaller enterprises regardless of what products or services they sell.
   c. add confusion and hamper communication between firms, suppliers, business customers, and strategic partners.
   d. All of the above.

3. The sole proprietorship
   a. is the easiest and least expensive form of business to start.
   b. has the advantage of tax benefits if losses are experienced and of reaping all the profits if successful.
   c. has the disadvantage of facing unlimited liability.
   d. All of the above.

4. Which of the following is a disadvantage of sole proprietorships?
   a. They provide the owner with control and independence.
   b. The business may cease when the owner dies.
   c. The owner reaps all the profits.
   d. Business losses can be deducted from personal income.

5. Which of the following is an advantage of sole proprietorships?
   a. The company's financial resources are usually limited.
   b. Management talent may be limited.
   c. The company's plans and financial performance remain private.
   d. The owner is liable for the debts and damages incurred by the business.

6. Which of the following statements is true?
   a. A limited partnership is owned by at least one general partner who runs the business and limited partners who are passive investors generally liable for no more than the amount of their investment.
   b. A general partnership is owned by general partners who are equally liable for the business' debts.
   c. Cooperatives are associations of people or small companies with similar interests, formed to obtain greater bargaining power or other economies of scale.
   c. All of the above are true.

7. In a master limited partnership
   a. an organization sells shares (partnership interests) to investors on public markets.
   b. the master partner retains at least 50-percent ownership and runs the business; the minority partners have no management voice.
   c. the master partner must provide minority partners with detailed operating and financial data on a regular basis.
   d. All of the above.

8. A corporation
   a. has a legal status and obligations independent of its owners.
   b. is characterized by a separation of ownership and management.
   c. can be a small company, and most small corporations are privately held, which means that the company's stock is not traded publicly.
   d. All of the above.

9. Which of the following is *not* an advantage of corporations?
   a. They have the power to raise large sums of money.
   b. They have to disclose financial information.
   c. They offer shareholders protection from liability.
   d. They have a legal life independent of the owners.

10. Which of the following statements is *false*?
    a. A multinational or transnational corporation is a corporation that spans national boundaries.
    b. A closely held corporation is a corporation that actively sells stock on the open market.
    c. An S corporation is a corporation with no more than 35 shareholders that may be taxed as a partnership.
    d. The limited liability corporation is a hybrid of a publicly held corporation and a partnership in which owners are taxed as partners but enjoy the benefits of limited liability.

11. Which of the following statements is true?
    a. Preferred stock guarantees holders fixed dividends while common stock usually pays dividends only if the corporation makes a profit.
    b. A proxy is a document authorizing another person to vote on behalf of a shareholder in a corporation.
    c. The chief executive officer (CEO) is a person appointed by a corporation's board of directors to carry out the board's policies and supervise the activities of the corporation.
    d. All of the above are true.

12. Which of the following statements is *false*?
    a. A vertical merger is the combination of companies that are direct competitors in the same industry.

b.   A divestiture is the sale of part of a company.
c.   An acquisition is a combination of two companies in which one company purchases the other and assumes control of its property and liabilities.
d.   A merger is a combination of two or more companies in which the old companies cease to exist and the new enterprise is created.

13. When two unrelated businesses come together to form a new corporation, this is called a
   a.   spin-off.
   b.   conglomerate merger.
   c.   horizontal merger.
   d.   divestiture.

14. A food processing company buying a chain of grocery stores is an example of a
   a.   horizontal merger.
   b.   vertical merger.
   c.   conglomerate merger.
   d.   spin-off.

15. Which of the following statements is true?
   a.   A hostile takeover is a situation in which an outside party buys enough stock in a corporation to take control against the wishes of the board of directors and corporate officers.
   b.   A tender offer is an invitation made directly to shareholders by an outside party who wishes to buy a company's stock at a price above the current market price.
   c.   A divestiture occurs when a firm sells off a part of the company that is unrelated to its core business or is an under-performing part of the business.
   d.   All of the above are true

JEOPARDY
You have 5 seconds to complete the question to each of the following answers.

	Sole Proprietorships and Partnerships	Corporations	Mergers and Acquisitions
$100	One advantage of sole proprietorships. What is_____ _____?	One advantage of corporations. What is_____ _____?	A combination of two or more companies in which the old company ceases to exist and a new enterprise is created. What is_____ _____?
$200	One disadvantage of sole proprietorships. What is_____ _____?	One disadvantage of corporations. What is_____ _____?	A combination of two companies in which one company purchases the other and assumes control of its property and liabilities. What is_____ _____?
$300	One advantage partnerships have over sole proprietorships. What is_____ _____?	The three groups that govern a corporation. What are_____ _____?	A combination of companies that are in unrelated businesses. What is_____ _____?

$400	One disadvantage of partnerships. What is_____ ?	Corporations whose stock is widely held and available for sale to the general public What is_____ ?	A strategy whereby a firm sells one or more of its business units. What is_____ ?
$500	A partnership composed of one or more general partners and one or more partners whose liability is usually limited to the amount of their capital invested. What is_____ ?	Corporations with no more than 35 shareholders that may be taxed as a partnership What is_____ ?	A situation in which an outside party buys enough stock in a corporation to take control against the wishes of the board of directors and corporate officers. What is_____ ?

MATCH THE TERMS AND CONCEPTS TO THEIR DEFINITIONS

a. Industrial Revolution
b. production era
c. marketing concept
d. sole proprietorship
e. unlimited liability
f. general partnership
g. limited partnership
h. limited partner
i. general (or active) partner
j master limited partnership
k. corporation
l. limited liability
m. tender offer
n. double taxation
o. closely held (or private) corporation

p. publicly held (or public) corporation
q. S corporation
r. limited liability corporation, or LLC
s. professional corporation
t. multinational or transnational corporation
u. corporate governance
v. articles of incorporation
w. bylaws
x. stockholder (or shareholder)
y. stock
z. preferred stock
aa. common stock
bb. proxy

cc. initial public offering (IPO)
dd. board of directors
ee. chief executive officer (CEO)
ff. strategic alliance
gg. joint venture
hh. employee stock ownership plan (ESOP)
ii. institutional investors
jj. merger
kk. acquisition
ll. horizontal merger
mm. vertical merger
nn. conglomerate merger
oo. divestiture
pp. spin-off

_____ 1. Type of partnership consisting of limited partners and an active or managing partner.

_____ 2. Corporation whose stock is widely held and available for sale to the general public.

_____ 3. Governing body of a corporation that reports to its shareholders and delegates power to run its day-to-day operations, but remains responsible for sustaining its assets.

_____ 4. Owner of shares of stock in a corporation.

_____ 5. Merger between firms that are customers and/or suppliers to one another.

_____ 6. Offer to buy shares made by a prospective buyer directly to a target corporation's shareholders, who then make individual decisions about whether to sell.

_____ 7. Idea that a business must focus on identifying and satisfying consumer wants in order to be profitable.

_____ 8. Form of corporation spanning national boundaries.

_____ 9. Strategy of setting up one or more corporate units as new, independent corporations.

_____ 10. Strategic alliance in which the collaboration involves joint ownership of new venture.

_____ 11. Legal principle holding owners responsible for paying off all debts of a business.

_____ 12. Large investors, such as mutual funds and pension funds, that purchase large blocks of corporate stock.

_____ 13. Business that is legally considered an entity separate from its owners and is liable for its own debts; owners' liability extends to the limits of their investments.

_____ 14. Corporation whose stock is held by only a few people and is not available for sale to the general public.

_____ 15. Document detailing corporate rules and regulations, including election and responsibilities of directors and procedures for issuing new stock.

_____ 16. The purchase of one company by another.

_____ 17. Major mid-eighteenth century change in production characterized by a shift to the factory system, mass production, and the specialization of labor.

_____ 18. Stock that pays dividends and guarantees corporate voting rights, but offers last claims over assets.

_____ 19. Partner who actively manages a firm and who has unlimited liability for its debts.

_____ 20. Hybrid of a publicly held corporation and a partnership in which owners are taxed as partners but enjoy the benefits of limited liability.

_____ 21. Period during the early twentieth century in which U.S. business focused primarily on improving productivity and manufacturing efficiency.

_____ 22. Share of ownership in a corporation.

_____ 23. Strategy whereby a firm sells one or more of its business units.

_____ 24. Merger involving firms in the same industry.

_____ 25. Business with two or more owners who share in both the operation of the firm and in financial responsibility for its debts.

_____ 26. Roles of shareholders, directors, and other managers in corporate decision making.

_____ 27. Hybrid of a closely held corporation and a partnership, organized and operated like a corporation but treated as a partnership for tax purposes.

_____ 28. Authorization granted by a shareholder for someone else to vote his or her shares.

_____ 29. Stock that guarantees its holders fixed dividends and priority claims over assets but no corporate voting rights.

_____ 30. Business owned and usually operated by one person who is responsible for all of its debts.

_____ 31. Document detailing the corporate governance of a company, including its name and address, its purpose, and the amount of stock it intends to issue.

_____ 32. Form of organization that sells shares to investors who receive profits and pay taxes on individual income from profits.

_____ 33. The union of two corporations to form a new corporation.

_____ 34. Form of ownership allowing professionals to take advantage of corporate benefits while granting them limited business liability and unlimited professional liability.

_____ 35. Arrangement in which a corporation holds its own stock in trust for its employees, who gradually receive ownership of the stock and control its voting rights.

_____ 36. First offer of shares in a closely held corporation to outside investors.

_____ 37. Partner who does not share in a firm's management and is liable for its debts only to the limit of his or her investment.

_____ 38. Situation in which taxes may be payable both by a corporation on its profits and by shareholders on dividend incomes.

_____ 39. Strategy in which two or more organizations collaborate on a project for mutual gain.

_____ 40. Legal principle holding investors liable for a firm's debts only to the limits of their personal investments in it.

_____ 41. Top manager hired by the board of directors to run a corporation.

_____ 42. Merger between firms in unrelated businesses.

WORD SCRAMBLE

1. _____   2. _____ _____   3. _____
   tarpsnerpih   lose   shipprotorprie   portonaicor

LEARNING OBJECTIVES--POTENTIAL SHORT ANSWER OR ESSAY QUESTIONS

Learning Objective #1: "Trace the history of business in the United States."

Learning Objective #2: "Identify the *major forms of business ownership*."

Learning Objective #3: "Explain *sole proprietorships* and *partnerships* and discuss the advantages and disadvantages of each."

Learning Objective #4: "Describe *corporations*, discuss their advantages and disadvantages, and identify different kinds of corporations."

Learning Objective #5: **"Describe the basic issues involved in creating and managing a corporation."**

Learning Objective #6: **"Identify recent trends and issues in corporate ownership."**

Learning Objective #7: **"Discuss *mergers, acquisitions, divestitures,* and *spin-offs.*"**

CRITICAL THINKING QUESTIONS

1. As an up-and-coming business consultant you advise people, for a small fee, who are interested in starting their own businesses. You provide advice with respect to the legal form that their business ought to take, given their individual circumstances. Which form of business would you recommend to the following clients? Why?

    a. Marcia Kruse has been a very dependable manager of a large grocery store's floral shop for years. She has enjoyed working directly with the public and gets along with everyone. She is good at designing floral arrangements but doesn't particularly like doing paper work. Although she enjoys her current position and its security, her desire for a bigger challenge and an opportunity to more fully express her independence has had her thinking about her own floral shop for years. She is very confident that her own floral shop would be very prosperous. However, she lacks some of the financial resources to get started.

b. Allen Olsen is a talented computer scientist and software designer who has developed a name for himself in Silicon Valley. He has recently become troubled with the apparent lack of willingness on the part of his current employer to take the long-term monetary risks necessary to invest in his latest software development ideas. He claims that the short-sightedness by his employer may result in the company losing out on a vast new market for software technology and huge potential profits. He is willing to put up much of his own money to invest in the creation of a new company but he is not willing to lose all that he has gained over the years. What he can invest in the creation of a new business is still far from the funds necessary to undertake the research and development required to develop this next generation of software capabilities. Moreover, he wants to undertake only the research and development, not the day-to-day management of the firm.

c. Sam Jackson is a highly motivated young man who wants to be his own boss. He has been making his current boss a lot of money as a house painter for quite some time. Because of his reputation in the community of being an excellent and dependable painter, he is convinced he could make even more money for himself running his own house painting business. He already has the equipment and the funds necessary to get started. His insurance and operating expenses are expected to be relatively very small.

2. Suppose you are interested in creating a corporation. What are the three basic steps in doing so?

BRAIN TEASER

1. Antitrust laws in the United States grant the federal government the power to prevent mergers and acquisitions if it can be shown they would significantly reduce competition. In recent years, the federal government has been more lenient in its antitrust enforcement, allowing more mergers and acquisitions than in earlier years. Thinking in terms of an increasingly global economy, what reasoning could justify this more lenient approach to antitrust enforcement?

ANSWERS

True-False--*Answers*

1. True
2. True
3. True
4. False: A major disadvantage of *sole proprietorships and partnerships* is unlimited liability.
5. True
6. False: A *limited* partnership is owned by at least one general partner who runs the business and limited partners who are passive investors and generally liable for no more than the amount of their investment.
7. True
8. True
9. False: *Closely held (or private)* corporations withhold their stock from public sale.
10. True
11. False: No other form of business can match the success of the *corporation* in bringing together money, resources, and talent; in accumulating assets; and in creating wealth.
12. True
13. False: *Preferred* stock guarantees holders fixed dividends while *common* stock usually pays dividends only if the corporation makes a profit.
14. True
15. False: An *employee stock ownership program* is an arrangement in which a corporation holds its own stock in trust for its employees, who gradually receive ownership of the stock and control its voting rights.
16. True
17. False: *A merger* occurs when two firms combine to create a new company; *an acquisition* occurs when one firm buys another outright.
18. False: A *vertical* merger combines two companies where one is a supplier to, or a customer of, the other.

Multiple Choice--*Answers*

1. d	5. c	9. b	13. b
2. b	6. d	10. b	14. b
3. d	7. d	11. d	15. d
4. b	8. d	12. a	

Jeopardy—*Answers*

	Sole Proprietorships and Partnerships	Corporations	Mergers and Acquisitions
$100	they are easy to establish; they provide the owner with control and independence; the owner reaps all the profits; losses can be deducted from personal income taxes; or the company's plans and financial performance remain private.	they have the power to raise large sums of capital, they offer shareholders protection from liability, or they have an unlimited life span.	a merger

$200	the company's financial resources are usually limited; management talent may be limited; the owner is liable for the debts and damages incurred by the business; or the business may cease when the owner dies.	they have to disclose financial information or their profits are taxed twice.	an acquisition
$300	they increase the diversity of skills; they may have better luck at obtaining financing; or there are greater chances the business will endure because new partners can be drawn into the business to replace those who die or retire.	shareholders, the board of directors, and the corporate officers	a conglomerate merger
$400	the active partners face unlimited liability or there is the potential for interpersonal problems.	a publicly held corporation or public corporation	a divestiture
$500	a limited partnership	an S corporation	a hostile takeover

Match the Terms and Concepts to Their Definitions--*Answers*

1. g	7. c	13. k	19. i	25. f	31. v	37. h
2. p	8. t	14. o	20 r	26. u	32. j	38. n
3. dd	9. pp	15. w	21. b	27. q	33. jj	39. ff
4. x	10. gg	16. kk	22. y	28. bb	34. s	40. l
5. mm	11. e	17. a	23. oo	29. z	35. hh	41. ee
6. m	12. ii	18. aa	24. ll	30. d	36. cc	42. nn

Word Scramble--*Answers*

1. partnership   2. sole proprietorship   3. corporation

Learning Objectives--Potential Short Answer or Essay Questions--*Answers*

Learning Objective #1:

    Modern U.S. business structures reflect a pattern of development over centuries. Throughout much of the colonial period, sole proprietors supplied raw materials to English manufacturers. The rise of the factory system during the *Industrial Revolution* brought with it *mass production* and *specialization of labor*. During the *entrepreneurial era* in the nineteenth century, huge corporations—and monopolies—emerged. During the *production era* of the early twentieth century, companies grew by emphasizing output and production. During the *marketing era* of the 1950s and 1960s, businesses began focusing on sales staff, advertising, and the need to produce what consumers wanted. The *global perspective* of business emerged in the 1980s and continues today. The most recent developments are pointing toward an *Internet era* as perhaps the next big period in the evolution of business.

Learning Objective #2:

The most common forms of business ownership are the *sole proprietorship*, the *partnership*, the *cooperative*, and the regular *corporation*. Each form has several advantages and disadvantages. The form under which a business chooses to organize is crucial because it affects both long-term strategy and day-to-day decision making. In addition to advantages and disadvantages, entrepreneurs must consider their preferences and long-range requirements.

Learning Objective #3:

Sole proprietorships, the most common form of business, consist of one person doing business. Although sole proprietorships offer freedom and privacy and are easy to form, they lack continuity and present certain financial risks. For one thing, they feature *unlimited liability*: The sole proprietor is liable for all debts incurred by the business. *General partnerships* are proprietorships with multiple owners. *Limited partnerships* allow for limited partners who can invest without being liable for debts incurred by general or active partners. In *master limited partnerships*, master partners can sell shares and pay profits to investors. Partnerships have access to a larger talent pool and more investment money than sole proprietorships, but they may be dissolved if conflicts between partners cannot be settled.

Learning Objective #4:

Corporations are independent legal entities that are usually run by professional managers. The corporate form is used by most large businesses because it offers continuity and opportunities for raising money. It also features financial protection through *limited liability*: The liability of investors is limited to their personal investments. However, the corporation is a complex legal entity subject to *double taxation:* In addition to taxes paid on corporate profits, investors must pay taxes on earned income. The most common types are *closely held corporations* (also called *private corporations*), *publicly held corporations* (also called *public corporations*), *S corporations*, *limited liability corporations* (*LLCs*), *professional corporations*, and *multinational* or *transnational corporations*.

Learning Objective #5:

Creating a corporation generally requires legal assistance to file *articles of incorporation*, to establish corporate *bylaws*, and to comply with government regulations. Corporations issue *stock* that is controlled by their owners. A closely held corporation can raise capital and become a publicly traded corporation through an *initial public offering*, or *IPO*, of stock to outside investors. Managers must understand stockholders' rights as well as the rights and duties of the *board of directors*.

Learning Objective #6:

Recent trends in corporate ownership include *joint ventures* or *strategic alliances* (in which two or more organizations collaborate on an enterprise), *employee stock ownership plans* (*ESOPs*) (by which employees buy large shares of their employer companies), and *institutional ownership* of corporations (by groups such as mutual and pension funds).

Learning Objective #7:

Mergers and acquisitions (M&As) are becoming increasingly popular strategies for firms today. Common forms of mergers include *horizontal*, *vertical*, and *conglomerate mergers*. Firms sometimes engage in *divestitures* to improve profitability and may create *spin-offs* to raise new capital.

Critical Thinking Questions--*Answers*

1. a. General partnership. A very reliable and very dependable partner (remember there is unlimited liability) who likes to do paperwork and who has the needed funds to get started would be ideal.
    b. Corporation. There is a need for large sums of money. He wants limited liability and doesn't want to run the company on a day-to-day basis although he would want enough control over the stock to influence investment decisions. Moreover, his reputation should help the chances of selling stock in the first place and for the corporation to raise funds later.
    c. Sole proprietorship. Because he wants to be his own boss, there is little need for outside sources of funds and virtually no chance of losing personal property in the event of business failure.

2. In its simplest form, the process of creating a corporation consists of three basic steps:

    1. *Consult an attorney.* Although it is possible to establish a corporation without legal guidance, most people soon realize that the process involves, among other things, satisfying various government rules and regulations.
    2. *Select a state in which to incorporate.* As noted, many companies choose Delaware for tax purposes. It usually makes sense, however, for a smaller company to incorporate in the state in which it will conduct most of its business.
    3. *File articles of incorporation and corporate bylaws.* Articles of incorporation specify such information as the firm's name and address, its purpose, the amount of stock it intends to issue, and other legally required information. Bylaws detail methods for electing directors and define terms and basic responsibilities. They also describe the process of issuing new stock and address such issues as stock ownership and stockholders' rights.

Brain Teaser—*Answer*

1. Because we live in an ever more globally competitive environment, the federal government has allowed more concentration (bigger companies) in American industry. It is argued that this will allow those industries to experience greater economies of scale that reduce their costs and enhance their price competitiveness in the global economy. That is, it may be necessary to allow more concentration in American industries in order for those industries to compete, or to survive, in the global economy. Moreover, it may now be more necessary to measure the degree of competitiveness in an industry in the context of the global economy as opposed to looking at the size and number of firms that exist in our domestic economy. Moreover, there is less concern today that concentration in an industry will result in higher "monopoly" prices because of the competition from abroad.

Chapter 3
Understanding the Global Context of Business

LEARNING OBJECTIVES
After studying this chapter, you should be able to:

1. Describe the rise of international business, identify the major world marketplaces, and discuss the United States' major trading partners.
2. Explain how different forms of *competitive advantage, import-export balances, exchange rates,* and *foreign competition* determine the ways in which countries and businesses respond to the international environment.
3. Discuss the factors involved in deciding to do business internationally and in selecting the appropriate *levels of international involvement* and *international organizational structure.*
4. Describe some of the ways in which *social, cultural, economic, legal,* and *political differences* among nations affect international business.

TRUE-FALSE
Indicate whether the statement is generally true or false by placing a "T" or "F" in the space provided. If it is a false statement, correct it so that it becomes a true statement.

_____ 1. The contemporary world economy revolves around three major marketplaces: North America, Europe, and Africa.

_____ 2. Canada is the United States' largest trading partner.

_____ 3. If a nation has a comparative advantage in the production of a good, this means that the nation is relatively more efficient at producing that good than any other nation.

_____ 4. The balance of payments refers to the amount of goods a nation imports and exports; the balance of trade refers to the amount of money flowing in and out of the country.

_____ 5. A strong dollar would increase exports from the United States and reduce its imports, creating a trade surplus.

_____ 6. Key factors for a business considering international expansion is the business climate in other nations, assessing demand for the company's product abroad, and determining whether the product will have to be adapted for international consumption?

_____ 7. After a firm decides to expand internationally, it must decide whether to either be an exporter or importer, to organize as an international firm, or to operate as a multinational firm.

_____ 8. A licensing arrangement is a cooperative partnership in which firms choose foreign individuals to manufacture or market their products in another country.

_____ 9. A strategic alliance (or joint venture) is an arrangement in which a company finds a foreign partner to contribute approximately half of the resources needed to establish and operate a new business in the partner's country.

_____ 10. Importing is the investment of money by foreign companies in domestic business enterprises.

_____ 11. Cultural differences are not that important anymore when doing international business.

_____ 12. An international business needs to learn as much as possible about the culture of the foreign countries it does business with.

_____ 13. A subsidy is a government payment to help a domestic business compete with foreign firms.

_____ 14. A quota is a tax on an imported product; a tariff is a limit on the quantity allowed to enter the country.

_____ 15. Business practice laws can differ significantly among nations.

MULTIPLE CHOICE

Circle the one best answer for each of the following questions.

1. Globalization has accelerated due to
   a. governments and businesses becoming more aware of the benefits of globalization to their countries and shareholders.
   b. new technologies that have made international travel, communication, and commerce easier, faster, and cheaper.
   c. competitive pressures forcing firms to enter foreign markets just to keep pace with competitors.
   d. All of the above.

2. Which of the following statements is *false*?
   a. According to the World Bank, a low-income country has a per capita income of less than $9,386 but more than $765.
   b. Even if a nation does not have an absolute advantage, it is still beneficial for that nation to participate in international trade if it has a comparative advantage.
   c. Nations trade with each because they are better off by doing so.
   d. Globalization is becoming increasingly more prevalent.

3. One of the conditions for a country to experience a national competitive advantage in the production of a product is
   a. an inadequate quantity of natural resources to produce that product.

   b.   the presence of consumers who are not particular about quality or innovation.
   c.   strong local or regional suppliers and/or industrial customers.
 d.   the presence of firms and industries that do not stress cost reduction, product quality, and higher productivity, and are not particularly innovative.

4.   An increase in the value of the U.S. dollar (a "stronger" dollar) would
   a.   reduce the relative price of American-made goods for foreigners.
   b.   increase the relative price of foreign-made goods for Americans.
   c.   increase U.S. imports.
   d.   create a trade surplus for the United States.

5.   Which of the following is true concerning business involvement in the global economy?
   a.   An *importer* is a firm that makes products in one country and then distributes and sells them in others.
   b.   An *international firm* conducts a significant portion of its business abroad.
   c.   A *multinational firm* is a very large corporation that has been successful in out-competing foreign firms in its home market but does not compete in foreign markets.
   d.   All of the above.

6.   Licensing is
   a.   purchasing goods or services from another country and bringing them into one's own country.
   b.   an agreement to produce and market another company's product in exchange for a royalty or fee.
   c.   an arrangement in which a company finds a foreign partner to contribute approximately half of the resources needed to establish and operate a new business in the partner's country.
   d.   sending some managers from the home office to run overseas operations.

7.   Investment of money by foreign companies in domestic business enterprises is
   a.   exporting.
   b.   licensing.
   c.   foreign direct investment (FDI).
   d.   a subsidy.

8.   To improve international competitiveness, firms need to
   a.   learn as much as possible about the cultures of foreigners they work with.
   b.   keep an open mind, avoid stereotyping, and learn how to show respect in another culture.
   c.   learn as much as possible about the economic, legal, and political differences among nations.
   d.   do all of the above.

9.   Which of the following statements is true?
   a.   Protectionism typically increases employment for a nation as a whole over time.
   b.   Dumping is charging less than the actual cost of production.
   c.   A quota is a tax on an imported good, while a tariff is a limit on the quantity allowed to enter the country.
   d.   Rarely are trade barriers politically popular.

10.   Which of the following is *not* a trade barrier (a form of protectionism)?
   a.   Local content requirements
   b.   Embargoes
   c.   Foreign direct investment (FDI)
   d.   Subsidies

11. Which of the following is *not* an argument in favor of protectionism?
    a. Protectionism preserves domestic jobs.
    b. Protectionism helps weak domestic industries stay afloat.
    c. Protectionism allows a nation to retaliate against unfair foreign competition.
    d. All of the above are arguments in favor of protectionism.

JEOPARDY

You have 5 seconds to complete the question to each of the following answers.

	International Trade Barriers	Arguments For and Against Protectionism	Forms of International Business Activity
$100	Taxes levied on imports. What are_____?	A major argument against protectionism pertaining to prices. What is_____?	Selling a product outside the country. What is_____?
$200	Fixed limits on the quantity of imports a nation will allow for a specific product. What are_____?	A major argument in favor of protectionism pertaining to the effect on domestic economies. What is_____?	Foreign individual or organization that agrees to represent an exporter's interest. What is_____?
$300	Government payments to help domestic businesses compete with foreign firms. What are_____?	A major argument in favor of protectionism pertaining to jobs. What is_____?	An agreement to produce and market another company's product in exchange for a royalty or fee. What is_____?
$400	Government order banning exportation and/or importation of a particular product or all products from a particular country. What is_____?	A major argument against protectionism pertaining to jobs. What is_____?	Arrangement in which a firm finds a foreign partner to contribute about half of the resources needed to establish and operate a new business in the partner's country. What is_____?
$500	The effect of trade barriers on the price of both domestic and foreign goods. What is_____?	A major argument in favor of protectionism pertaining to unfair competition. What is_____?	A special form of licensing that is also growing in popularity. What is_____?

MATCH THE TERMS AND CONCEPTS TO THEIR DEFINITIONS

a. globalization
b. per capita income
c. import
d. export
e. absolute advantage
f. comparative advantage

l. exchange rate
m. Euro
n. exporter
o. importer
p. international firm
q. multinational firm

v. foreign direct investment
w. quota
x. embargo
y. tariff
z. subsidy
aa. protectionism

g. national competitive advantage   r.   independent agent   bb. local content law
h. balance of trade   s.   licensing arrangement   cc. business practice laws
i. trade deficit   t.   royalty   dd. cartel
j   trade surplus   u.   strategic alliance (or   ee. dumping
k. balance of payments   joint venture)

_____ 1. Product made or grown domestically but shipped and sold abroad.

_____ 2. Firm that buys products in foreign markets and then imports them for resale in its home country.

_____ 3. Arrangement in which a firm buys or establishes tangible assets in another country.

_____ 4. Economic value of all products a country imports minus the economic value of all products it exports.

_____ 5. The ability to produce some products more efficiently than others.

_____ 6. Practice of selling a product abroad for less than the cost of production.

_____ 7. Firm that designs, produces, and markets products in many nations.

_____ 8. International competitive advantage stemming from a combination of factor conditions; demand conditions; related and supporting industries; and firm strategies, structures, and rivalries.

_____ 9. Average income per person in a country.

_____ 10. Arrangement in which a company finds a foreign partner to contribute approximately half of the resources needed to establish and operate a new business in the partner's country.

_____ 11. Flow of all money into or out of a country.

_____ 12. Laws or regulations governing business practices in given countries.

_____ 13. Government order banning exportation and/or importation of a particular product or all products from a particular country.

_____ 14. Situation in which a country's imports exceed its exports, creating a negative balance of trade.

_____ 15. Firm that distributes and sells products to one or more foreign countries.

_____ 16. Process by which the world economy is becoming a single interdependent system.

_____ 17. Payment made to a license holder in return for the right to market the licenser's product.

_____ 18. Law requiring that products sold in a particular country be at least partly made there.

_____ 19. Foreign individual or organization that agrees to represent an exporter's interests.

_____ 20. Situation in which a country's exports exceed its imports, creating a positive balance of trade.

_____ 21. Product made or grown abroad but sold domestically.

_____ 22. Restriction on the number of products of a certain type that can be imported into a country.

_____ 23. Practice of protecting domestic business against foreign competition.

_____ 24. Rate at which the currency of one nation can be exchanged for the currency of another country.

_____ 25. Tax levied on imported products.

_____ 26. The ability to produce something more efficiently than any other country can.
_____ 27. Association of producers whose purpose is to control supply and prices.

_____ 28. Common currency created by the European Union.

_____ 29. Arrangement in which firms choose foreign individuals or organizations to manufacture or market their products in another country.

_____ 30. Firm that conducts a significant portion of its business in foreign countries.

_____ 31. Government payment to help a domestic business compete with foreign firms.

WORD SCRAMBLE

1. _____   2. _____   3. _____   _____
   riftaf   toqua   tarcompaive   ageadvant

LEARNING OBJECTIVES--POTENTIAL SHORT ANSWER OR ESSAY QUESTIONS

Learning Objective #1: "Describe the rise of international business, identify the major world marketplaces, and discuss the United States' major trading partners."

Learning Objective #2: "Explain how different forms of *competitive advantage, import-export balances, exchange rates*, and *foreign competition* determine the ways in which countries and businesses respond to the international environment."

Learning Objective #3: "Discuss the factors involved in deciding to do business internationally and in selecting the appropriate *levels of international involvement* and *international organizational structure*."

Learning Objective #4: "Describe some of the ways in which *social, cultural, economic, legal*, and *political differences* among nations affect international business."

CRITICAL THINKING QUESTIONS

1. From a national perspective, do the benefits (pros) of international trade outweigh the costs (cons), or do the costs outweigh the benefits over time? In other words, does protectionism promote the general welfare? If not, then why do some politicians push for protectionist policies (trade barriers)?

2. Why is a weaker dollar good for American business but not necessarily good for the American consumer?

BRAIN TEASER

1. Given that either a tariff or a quota is going to be imposed, which would an international business prefer and why? Which would the imposing government prefer and why?

ANSWERS

True-False--*Answers*

1. False: The contemporary world economy revolves around three major marketplaces: North America, Europe and, *Asia.*
2. True
3. True
4. False: The *balance of trade* refers to the amount of goods a nation imports and exports; the *balance of payments* refers to amount of money flowing in and out of the country.
5. False: A strong dollar would *decrease* the United States exports and *increase* its imports, creating a *trade deficit.*
6. True
7. True
8. True
9. True
10. False: *Foreign direct investment (FDI)* is the investment of money by foreign companies in domestic business enterprises.
11. False: Cultural differences *remain extremely* important when doing international business.
12. True
13. True
14. False: A *tariff* is a tax on an imported product; a *quota* is a limit on the quantity allowed to enter the country.
15. True

Multiple Choice--*Answers*

1. d	5. b	9. b
2. a	6. b	10. c
3. c	7. c	11. c
4. c	8. D	

Jeopardy--*Answers*

	Trade Barriers	Arguments For and Against Protectionism	Forms of International Business Activity
$100	tariffs	Protectionism creates higher prices for both domestic and foreign goods.	exporting
$200	quotas	Protectionism boosts domestic economies by restricting foreign competition.	an independent agent
$300	subsidies	Protectionism boosts domestic jobs.	licensing
$400	embargo	The cost of saving jobs is enormous, and some jobs may be lost due to higher import prices.	a joint venture (or strategic alliance)
$500	higher prices for both domestic and foreign goods	Nations must sometimes retaliate against foreign trade restrictions.	franchising.

Match the Terms and Concepts to Their Definitions--*Answers*

1. d	6. ee	11. k	16. a	21. c	26. e	31. z
2. o	7. q	12. cc	17. t	22. w	27. dd
3. v	8. g	13. x	18. bb	23. aa	28. m
4. h	9. b	14. i	19. r	24. l	29. s
5. f	10. u	15. n	20. j	25. y	30. p

Word Scramble--*Answers*

1. tariff   2. quota   3. comparative advantage

Learning Objectives--Potential Short Answer or Essay Questions--*Answers*

Learning Objective #1:

More and more firms are engaged in international business. The term *globalization* refers to the process by which the world economy is fast becoming a single interdependent system. The three major marketplaces for international business are *North America* (the United States, Canada, and Mexico), *Western Europe* (which is dominated by Germany, the United Kingdom, France, and Italy), and the *Pacific Rim* (where the dominant country, Japan, is surrounded by such rapidly advancing nations as South Korea, Taiwan, Hong Kong, and China). The United States' major trading partners include Canada, Mexico, Japan, the United Kingdom, Taiwan, and Germany.

Learning Objective #2:

The different forms of competitive advantage are critical to international business. With an *absolute advantage*, a country engages in international trade because it can produce a product more efficiently than any other nation. *Comparative advantages* exist when they can produce some items more efficiently than they can produce other items. *National competitive advantage* stems from a combination of factor conditions; demand conditions; related and supporting industries; and firm strategies, structures, and rivalries. The *import-export balance*, including the *balance of trade* and the *balance of payments*, and *exchange rate differences* in national currencies affect the international economic environment and are important elements of international business.

Learning Objective #3:

In deciding whether to do business internationally, a firm must determine whether a market for its product exists abroad and, if so, whether it has the skills and knowledge to manage such a business. It must also assess the business climates of other nations to make sure that they are conducive to international operations.

A firm must also decide on its level of international involvement. It can choose to be an *exporter* or *importer*, to organize as an *international firm*, or to operate as a *multinational firm*. The choice will influence the organizational structure of its international operations, specifically, its use of *independent agents, licensing arrangements* (including *franchising*), *branch offices, strategic alliances*, and *direct investment*.

Learning Objective #4:

Social and *cultural differences* that can serve as barriers to trade include language, social values, and traditional buying patterns. Differences in economic systems may force businesses to establish close relationships with foreign governments before they are permitted to do business abroad. *Quotas, tariffs, subsidies*, and *local content laws* offer protection to local industries. Differences in *business practice laws* can make standard business practices in one nation illegal in another.

Critical Thinking Questions--*Answers*

1. The evidence is clear that the costs (cons) associated with protectionist policies outweigh the benefits (pros) for a *nation*. However, free trade does hurt some specific individuals (those who own or work for domestic businesses which cannot compete internationally). It is these individuals we would expect to make a case for protectionism and to lobby government for trade barriers. Some politicians may succumb to that political pressure or are unaware of the fact that the costs do outweigh the benefits. Nonetheless, it is generally true that the costs for the nation as a whole in the form of higher prices consumers must pay for both domestic and foreign products do outweigh the benefits that accrue to selected protected industries and their workers over time.

2. A weaker dollar reduces the relative price of American exports to foreigners. They would, therefore, buy more of our exports. This is beneficial to American firms that export their products around the globe. However, at the same time, a weaker dollar will hurt many American consumers because imported products will become more expensive.

Brain Teaser--*Answer*

1. An international business would prefer a quota because a tariff implies a tax that must be paid to the imposing government. With a quota, there is no such tax payment. However, the imposing government would prefer a tariff because of the tax revenues it generates.

Chapter 4
Conducting Business Ethically and Responsibly

LEARNING OBJECTIVES
After studying this chapter, you should be able to:

1. Explain how individuals develop their personal *codes of ethics* and why ethics are important in the workplace.
2. Distinguish *social responsibility* from *ethics*, identify *organizational stakeholders*, and trace the evolution of social responsibility in U.S. business.
3. Show how the concept of social responsibility applies both to environmental issues and to a firm's relationships with customers, employees, and investors.
4. Identify four general *approaches to social responsibility* and describe the four steps that a firm must take to implement a *social responsibility program*.
5. Explain how issues of social responsibility and ethics affect small business.

TRUE-FALSE
Indicate whether the statement is generally true or false by placing a "T" or "F" in the space provided. If it is a false statement, correct it so that it becomes a true statement.

_____ 1. What constitutes ethical and unethical behavior is determined partly by the individual and partly by culture.

_____ 2. Socially responsible behavior and ethical business practices rarely increase the profits of businesses.

_____ 3. Probably the single least effective way to improve ethical behavior within an organization is to start with top management support.

_____ 4. Two of the most common approaches to formalizing ethical business practices are *adopting written codes of conduct* and *instituting ethics programs*.

_____ 5. Determining what is right in any given situation can be difficult.

_____ 6. Trust is indispensable to any business.

_____ 7. Most companies that strive to be responsible to their stakeholders concentrate first and foremost on five main groups: *customers*, *employees*, *investors*, *suppliers*, and their *local communities*.

_____ 8. An ethical business rarely experiences conflicts in balancing stakeholders' interests.

_____ 9. Many observers argue that today's businesses are less sensitive to their social responsibilities.

_____ 10. Air, water, and land pollution are no longer significant social problems.

_____ 11. Very few companies have acted on their own to reduce the pollution they produce, to recycle waste materials, or to safely dispose of hazardous wastes.

_____ 12. Consumers have the right to fair prices, good service, the right to complain, and the right to return products unused for a full refund.

_____ 13. Consumerism was a movement that began in the 1960s designed to protect the rights of consumers in their dealings with businesses.

_____ 14. Collusion occurs when two or more firms agree to collaborate on such wrongful acts as price fixing.

_____ 15. In recent years, increased attention has been given to ethics in advertising and product information.

_____ 16. Whistle-blowing occurs when an employee who detects and tries to put an end to a company's unethical, illegal, or socially irresponsible actions publicizes them.

_____ 17. Investors can be cheated in many ways, but most scams fall into two categories: (1) misrepresenting company resources; and (2) diverting earnings or assets so that the investor's rightful return is reduced.

_____ 19. The highest degree of social responsibility that a firm can take is the *defensive stance.*

MULTIPLE CHOICE
Circle the one best answer for each of the following questions.
1. Which of the following is one of the steps suggested in the textbook for applying ethical judgments to situations that may arise during the course of business?
    a. Gather the relevant factual information.
    b. Determine the most appropriate moral values.
    c. Make an ethical judgment based on the rightness and wrongness of the proposed activity or policy.
    d. All of the above.

2. Which of the following is *not* one of the four fundamental ethical norms?
    a. Self-interest
    b. Utility
    c. Justice
    d. Caring

3. Written codes of ethical conduct established by businesses are designed to do all of the following *except*
    a. increase public confidence in a firm or its industry.
    b. increase government regulation.
    c. improve internal operations by providing consistent standards of both ethical and legal conduct.
    d. help managers respond to problems that arise as a result of unethical or illegal behavior.

4. Which of the following is a stakeholder group to which business has a responsibility?
    a. Consumers, and society in general
    b. Investors
    c. Employees
    d. All of the above.

5. Which of the following statements is true?
    a. One way companies can evaluate their ethical standards is by conducting a social audit.
    b. The only real stakeholders to a company are investors.
    c. The idea that business has certain obligations to society beyond the pursuit of profits faded in the1980s.
    d. Rarely do businesses profit from socially responsible behavior.

6. Which of the following statements is *false*?
    a. Socially responsible business behavior is a concept that dates back to at least the latter 1800s.
    b. Government laws and regulations designed to prevent pollution have in practice only made pollution worse.
    c. Sometimes costs of production, and therefore, prices are higher when businesses take the steps necessary to pollute less.
    d. The three major kinds of pollution are air, water, and land pollution.

7. Which one of the different phases in the evolution of social responsibility gave rise to the nation's first laws regulating basic business practices?
    a. The Entrepreneurial Era of the latter 1800s
    b. The Great Depression Era of the 1930s
    c. The Era of Social Activism of the 1960s and 1970s
    d. The Self-Interest Era of the 1980s

8. Consumerism
    a. began in the 1960s.
    b. is a movement that pressures businesses to consider consumer needs and interests.
    c. prompted many businesses to create consumer-affairs departments to handle customer complaints and many state and local agencies to set up bureaus to offer consumer information and assistance.
    d. did all of the above.

9. Which of the following is *not* one of President John F. Kennedy's "bills of rights" for consumers?
    a.   The right to a fair price
    b.   The right to be informed about all relevant aspects of a product
    c.   The right to safe products
    d.   The right to choose what one buys

10. Government product labeling requirements, on canned goods, for example, demonstrate a response to which of the following consumer rights?
    a.   The right to be heard
    b.   The right to be informed about all relevant aspects of a product
    c.   The right to choose what one buys
  e.   The right to complain
  f.

11. Investors
    a.   can be cheated if they are not provided the rate of return on their funds that they expected.
    b.   can be cheated if companies or individuals misrepresent the value of an investment, or if company funds are diverted by managers for their personal use.
    c.   are very rarely ever cheated.
    d.   All of the above.

12. Questionable business practices include
    a.   insider trading.
    b.   paying excessive salaries to senior managers.
    c.   not conforming to generally accepted accounting practices.
    d.   all of the above.

13. A company that has little regard for ethical conduct and will generally go to great lengths to hide wrongdoing would be practicing the
    a.   *obstructionist stance* to social responsibility.
    b.   *defensive stance* to social responsibility.
    c.   *accommodative stance* to social responsibility.
    d.   *proactive stance* to social responsibility .

JEOPARDY

You have 5 seconds to complete the question to each of the following answers.

	Ethics and Ethical Behavior	**Stakeholder Groups, Pollution, and Consumerism**	**Implementing Social Responsibility Programs**
$100	Beliefs about what are right and wrong or good and bad in actions that affect others. What are_____ _____?	Stakeholder groups to which businesses have a responsibility. What are_____ _____?	The highest degree of social responsibility that a firm can exhibit. What is_____ _____?
$200	Behavior conforming to generally accepted social norms concerning beneficial and harmful actions. What is_____ _____?	The contemporary view of social responsibility by business. What is_____ _____?	The first step in managing a social responsibility program. What is_____ _____?

$300	Four basic ethical norms. What are_____ _____?	Three types of pollution. What are_____ _____?	The second step in managing a social responsibility program. What is_____ _____?
$400	Two common approaches to formalizing commitment to ethical business practices. What are_____ _____?	The four consumer "bill of rights." What are _____ _____?	The third step in managing a social responsibility program What is_____ _____?
$500	A three-step procedure in applying ethical judgments to business situations. What is_____ _____?	The consumer right violated if a tire company sells tires that may blow-out unexpectedly. What is_____ _____?	The forth step in managing a social responsibility program What is_____ _____?

MATCH THE TERMS AND CONCEPTS TO THEIR DEFINITIONS

a.   ethics
b.   ethical behavior
c.   unethical behavior
d.   business ethics
e.   social responsibility

f.   organizational stakeholders
g.   consumerism
h.   collusion
i.   whistleblower
j.   check kiting

k.   obstructionist stance
l.   defensive stance
m.   accommodative stance
n.   proactive stance
o.   social audit

_____   1.   Behavior that does not conform to generally accepted social norms concerning beneficial and harmful actions.

_____   2.   Approach to social responsibility by which a company, if specifically asked to do so, exceeds legal minimums in its commitments to groups and individuals in its social environment.

_____   3.   Employee who detects and tries to put an end to a company's unethical, illegal, or socially irresponsible actions by publicizing them.

_____   4.   The attempt of a business to balance its commitments to groups and individuals in its environment, including customers, other businesses, employees, and investors.

_____   5.   Approach to social responsibility that involves doing as little as possible and may involve attempts to deny or cover up violations.

_____   6.   Form of social activism dedicated to protecting the rights of consumers in their dealings with businesses.

_____   7.   Beliefs about what is right and wrong or good and bad in actions that affect others.

_____   8.   Systematic analysis of a firm's success in using funds earmarked for meeting its social responsibility goals.

_____   9.   Ethical or unethical behaviors by a manager or employer of an organization.

_____ 10. Illegal agreement between two or more companies to commit a wrongful act.

_____ 11. Approach to social responsibility by which a company meets only minimum legal requirements in its commitments to groups and individuals in its social environment.

_____ 12. Those groups, individuals, and organizations who are directly affected by the practices of an organization and who therefore have a stake in its performance.

_____ 13. Illegal practice of writing checks against money that has not yet been credited at the bank on which the checks are drawn.

_____ 14. Behavior conforming to generally accepted social norms concerning beneficial and harmful actions.

_____ 15. Approach to social responsibility by which a company actively seeks opportunities to contribute to the well being of groups and individuals in its social environment.

WORD SCRAMBLE

1. _____   2. _____   3. _____
      thesic   simsumconer   listlewhobwer

LEARNING OBJECTIVES--POTENTIAL SHORT ANSWER OR ESSAY QUESTIONS

Learning Objective #1: **"Explain how individuals develop their personal *codes of ethics* and why ethics are important in the workplace."**

Learning Objective #2: **"Distinguish *social responsibility* from ethics and trace the evolution of social responsibility in U.S. business."**

Learning Objective #3: "Show how the concept of social responsibility applies both to environmental issues and to a firm's relationships with customers, employees, and investors."

Learning Objective #4: "Identify four general *approaches to social responsibility* and describe the four steps a firm must take to implement a *social responsibility program.*"

Learning Objective #5: "Explain how issues of social responsibility and ethics affect small businesses."

CRITICAL THINKING QUESTIONS

1. Why might a business experience an increase in its profits even though it voluntarily undertakes a costly antipollution effort, or undertakes some other kind of costly but socially responsible behavior?

2. What role must top management play in promoting socially and ethically responsible behavior by its employees?

3. What are some steps management must take to foster a company-wide sense of social responsibility?

BRAIN TEASER

1. Discrimination is considered by virtually everyone to be unethical. Is the fact that men as a group are paid more than women as a group sufficient to prove that gender discrimination exists? If not, then when do we know when gender discrimination exists in the workplace?

ANSWERS

True-False--*Answers*

1. True
2. False: Socially responsible behavior and ethical business practices *usually* increase the profits of businesses *over time.*
3. False: Probably the single *most* effective way to improve ethical behavior within an organization is to start with top management support.
4. True
5. True
6. True
7. True
8. False: An ethical business *usually* experiences conflicts in balancing stakeholders' interests.
9. False: Many observers argue that today's businesses are *more* sensitive to their social responsibilities *(especially considering the increased global competitiveness among businesses and the heightened campaigning on the part of environmentalists and other activists).*
10. False: Air, water, and land pollution are *still* significant social problems.
11. False: *Many* companies have acted on their own to reduce the pollution they produce, to recycle waste materials, *and* to safely dispose of hazardous wastes.
12. False: Consumers have the right to *safe products, the right to be informed, the right to be heard,* and *the right to choose.*
13. True
14. True
15. True
16. True
17. True
18. True
19. False: The highest degree of social responsibility that a firm can take is the *proactive stance.*

Multiple Choice--*Answers*

1. d	5. a	9. a	13. a
2. a	6. b	10. b	
3. b	7. a	11. b	
4. d	8. d	12. d	

Jeopardy---*Answers*

	Ethics and Ethical Behavior	**Stakeholder Groups, Pollution, and Consumerism**	**Implementing Social Responsibility Programs**
$100	ethics	customers, employees, investors, suppliers, and the local communities	the proactive stance to implementing social responsibility programs
$200	ethical behavior	an enlightened view stressing the need for a greater social role for business	"Top management must embrace a strong stand on social responsibility and develop a policy statement outlining that commitment."
$300	utility, rights, justice, and caring	air, water, and land	"A committee of top managers must develop a plan detailing the level of management support."
$400	adopting written codes of conduct and instituting ethics programs	the right to safety, to be informed, to be heard, and to choose	"One executive must be put in charge of the firm's social responsibility agenda."
$500	gather the relevant factual information, determine the most appropriate moral values, and then make an ethical judgment.	the right to safe products	"The organization must conduct occasional social audits."

Match the Terms and Concepts to Their Definitions--*Answers*

1. c	6. g	11. l
2. m	7. a	12. f
3. i	8. o	13. j
4. e	9. d	14. b
5. k	10. h	15. n

Word Scramble--*Answers*

1. ethics   2. consumerism   3. whistleblower

Learning Objectives--Potential Short Answer or Essay Questions--*Answers*

Learning Objective #1:

   Individual *codes of ethics* are derived from social standards of right and wrong. *Ethical behavior* is behavior that conforms to generally accepted social norms concerning beneficial and harmful actions. Because ethics affect the behavior of individuals on behalf of the companies that employ them, many firms are adopting formal statements of ethics. Unethical behavior can result in loss of business, fines, and even imprisonment.

Learning Objective #2:

   Social responsibility refers to an organization's response to social needs. One way to understand social responsibility is to view it in terms of *stakeholders*—those groups, individuals, and organizations who are directly affected by the practices of an organization and who therefore have a stake in its performance. Until the second half of the nineteenth century, businesses often paid little attention to stakeholders. Since then, however, both public pressure and government regulation, especially as a result of the Great Depression of the 1930s and the social activism of the 1960s and 1970s, have forced businesses to consider the public welfare, at least to some degree. A trend toward increased social consciousness, including a heightened sense of environmental activism, has recently emerged.

Learning Objective #3:

Social responsibility toward the environment requires firms to minimize pollution of air, water, and land. Social responsibility toward customers requires firms to provide products of acceptable quality, to price products fairly, and to respect consumers' rights. Social responsibility toward employees requires firms to respect workers both as resources and as people who are more productive when their needs are met. Social responsibility toward investors requires firms to manage their resources and to represent their financial status honestly.

Learning Objective #4:

An *obstructionist stance* on social responsibility is taken by a firm which does as little as possible to address social or environmental problems and which may deny or attempt to cover up problems that may occur. The *defensive stance* emphasizes compliance with legal minimum requirements. Companies adopting the *accommodative stance* go beyond minimum activities, if asked. The *proactive stance* commits a company to actively seek to contribute to social projects. Implementing a social responsibility program entails four steps: (1) drafting a policy statement with the support of top management, (2) developing a detailed plan, (3) appointing a director to implement the plan, and (4) conducting *social audits* to monitor results.

Learning Objective #5:

Managers and employees of small businesses face many of the same ethical questions as their counterparts at larger firms. Small businesses face the same issues of social responsibility and the same need to decide on an approach to social responsibility. The differences are primarily differences of scale.

Critical Thinking Questions--*Answers*

1. Because, over time, the business will likely earn the reputation of being a very socially responsible business and experience a rather dramatic increase in its sales for that reason alone. Most people prefer to buy products produced by socially responsible companies—even if they cost a little more.

2. Top management must make an uncompromising commitment to ethical behavior and lead by example. If top management does not take it seriously, then no one else will either.

3. Implementing a social responsibility program entails four steps: (1) drafting a policy statement with the support of top management, (2) developing a detailed plan, (3) appointing a director to implement the plan, and (4) conducting *social audits* to monitor results.

Brain Teaser--*Answer*

1. The simple fact that men as a group are paid more than women as a group is not sufficient to prove that gender discrimination exists. This is because discrimination exists whenever equals are treated unequally or whenever unequals are treated equally. Men and women, as groups, are not equal in their education, training, and skill levels, and therefore their pay is different. But, gender discrimination does exist when men and women are equally productive and are paid unequally. Unfortunately, too often equally productive women are paid less than their male counterparts. (In addition, note that by this definition---which may be debatable—"reverse discrimination" exists whenever unequals are treated equally.)

Chapter *5*

Managing the Business Enterprise

LEARNING OBJECTIVES
After studying this chapter, you should be able to:

1. Explain the importance of setting *goals* and formulating *strategies* as the starting points of effective management.
2. Describe the four activities that constitute the *management process*.
3. Identify *types of managers* by level and area.
4. Describe the five basic *management skills*.
5. Describe the development and explain the importance of *corporate culture*.

TRUE-FALSE
Indicate whether the statement is generally true or false by placing a "T" or "F" in the space provided. If it is a false statement, correct it so that it becomes a true statement.

_____ 1. A statement of an organization's purpose is known as a vision.

_____ 2. Regardless of a company's purpose and mission, every firm has long-term, intermediate, and short-term goals.

_____ 3. Strategic goals are really long-term goals derived form a firm's mission statement.

_____ 4. Environmental analysis studies the strengths and weaknesses within a firm, whereas organizational analysis involves scanning the external environment for threats and weaknesses.

_____ 5. Typically, top managers develop strategic plans, middle managers develop tactical plans, and first-line mangers develop operational plans.

_____ 6. Tactical plans are plans that define the actions and the resource allocation necessary to achieve strategic objectives.

_____ 7. The four management functions are planning, organizing, firing, and controlling.

_____ 8 The three basic levels of management are *top, middle,* and *first-line management.*

_____ 9 First-line managers are those at the top of the organization's management hierarchy.

_____ 10. Middle managers develop plans to implement the goals of top managers and coordinate the work of first-line managers.

_____ 11. In addition to setting goals and assuming various roles, managers also employ skills that fall into five basic categories: technical, human relations, conceptual, decision-making, and time management.

_____ 12. Human relations skills are the ability to perform the mechanics of a particular job.

_____ 13. Top managers depend most on conceptual skills, first-line mangers least.

_____ 14. Mangers of the future will need to understand foreign markets, cultural differences, and the motives and practices of foreign rivals.

_____ 15. Corporate culture has little influence on management philosophy, style, and behavior.

_____ 16. Corporate culture is the shared experiences, stories, beliefs, and norms that characterize an organization.

MULTIPLE CHOICE

Circle the one best answer for each of the following questions.

1. Company goals
   a. provide direction and guidance for managers at all levels.
   b. reduce the firm's ability to allocate resources.
   c. confuse the sense of corporate culture.
   d. make it more difficult for managers to assess performance.

2. A goal set for a period of one to five years is
   a. an immediate goal.
   b. a short-term goal.
   c. an intermediate goal.
   d. a long-term goal.

3. Which of the following is true about plans?
   a. Strategic plans, which are developed by mid- and lower-level managers, set short-term targets for daily, weekly, or monthly performance.
   b. Tactical plans are shorter-range plans for implementing specific aspects of the company's strategic plans.
   c. Operational plans reflect decisions about resource allocations, company priorities, and the steps needed to meet long-term company objectives.
   d. All of the above.

4. Which type of plan do top managers usually develop?
    a. Operational plans
    b. Strategic plans
    c. Tactical plans
    d. Forecasting plans

5. The management process that monitors progress toward company goals, resets the course if goals or objectives change, and corrects deviations if goals or objectives are not being attained is called the
    a. planning function of management.
    b. organizing function of management.
    c. controlling function of management.
    d. directing function of management.

6. The order in which plans are undertaken is
    a. tactical, operational, and then strategic.
    b. strategic, tactical, and then operational.
    c. operational, strategic, and then tactical.
    d. operational, tactical, and then strategic.

7. Middle managers
    a. are responsible for the overall performance and effectiveness of the firm.
    b. spend most of their time working with and supervising employees at the bottom of the organization.
    c. set strategic goals and direct the firm toward the realization of the firm's mission statement.
    d. are responsible for implementing the strategies, policies, and decisions made by top managers.

8. Managers who hire and train employees, who evaluate performance, and who determine compensation are
    a. human resource managers
    b. operations managers
    c. finance managers
    d. information mangers

9. The skill that enables a manager to think in the abstract, to diagnose and analyze different situations, and to see beyond the present situation is a
    a. technical skill.
    b. time management skill.
    c. decision-making skill.
    d. conceptual skill.

10. Skills especially important for first-line managers are
    a. technical skills.
    b. time management skills.
    c. decision-making skills.
    d. conceptual skills.

11. Decision making involves
    a. defining the problem, gathering the facts, and identifying alternative solutions.
    b. evaluating alternative solutions and selecting the best one.
    c. implementing a chosen alternative, and periodically following up and evaluating the effectiveness of that choice.

    d.   All of the above.

12. Which of the following is one of the leading causes of wasted time reducing managers' ability to mange their time effectively?
    a.   Telephone calls and e-mails
    b.   Meetings.
    c.   Paperwork.
    d.   All of the above.

13. To use a firm's culture to its advantage, managers
    a.   themselves must have a clear understanding of the culture.
    b.   must transmit the culture to others in the organization.
    c.   need to reward and promote those who understand the culture and work toward maintaining it.
    d.   need to do all of the above.

14. Which of the following is an effective way management could deal with radical change within an organization?
    a.   Top management highlights extensive change as the most effective response to the company's problems.
    b.   Top management resists change in the company's vision or culture.
    c.   Top management maintains the company's original system of appraising and compensating employees.
    d.   All of the above.

JEOPARDY
You have 5 seconds to complete the question to each of the following answers.

	Goals and Plans	**The Management Process**	**Managers and Management Skills**
$100	A statement of the organization's purpose. What is_____ _____?	The four functions of management. What are_____ _____?	Managers responsible for implementing strategies and policies made by top management. What are_____ _____?
$200	A goal that relates to extended periods of time, typically 5 years or more. What is_____ _____?	Management process of determining what needs to be done and how best to do it. What is_____ _____?	Technical skills are especially important for these managers. What are_____ _____?
$300	A plan developed by mid- and lower-level managers that sets short-term targets. What is_____ _____?	Management process of guiding and motivating employees to meet the firm's objectives. What is_____ _____?	These skills are particularly important for top managers. What are_____ _____?
$400	A shorter-range plan for implementing specific aspects of the firm's strategic plans. What is_____	Management process of monitoring performance to ensure the firm is meeting its goals. What is_____	Assess the problem, evaluate alternatives, choose an alternative, and follow up and evaluate that choice. What are_____

	_____?	_____?	_____?
$500	These types of plans reflect decisions about resource allocation, company priorities, and the steps to meet strategic goals. What are _____ _____?	Management process of determining how best to arrange an organization's resources and activities into a coherent structure. What is_____ _____?	Global management skills require this. What is_____ _____?

MATCH THE TERMS AND CONCEPTS TO THEIR DEFINITIONS

a. goal
b. mission statement
c. long-term goals
d. intermediate goals
e. short-term goals
f. strategy formulation
g. strategic goals
h. environmental analysis

i. organizational analysis
j. strategic plans
k. tactical plans
l. operational plans
m. management
n. planning
o. organizing
p. controlling

q. top managers
r. middle managers
s. first-line managers
t. technical skills
u. human relations skills
v. conceptual skills
w. decision-making skills
x. corporate culture
y. directing

_____ 1. Goals set for a period of 1 to 5 years into the future.

_____ 2. Management process of monitoring an organization's performance to ensure that it is meeting its goals.

_____ 3. Management process of determining what an organization needs to do and how best to get it done.

_____ 4. Skills in defining problems and selecting the best courses of action.

_____ 5. Process of analyzing a firm's strengths and weaknesses.

_____ 6. Skills needed to perform specialized tasks.

_____ 7. Managers responsible to the board of directors and stockholders for a firm's overall performance and effectiveness.

_____ 8. The shared experiences, stories, beliefs, and norms that characterize an organization.

_____ 9. Organization's statement of how it will achieve its purpose in the environment in which it conducts its business.

_____ 10. Creation of a broad program for defining and meeting an organization's goals.

_____ 11. Process of planning, organizing, directing, and controlling an organization's resources to achieve its goals.

_____   12. Managers responsible for implementing the strategies, policies, and decisions made by top managers.

_____   13. Objective that a business hopes and plans to achieve.

_____   14. Managers responsible for supervising the work of employees.

_____   15. Generally short-range plans concerned with implementing specific aspects of a company's strategic plans.

_____   16. Long-term goals derived directly from a firm's mission statement.

_____   17. Skills in understanding and getting along with people.

_____   18. Management process of determining how best to arrange an organization's resources and activities into a coherent structure.

_____   19. Abilities to think in the abstract, diagnose and analyze different situations, and see beyond the present situation.

_____   20. Process of scanning the business environment for threats and opportunities.

_____   21. Goals set for an extended time, typically 5 years or more into the future.

_____   22. Goals set for the very near future, typically less than 1 year.

_____   23. Plans setting short-term targets for daily, weekly, or monthly performance.

_____   24. Plans reflecting decisions about resource allocations, company priorities, and steps needed to meet strategic goals.

_____   25. Management guiding and motivating employees to met the firm's objectives.

WORD SCRAMBLE

1. _____   2. _____   3. _____
   groaniginz   nangplin   trollconing

LEARNING OBJECTIVES--POTENTIAL SHORT ANSWER OR ESSAY QUESTIONS

Learning Objective #1: "Explain the importance of setting *goals* and formulating *strategies* as the starting points of effective management."

Learning Objective #2: **"Describe the four activities that constitute the *management process*."**

Learning Objective #3: **"Identify *types of managers* by level and area."**

Learning Objective #4: **"Describe the five basic *management skills*."**

Learning Objective #5: **"Describe the development and explain the importance of *corporate culture*."**

CRITICAL THINKING QUESTIONS

1. You are applying for a supervisory position in a local company. In preparing for the upcoming interview, what types of managerial skills should you stress that you possess?

2. Some experts argue that there are three leadership styles managers may adopt: autocratic, democratic, and laissez-faire (also called free-rein). The autocratic style is the most "bossy" style. Holding everything else the same, which type of leadership style do you think would be most appropriate in managing relatively unskilled workers? What about managing professionals?

BRAIN TEASER

1. Why do managers establish "procedures," "policies," and "rules"?

ANSWERS

True-False—*Answers*

1. False: A statement of an organization's purpose is known as a *mission statement*.
2. True
3. True
4. False: *Organizational analysis* studies the strengths and weaknesses within a firm, whereas *environmental analysis* involves scanning the external environment for threats and weaknesses.
5. True
6. False: *Strategic* plans are plans that define the actions and the resource allocation necessary to achieve strategic objectives.
7. False: The four management functions are planning, organizing, *directing*, and controlling.
8. True
9. False: First-line managers are those at the *bottom* of the organization's management hierarchy.
10. True
11. True
12. False: *Technical skills* are the ability to perform the mechanics of a particular job.
13. True
14. True
15. False: Corporate culture has *a big* influence on management philosophy, style, and behavior.
16. True

Multiple Choice--*Answers*

1. a	5. c	9. d	13. d
2. c	6. b	10. a	14. a
3. b	7. d	11. d	
4. b	8. a	12. d	

Jeopardy—*Answers*

	Goals and Plans	**The Management Process**	**Managers and Management Skills**
$100	a mission statement	planning, organizing, directing, and controlling	middle managers
$200	a long-term goal	planning	first-line managers
$300	an operational plan	directing	conceptual skills
$400	a tactical plan	controlling	the basic steps in decision-making
$500	strategic plans	organizing	the need to understand foreign markets, cultural differences, and the motives and practices of foreign rivals

Match the Terms and Concepts to Their Definitions--*Answers*

1. d	6. t	11. m	16. g	21. c
2. p	7. q	12. r	17. u	22. e
3. n	8. x	13. a	18. o	23. l
4. w	9. b	14. s	19. v	24. j

5. i   10. f   15. k   20. h   25. y

Word Scramble---*Answers*
1. organizing   2. planning   3. controlling

Learning Objectives--Potential Short Answer or Essay Questions--*Answers*

Learning Objective #1:

Goals—the performance targets of an organization—can be *long term, intermediate,* or *short term.* They provide direction for managers, help managers decide how to allocate limited resources, define the corporate culture, and help managers assess performance. *Strategies*—the methods that a company uses to meet its stated goals—involve three major activities: *setting strategic goals, analyzing the organization and its environment,* and *matching the organization and its environment.* These strategies are translated into *strategic, tactical,* and *operational plans.*

Learning Objective #2:

Management is the process of planning, organizing, directing, and controlling an organization's financial, physical, human, and information resources to achieve the organization's goals. *Planning* means determining what the company needs to do and how best to get it done. *Organizing* means determining how best to arrange a business's resources and the necessary jobs into an overall structure. *Directing* means guiding and motivating employees to meet the firm's objectives. *Controlling* means monitoring the firm's performance to ensure that it is meeting its goals.

Learning Objective #3:

Managers can be differentiated in two ways: by level and by area. By level, *top managers* set policies, formulate strategies, and approve decisions. *Middle managers* implement strategies, policies, and decisions. *First-line managers* usually work with and directly supervise employees. Areas of management include human resources, operations, marketing, information, and finance. Managers at all levels may be found in every area of a company.

Learning Objective #4:

Most managers agree that five basic management skills are necessary for success. *Technical skills* are associated with performing specialized tasks. *Human relations skills* are associated with understanding and getting along with other people. *Conceptual skills* are the abilities to think in the abstract, to diagnose and analyze different situations, and to see beyond present circumstances. *Decision-making skills* allow managers to define problems and to select the best course of action. *Time management skills* refer to the productive use that managers make of their time.

Learning Objective #5:

A strong, well-defined culture can help a business reach its goals and can influence management styles. In addition to having a clear understanding of *corporate culture,* managers must be able to communicate it effectively to others. Communication is especially important when organizations find it necessary to make changes in the culture. Top management must establish new values that reflect a vision of a new company, and these values must play a role in appraising and compensating employee performance.

Critical Thinking Questions--*Answers*

1. Although all of the basic managerial skills—technical, human relations, conceptual, decision-making, and time management skills—are necessary for effective management at all levels, technical skills are relatively more important at the supervisory level. This is because the supervisor is a first-line manager. However, because human relations skills are so important in management at any level, then you should stress your technical *and* human relations skills in the interview.

2. Unskilled workers are typically less sophisticated and motivated. A more autocratic style of leadership may prove more fruitful in "getting the job done." However, most professionals don't like being "bossed around." A more democratic or laissez-faire style is usually more appropriate and successful.

Brain Teaser--*Answer*

1. "Procedures," "policies," and "rules" are really programmed decisions. These types of decisions involve simple, frequently occurring problems or opportunities for which solutions have been determined previously. Such decisions are made quickly by making reference to a procedure, rule, or company policy, and managers need spend little time in identifying and evaluating alternatives. In sum, rules and procedures allow managers to spend their time more wisely on more important matters. They act as a built-in time-management tool for managers.

Chapter 6
Organizing the Business Enterprise

LEARNING OBJECTIVES
After studying this chapter, you should be able to:

1. Discuss the elements that influence a firm's *organizational structure.*
2. Explain *specialization* and *departmentalization* as the building blocks of organizational structure.
3. Distinguish between *responsibility, authority, delegation,* and *accountability,* and explain the differences between decision making in *centralized* and *decentralized organizations.*
4. Explain the differences between *functional, divisional, matrix,* and *international organizational structures.*
5. Describe the *informal organization* and discuss *intrapreneuring.*

TRUE-FALSE
Indicate whether the statement is generally true or false by placing a "T" or "F" in the space provided. If it is a false statement, correct it so that it becomes a true statement.

_____ 1. Key elements that work together in determining an organization's structure include the organization's purpose, mission, and strategy.

_____ 2. An organization chart depicts a company's structure and shows employees where they fit into its operations.

_____ 3. The first step in developing the structure of any business, large or small, involves two activities: "specialization" and "departmentalization."

_____ 4. Specialization involves determining how people performing certain tasks can best be grouped together; departmentalization involves determining who will do what.

_____ 5. Rarely do companies adopt different forms of departmentalization for their various levels of organization.

_____ 6. After jobs have been appropriately specialized and grouped into manageable departments, the next step in organizing is to establish the decision-making hierarchy.

_____ 7. "Authority" is the duty to perform an assigned task; "responsibility" is the power to make the decisions necessary to complete the task.

_____ 8. "Accountability" begins when a manager assigns a task to a subordinate; "delegation" falls to subordinates, who must then complete the task.

_____ 9. In a decentralized organization, upper-level managers hold most decision-making authority.

_____ 10. With relatively fewer layers of management, decentralized firms tend to reflect a tall organizational structure.

_____ 11. A flat organization has a narrow span of management and many layers of management.

_____ 12. When a large number of people report directly to one person, that person has a wide span of management control.

_____ 13. Three forms of authority are line authority, staff authority, and committee and team authority.

_____ 14. The four most common forms of organizational structure are the functional, divisional, matrix, and international structures.

_____ 15. A functional organization relies on product departmentalization.

_____ 16. Functional organization is the approach to organizational structure used by most small to medium-size firms.

_____ 17. In a matrix organizational structure, teams are formed in which individuals report to two or more managers.

_____ 18. There are many specific types of international organizational structures.

_____ 19. Formal organization is the everyday social interactions among employees that transcend formal jobs and job interrelationships.

_____ 20. Internal communication networks involve both formal and informal communication channels.

_____ 21. Intrapreneuring is the process of creating and maintaining the innovation and flexibility of a small-business environment within the confines of a large organization.

_____ 22. Regardless of how an organization divides its tasks, it will function more smoothly if employees are clear about who is responsible for each task, and who has the authority to make official decisions.

MULTIPLE CHOICE
Circle the one best answer for each of the following questions.

1. Which of the following is true?
   a. "Chain of command" refers to the reporting relationships within a company.
   b. Job specialization is a natural consequence of organizational growth.
   c. After jobs are specialized, they must be grouped into logical units, which is the process of departmentalization.
   d. All of the above.

2. Which of the following is *not* a form of departmentalization?
   a. Internal departmentalization
   b. Customer departmentalization
   c. Product departmentalization
   d. Functional departmentalization

3. Departmentalization according to types of customers likely to buy a given product is
   a. product departmentalization.
   b. geographic departmentalization.
   c. customer departmentalization.
   d. functional departmentalization.

4. Departmentalization according to groups' activities is
   a. process departmentalization.
   b. geographic departmentalization.
   c. customer departmentalization.
   d. functional departmentalization.

5. Departmentalization:
   a. can occur by function, geography, process, product, or customer.
   b. by process requires the same equipment and the same worker skills when producing different products.
   c. by geography is dividing the company according to the specific product or service being created.
   e. All of the above.

6. Establishing the decision-making hierarchy involves
   a. assigning tasks: determining who can make decisions and specifying how they should be made.
   b. performing tasks: implementing decisions that have been made.
   c. distributing authority: determining whether the organization is to be centralized or decentralized.
   d. All of the above.

7. Which of the following statements is true?
   a. Authority is the power to make decisions necessary to complete a task.
   b. Delegation is the obligation to complete a task.
   c. Accountability is the duty to perform an assigned task.
   d. Responsibility is assigning a task to a subordinate.

8. To overcome the problems associated with a lack of delegating, managers should
   a. recognize that if they want the job done right they should do it themselves.
   b. stop training workers where this training is designed to increase workers' responsibilities.
   c. recognize that if a subordinate performs well it also reflects favorably on themselves.
   d. All of the above.

9. Which of the following statements is true?
   a. A flat organization has a narrow span of management and many layers of management.
   b. Decentralized firms tend to reflect a flat organizational structure.
   c. If a manager has very few people reporting directly to her, then she has a wide span of management.
   d. All of the above.

10. Which of the following statements is true?
    a. The line-and-staff organization system has a clear chain of command but also includes groups of people who provide advice and specialized services.
    b. When several employees perform either the same simple task or a group of interrelated tasks, a wide span of control is possible and often desirable.
    c. A profit center is a separate company unit responsible for its own costs and profits.
    d. All of the above.

11. Which of the following statements is true?
    a. No formula exists for determining the ideal span of management control.
    b. Organizations that focus decision-making authority near the top of the chain of command are said to be decentralized.
    c. The most complicated chain-of-command is the line authority organization.
    d. All of the above are true.

12. An organizational structure in which corporate divisions operate as autonomous businesses under the larger corporate umbrella is a
    a. a functional organization.
    b. a matrix structure
    c. a divisional organization.
    d. an international organizational structure.

13. In a matrix organizational structure
    a. one manager usually has functional expertise, while the others have more of a product or project orientation.
    b. there is a lot of flexibility which allows for ready adaptability to changing circumstances.
    c. there is a lot of reliance on committee and team authority.
    d. All of the above.

14. Which of the following is true?
    a. The *boundaryless organization* relies almost exclusively on project-type teams, with little or no underlying functional hierarchy.
    b. The *team organization* works to integrate continuous improvement with continuous employee learning and development.
    c. The *virtual organization* has little or no formal organization.
    d. The *learning organization* is one in which traditional territories or structures are minimized or eliminated altogether.

15. Which of the following is true?
    a. The grapevine is an informal communication network that runs through an organization.
    b. Frequently, informal organization effectively alters a company's formal structure.
    c. Intrapreneuring is the process of creating and maintaining the innovation and flexibility of a small-business environment within the confines of a large organization.
    d. All of the above.

JEOPARDY
You have 5 seconds to complete the question to each of the following answers.

	Specialization and Departmentalization	The Decision-Making Hierarchy	Forms of Organizational Structure
$100	Diagram depicting a company's structure and showing employees where they fit into its operations. What is_____ _____?	After jobs have been appropriately specialized and grouped into manageable departments, the next step in organizing a business is to do this. What is_____ _____?	Form of business organization in which authority is determined by the relationship between group functions and activities. What is_____ _____?
$200	The process of identifying the specific jobs that need to be done and designating people who will perform them. What is_____ _____?	This occurs when a manager assigns a task to a subordinate. What is_____ _____?	Approaches to organizational structure developed in response to the need to compete in global markets. What is_____ _____?

$300	Process of grouping jobs into logical units. What is_____?	An organization where most decision-making authority is held by top management. What is_____?	Organizational structure in which corporate divisions operate as autonomous businesses under the larger corporate umbrella. What is_____?
$400	Departmentalization according to areas served by a business. What is_____?	With relatively fewer layers of management, decentralized firms tend to reflect this type of organizational structure. What is_____?	Organizational structure in which teams are formed and team members report to two or more managers. What is_____?
$500	Departmentalization according to groups' activities What is_____?	In tall organizations, this span of control is most common. What is_____?	An organization that has little or no formal structure. What is_____?

MATCH THE TERMS AND CONCEPTS TO THEIR DEFINITIONS

a. organizational structure
b. organization chart
c. chain of command
d. job specialization
e. departmentalization
f. profit center
g. customer departmentalization
h. product departmentalization
i. process departmentalization
j. geographic departmentalization
k. functional departmentalization
l. responsibility

m. authority
n. delegation
o. accountability
p. centralized organization
q. decentralized organization
r. flat organizational structure
s. tall organizational structure
t. span of control
u. line authority
v. line department
w. staff authority
x. staff members

y. committee and team authority
z. functional organization
aa. divisional organization
bb. division
cc. matrix structure
dd. international organizational structure
ee. grapevine
ff. intrapreneuring

_____ 1. Department that resembles a separate business in producing and marketing its own products.

_____ 2. Characteristic of centralized companies with multiple layers of management and relatively narrow spans of control.

_____ 3. Departmentalization according to groups' functions or activities.

_____ 4. The process of identifying the specific jobs that need to be done and designating the people who will perform them.

_____ 5. Departmentalization according to types of customers likely to buy a given product.

_____ 6. Informal communication network that runs through an organization.

_____ 7. Advisors and counselors who aid line departments in making decisions but do not have the authority to make final decisions.

_____ 8. Organization in which most decision-making authority is held by upper-level management.

_____ 9. Departmentalization according to production processes used to create a good or service.

_____ 10. Form of business organization in which authority is determined by the relationships between group functions and activities.

_____ 11. Power to make the decisions necessary to complete a task.

_____ 12. Diagram depicting a company's structure and showing employees where they fit into its operations.

_____ 13. Organizational structure in which authority flows in a direct chain of command from the top of the company to the bottom.

_____ 14. Approaches to organizational structure developed in response to the need to manufacture, purchase, and sell in global markets.

_____ 15. Authority granted to committees or work teams involved in a firm's daily operations.

_____ 16. Organization in which a great deal of decision-making authority is delegated to levels of management at points below the top.

_____ 17. Process of grouping jobs into logical units.

_____ 18. Number of people supervised by one manager.

_____ 19. Assignment of a task, responsibility, or authority by a manager to a subordinate.

_____ 20. Process of creating and maintaining the innovation and flexibility of a small-business environment within the confines of a large organization..

_____ 21. Organizational structure in which corporate divisions operate as autonomous businesses under the larger corporate umbrella.

_____ 22. Departmentalization according to areas served by a business.

_____ 23. Specification of the jobs to be done within an organization and the ways in which they relate to one another.

_____ 24. Separate company unit responsible for its own costs and profits.

_____ 25. Authority based on expertise that usually involves advising line managers.

_____ 26. Liability of subordinates for accomplishing tasks assigned by managers.

_____ 27. Organizational structure in which teams are formed and team members report to two or more managers.

_____ 28. Department directly linked to the production and sales of a specific product.

_____ 29. Reporting relationships within a company.

_____ 30. Departmentalization according to specific products being created.

_____ 31. Characteristic of decentralized companies with relatively few layers of management and relatively wide spans of control.

_____ 32. Duty to perform an assigned task.

WORD SCRAMBLE

1. _____   2. _____   3. _____
    napgrevie   talmentraizdepation   atabiclouncity

LEARNING OBJECTIVES--POTENTIAL SHORT ANSWER OR ESSAY QUESTIONS

Learning Objective #1: **"Discuss the elements that influence a firm's *organizational structure*."**

Learning Objective #2: **"Explain *specialization* and *departmentalization* as the building blocks of organizational structure."**

Learning Objective #3: **"Distinguish between *responsibility, authority, delegation,* and *accountability*, and explain the differences between decision making in *centralized* and *decentralized organizations*."**

Learning Objective #4: **"Explain the differences between** *functional,* *divisional,* *matrix,* **and** *international organizational structures.***"**

Learning Objective #5: **"Describe the** *informal organization* **and discuss** *intrapreneuring.***"**

CRITICAL THINKING QUESTIONS

1. Why are the flatter organizational structures observed in corporations today more often accompanied by more democratic styles of leadership (as opposed to autocratic—"I'm the boss"—styles of leadership)?

2. At lunch, someone comments that the downsizing (and the flattening of organizations) that has taken place in corporate America is the result of greed on the part of those corporations. Another person replies that, because of the increasing globalization of markets and production, much of the downsizing is due to the increased competition facing American corporations from abroad. You are asked to respond? How do you reply?

BRAIN TEASER

1. Why might downsizing without reorganizing (restructuring; "re-engineering") be counterproductive?

ANSWERS

True-False—*Answers*

1. True
2. True
3. True
4. False: *Departmentalization* involves determining how people performing certain tasks can best be grouped together; *specialization* involves determining who will do what.
5. False: *Often* companies adopt different forms of departmentalization for their various levels of organization—*especially larger companies.*
6. True
7. False: *Responsibility* is the duty to perform an assigned task; *authority* is the power to make the decisions necessary to complete the task.
8. False: *Delegation* begins when a manager assigns a task to a subordinate; *accountability* falls to subordinates, who must then complete the task.
9. False: In a *centralized* organization, upper-level managers hold most decision-making authority.
10. False: With relatively fewer layers of management, decentralized firms tend to reflect a *flat* organizational structure.
11. False: A *tall* organization has a narrow span of management and many layers of management.
12. True
13. True
14. True
15. False: A *divisional* organization relies on product departmentalization.
16. True
17. True
18. True
19. False: *Informal* organization is the everyday social interactions among employees that transcend formal jobs and job interrelationships.
20. True
21. True
22. True

Multiple Choice--*Answers*

1. d	5. a	9. b	13. d
2. a	6. d	10. d	14. c
3. c	7. a	11. a	15. d
4. d	8. c	12. c	

Jeopardy—*Answers*

	Specialization and Departmentalization	The Decision-Making Hierarchy	Forms of Organizational Structure
$100	an organization chart	to establish the decision-making hierarchy	a functional organization
$200	specialization	delegation	an international organizational structure
$300	departmentalization	a centralized organization	a divisional organization
$400	geographic departmentalization	a flat organizational structure	a matrix structure
$500	functional departmentalization	a narrow span of control	a virtual organization

Match the Terms and Concepts to Their Definitions--*Answers*

1. bb	6. ee	11. m	16. q	21. aa	26. o	31. r
2. s	7. x	12. b	17. e	22. j	27. cc	32. l
3. k	8. p	13. u	18. t	23. a	28. v	
4. d	9. i	14. dd	19. n	24. f	29. c	
5. g	10. z	15. y	20. ff	25. w	30. h	

Word Scramble--*Answers*

1. grapevine   2. departmentalization   3. accountability

Learning Objectives--Potential Short Answer or Essay Questions--*Answers*

Learning Objective #1:

Every business needs structure to operate. *Organizational structure* varies according to a firm's mission, purpose, and strategy. Size, technology, and changes in environmental circumstances also influence structure. In general, although all organizations have the same basic elements, each develops the structure that contributes to the most efficient operations.

Learning Objective #2:

The building blocks of organizational structure are *job specialization* and *departmentalization*. As a firm grows, it usually has a greater need for people to perform specialized tasks (specialization). It also has a greater need to group types of work into logical units (departmentalization). Common forms of departmentalization are *customer, product, process, geographic,* and *functional.* Large businesses often use more than one form of departmentalization.

Learning Objective #3:

Responsibility is the duty to perform a task; *authority* is the power to make the decisions necessary to complete tasks. *Delegation* begins when a manager assigns a task to a subordinate; *accountability* means that the subordinate must complete the task. *Span of control* refers to the number of people who work for any individual manager. The more people supervised, the wider the span of control. Wide spans are usually desirable when employees perform simple or unrelated tasks. When jobs are diversified or prone to change, a narrower span is generally preferable.

In a *centralized organization*, only a few individuals in top management have real decision-making authority. In a *decentralized organization*, much authority is delegated to lower-level management. When both *line* and *line-and-staff systems* are involved, line departments generally have authority to make decisions, whereas *staff departments* have a responsibility to advise. A relatively new concept, *committee and team authority*, empowers committees or work teams involved in a firm's daily operations.

Learning Objective #4:

In a *functional organization*, authority is usually distributed among such basic functions as marketing and finance. In a *divisional organization*, the various divisions of a larger company, which may be related or unrelated, operate in a relatively autonomous fashion. In *matrix organizations*, in which individuals report to more than one manager, a company creates teams to address specific problems or to conduct specific projects. A company that has divisions in many countries may require an additional level of *international organization* to coordinate those operations.

Learning Objective #5:

The informal organization consists of the everyday social interactions among employees that transcend formal jobs and job interrelationships. To foster the innovation and flexibility of a small business within the big-business environment, some large companies encourage *intrapreneuring—*

creating and maintaining the innovation and flexibility of a small-business environment within the confines of a large bureaucratic structure.

Critical Thinking Questions--*Answers*

1. The flatter organizations, where middle management positions are minimized, requires more direct communication, cooperation, and input from employees. Managers that pursue a more democratic style of leadership encourage input from employees. This style of management leadership may also use teams to provide input into the decision-making process. This is a more fruitful style of management because by empowering employees with greater responsibility and input into decision making, these same employees will be more apt to see to it that the group's decision succeeds. As a result, the manger, as a manager, also succeeds.

2. It may be true (and it may not be true) that some corporations are concentrating too much on short-run profit-maximization and are, therefore, looking for ways to reduce costs by downsizing and flattening the organization (even though long-term thinking may question this wisdom). However, it is also true that there is increased competition facing corporate America from abroad. This greater competition has forced many American corporations to look for more effective ways to organize, to reduce costs, to increase quality, and to increase their price competitiveness in the global economy. The greater competition from abroad forcing American firms to seek out more cost-effective means of production will not likely go away. Whether downsizing your staff is appropriate to achieve a competitive advantage is debatable.

Brain Teaser--*Answer*

1. Downsizing without reorganizing the work processes can lead to an organization so nervous about who will be laid off next that employees begin to think only of themselves and become unwilling to take risks that might benefit the firm. In addition, downsizing can cripple a company's long-term ability to meet customer needs. So, if a firm downsizes, it should also reorganize. The benefits of reorganizing include new opportunities for existing employees and better communication within the firm.

Chapter 7

Understanding Entrepreneurship and the Small Business

LEARNING OBJECTIVES

After studying this chapter, you should be able to:

1. Define small business and explain its importance to the U.S. economy.
2. Explain which *types of small business* best lend themselves to success.
3. Define *entrepreneurship* and describe some basic *entrepreneurial characteristics*.
4. Describe the *start-up decisions* made by small businesses and identify sources of *financial aid* and *management advice* available to such enterprises.
5. Identify the advantages and disadvantages of *franchising*.

TRUE-FALSE

Indicate whether the statement is generally true or false by placing a "T" or "F" in the space provided. If it is a false statement, correct it so that it becomes a true statement.

_____ 1. Although the term "small business" defies easy definition, it is an independently owned and managed business that does not dominate its market.

_____ 2. The Small Business Administration (SBA) is a government agency that serves as a resource and advocate for small firms.

_____ 3. Small companies tend to be innovative, partly because company owners are more accessible and partly because these companies offer more opportunity for individual expression.

_____ 4. Running a small business takes a lot of hard work, drive, and dedication, and being a successful corporate employee doesn't necessarily translate into being a successful small-business owner.

_____ 5. Small businesses do not provide for very many new jobs.

_____ 6. Service businesses are the fastest growing segment of small-business enterprise.

_____ 7. Small businesses have accounted for a small fraction of the nation's new product developments.

_____ 8. "Entrepreneurs" want to remain small and simply support a lifestyle with their businesses; whereas "small-business" owners are motivated to grow and to expand their businesses.

_____ 9. Female entrepreneurs make up one of the fastest-growing segments in the small-business economy.

_____ 10. You can start a new business from scratch, by buying out an existing business, or by investing in a franchise.

_____ 11. Beyond personal funds, two other sources of start-up funds are venture capital companies and small-business investment companies.

_____ 12. Hoping to boost their economies and create jobs, state and local governments have launched many programs to help small businesses.

_____ 13. SBA loans are a major source of small-business financing.

_____ 14. Management advice from advisory boards, management consultants, the SBA, and networking is unfortunately usually not available to small-business owners.

_____ 15. A franchisee is the seller of a franchise, whereas a franchiser is the buyer of the franchise.

_____ 16. One disadvantage of a franchise is wide name recognition and mass advertising of the good or service sold.

_____ 17. One advantage of a franchise is the managerial support provided by the franchiser.

_____ 18. One disadvantage of a franchise is the possible continued obligation to contribute percentages of sales revenues to parent corporations.

MULTIPLE CHOICE

Circle the one best answer for each of the following questions.

1. Which of the following statements is true?
    a. Small businesses are a very important part of the U.S. economy.
    b. Small-business owners (as opposed to entrepreneurs) intend to grow their businesses very rapidly to earn very large profits.
    c. Very few of the products made by big manufacturers are sold to consumers by small businesses.
    d. All of the above.

2. Small businesses are characterized by
    a. being innovative.
    b. having relatively little influence in their markets.
    c. their owners working hard to perform a variety of job functions.
    d. All of the above.

3. Which of the following is *false* about small businesses in our economy?
    a. Small businesses provide jobs for a significant part of the labor force.
    b. Small businesses rarely sell services.
    c. Small businesses supply many of the needs of large corporations.
    d. Small businesses provide for many new innovations and product developments.

4. In which of the following sectors of our economy are small businesses least likely to be found?
    a. Services
    b. Retailing
    c. Finance and Insurance
    d. Manufacturing

5. Which of the following is true about entrepreneurs?
    a. An entrepreneur is any small–business owner.
    b. Entrepreneurs assume the risk of business ownership with a primary goal of growth and expansion.
    c. Entrepreneurs are rarely concerned about good personal customer relations.
    d. Entrepreneurs avoid risk whenever possible and cautiously respond to surprises.

6. Factors that account for the rapid start-up of new small businesses include
    a. the emergence of e-commerce.
    b. increased opportunities for minorities and women.
    c. new opportunities in global enterprise.
    d. All of the above.

7. Which of the following is *not* one of the reasons for small business failure?
    a. Managerial incompetence or inexperience.
    b. Effective control systems.
    c. Insufficient capital.
    d. Neglect.

8. Small business success can be attributed to
   a. luck.
   b. hard work, drive, and dedication.
   c. a high demand for the good or service produced.
   d. All of the above.

9. A way to get into business for yourself is to
   a. start a new company from scratch.
   b. buy out an existing business.
   c. invest in a franchise.
   d. do all of the above.

10. When starting a small business
    a. the first step is the individual's commitment to becoming a business owner.
    b. one needs to select the good or service to be offered for sale.
    c. one must understand the true nature of the enterprise in which they are to be engaged.
    d. All of the above.

11. Which of the following statements is true?
    a. If you apply to several banks for financing and are turned down by all of them, you may be able to qualify for a loan backed by the SBA.
    b. Venture capital companies are federally licensed to borrow money from the SBA and to invest it in or lend it to small businesses.
    c. Small-business investment companies are groups of small investors seeking to make profits on companies with rapid growth potential.
    d. All of the above.

12. When small businesses are loaned funds put up jointly by banks and the SBA, this is
    a. a guaranteed loans program.
    b. an immediate participation loans program.
    c. a local development companies program.
    d. a venture capital loans program.

13. An SBA program in which retired executives work with small businesses on a volunteer basis is the
    a. Active Corps of Executives.(ACE)
    b. Small Business Institute (SBI)
    c. Service Corps of Retired Executives (SCORE)
    d. Small Business Development Center (SBDC)

14. Which of the following is true?
    a. Strategic alliances are becoming a popular method for financing business growth.
    b. ACE (Active Corp of Executives) and SCORE (Service Corps of Retired Executives) are good resources for small business management advice.
    c. The Small Business Institute (SBI) is a SBA program in which college and university students and instructors work with small-business owners to help solve specific problems.
    d. All of the above.

15. Which of the following statements is *false*?
    a. Franchising is very common.
    b. A franchise enables one to use a larger company's trade name and sell its products or services in a specific territory.
    c. A franchisee never has to pay the franchiser a percentage of sales revenues.
    d. A franchise may constrain the franchisee's independence.

16. Which of the following is *false* about a franchise?
    a. Owning a franchise rarely involves any considerable start-up expense.
    b. A franchisee has the advantage of training and managerial support from the franchiser.
    c. A franchisee may have the advantage of financial support from the franchiser.
    d. A franchisee has the advantage of wide name recognition and mass advertising provided by the franchiser.

17. Which of the following is *false*?
    a. If an entrepreneur is good at launching a business, then he/she is assured of success in managing the business over the long term.
    b. One way companies expand their business is by franchising their concepts to others.
    c. Local chambers of commerce and the National Federation of Independent Businesses (NFIB) facilitate networking.
    d. By using the Internet, smaller firms can compete with bigger firms.

JEOPARDY

You have 5 seconds to complete the question to each of the following answers.

	Terms and Concepts	**Small Businesses**	**Small-Business Assistance**
$100	A company that is independently owned and operated, is not dominant in its field, and meets certain criteria for the number of employees and annual sales. What is_____ _____?	These businesses are the fastest growing segment of small-business enterprise. What are_____ _____?	A group of small investors that invest money in companies with rapid growth potential. What is_____ _____?
$200	A document that tells potential lenders why money is needed, how it will be used, and when it will be repaid. What is_____ _____?	Three ways of getting into business for yourself. What are_____ _____?	A government-regulated investment company that borrows money from the SBA to invest in or lend to a small business. What is_____ _____?
$300	SBA program in which small businesses are loaned funds put up jointly by banks and the SBA. What is_____ _____?	One reason for the rapid rise in the creation of new small businesses. What is_____ _____?	A program in which the SBA guarantees to repay 75 percent to 85 percent of small-business commercial loans up to $750,000. What is_____ _____?

$400	A person that strives for rapid growth and expansion of his/her business and accepts both risks and opportunities. What is_____ ?	The advantages of a franchise. What are_____ ?	A program in which the SBA works with local for-profit or not-for-profit organizations seeking to boost a community's economy. What is_____ ?
$500	A supplier that grants a franchise to an individual or group in exchange for payments. What is_____ ?	The disadvantages of a franchise. What are_____ ?	SBA program designed to consolidate information from various disciplines and make it available to small businesses What is_____ ?

MATCH THE TERMS AND CONCEPTS TO THEIR DEFINITIONS

a. Small Business Administration (SBA)
b. small business
c. entrepreneur
d. venture capital company
e. small-business investment company (SBIC)
f. minority enterprise small-business investment company (MESBIC)
g. guaranteed loans program
h. immediate participation loans program
i. local development companies (LDCs) program
j. management consultant
k. Service Corps of Retired Executives (SCORE)
l. Active Corps of Executives (ACE)
m. Small Business Institute (SBI)
n. Small Business Development Center (SBDC)
o. networking
p. franchise

_____ 1. Businessperson who accepts both the risks and the opportunities involved in creating and operating a new business venture.

_____ 2. SBA program in which college and university students and instructors work with small-business owners to help solve specific problems.

_____ 3. Interactions among businesspeople for the purpose of discussing mutual problems and opportunities and perhaps pooling resources.

_____ 4. Federally sponsored company that specializes in financing businesses that are owned and operated by minorities.

_____ 5. Program in which the SBA works with local for-profit or nonprofit organizations seeking to boost a community's economy.

_____ 6. Independently owned and managed business that does not dominate its market.

_____ 7. Arrangement in which a buyer (franchisee) purchases the right to sell the good or service of the seller (franchiser).

_____ 8. SBA program in which currently employed executives work with small businesses on a volunteer basis.

_____   9. A government-regulated investment company that borrows money from the SBA to invest in or lend to a small business.

_____   10. Program in which small businesses are loaned funds put up jointly by banks and the SBA.

_____   11. Group of small investors that invest money in companies with rapid growth potential.

_____   12. SBA program designed to consolidate information from various disciplines and make it available to small businesses.

_____   13. SBA program in which retired executives work with small businesses on a volunteer basis.

_____   14. Federal agency charged with assisting small businesses.

_____   15. Program in which the SBA guarantees to repay 75 percent to 85 percent of small-business commercial loans up to $750,000.

_____   16. Independent outside specialist hired to help managers solve business problems.

WORD SCRAMBLE

1. _____   2. _____   3. _____

   sanchfire   rowkingnet   trepreneuren

LEARNING OBJECTIVES--POTENTIAL SHORT ANSWER OR ESSAY QUESTIONS

Learning Objective #1: "Define *small business* and explain its importance to the U.S. economy."

Learning Objective #2: "Explain which *types of small business* best lend themselves to success."

Learning Objective #3: "Define *entrepreneurship* and describe some basic *entrepreneurial characteristics*."

Learning Objective #4: "Describe the *start-up decisions* made by small businesses and identify sources of *financial aid* and *management advice* available to such enterprises."

Learning Objective #5: "Identify the advantages and disadvantages of *franchising*."

CRITICAL THINKING QUESTIONS

1. What are some of the steps one needs to undertake in starting up a new business?

2. What are some of the questions that need to be addressed before signing a franchise agreement?

BRAIN TEASER

1. State and local governments launch hundreds of programs to help small businesses boost their local economies. These programs help to create jobs for these local economies. However, constituents must pay taxes to fund these programs. Are these programs worth these tax dollars? Why or why not?

ANSWERS

True-False--*Answers*
1. True
2. True
3. True

4. True
5. False: Small businesses *are a principle source of* new jobs.
6. True
7. False: Small businesses have accounted for a *large* fraction of the nation's new product developments.
8. False: *Small-business owners* want to remain small and simply support a lifestyle with their businesses; whereas *entrepreneurs are* motivated to grow and to expand their businesses.
9. True
10. True
11. True
12. True
13. False: SBA loans are *not* a major source of small-business financing.
14. False: Management advice from advisory boards, management consultants, the SBA, and networking *is usually readily* available to small-business owners.
15. False: A franchisee is the *buyer* of a franchise, whereas a franchiser is the *seller* of the franchise.
16. False: One *advantage* of a franchise is wide name recognition and mass advertising of the good or service sold.
17. True
18. True

Multiple Choice--*Answers*

1. a	5. b	9. d	13. c	17. a
2. d	6. d	10. d	14. d	
3. b	7. b	11. a	15. c	
4. d	8. d	12. b	16. a	

Jeopardy---*Answers*

	Terms and Concepts	Small Businesses	Small-Business Assistance
$100	a small business	small businesses that sell services	a venture capital company
$200	a business plan	starting a new company from scratch, buying out an existing business, or investing in a franchise	a small-business investment company (SBIC)
$300	the SBA's guaranteed loans program	the emergence of e-commerce, the increase in entrepreneurs who cross-over from big business, increased opportunities for minorities and women, new opportunities in global enterprise, or the improved rates of survival among small businesses	the SBA's guaranteed loans program.
$400	an entrepreneur	wide name recognition and mass advertising, financial help, and managerial training and support	the SBA's local development companies (LDCs) program

$500	a franchiser	a considerable start-up expense, requirements to pay a percentage of sales revenues to the franchiser, and constraints on the owner's independence	a Small Business Development Center (SBDC)

Match the Terms and Concepts to Their Definitions--*Answers*

1. c	6. b	11. d	16. j
2. m	7. p	12. n	
3. o	8. l	13. k	
4. f	9. e	14. a	
5. i	10. h	15. g	

Word Scramble--*Answers*

1.   franchise   2.   networking   3.   entrepreneur

Learning Objectives--Potential Short Answer or Essay Questions--*Answers*

Learning Objective #1:

A *small business* is independently owned and managed and does not dominate its market. Small businesses are crucial to the economy because they create new jobs, foster *entrepreneurship* and *innovation*, and supply goods and services needed by larger businesses.

Learning Objective #2:

Services are the easiest operations for small business owners to start because they require low levels of resources. They also offer high returns on investment and tend to foster innovation. Retailing and wholesaling are more difficult because they usually require some experience, but they are still attractive to many entrepreneurs. Construction and financial and insurance operations are also common sectors for small business. As the most resource-intensive areas of the economy, transportation and manufacturing are the areas least populated by small firms.

Learning Objective #3:

Entrepreneurs are small business owners who assume the risk of business ownership. Unlike small business owners, they seek growth and expansion as their primary goal. Most successful entrepreneurs share a strong desire to be their own bosses and believe that building businesses will help them gain control over their lives and build for their families. Many also enjoy taking risks and committing themselves to the necessary time and work. Finally, most report that freedom and creative expression are important factors in the decision to own and operate their own businesses.

Learning Objective #4:

The Internet is rewriting the rules of business start-up. But in deciding to go into business, the entrepreneur must still first choose between buying an existing business and starting from scratch. Both approaches involve practical advantages and disadvantages. A successful existing business has working relationships with other businesses and has already proved its ability to make a profit. New businesses, on the other hand, allow owners to plan and work with clean slates, but it is hard to make projections about the business's prospects.

Although small business owners generally draw heavily on their own resources for financing, they can get financial aid from venture capital firms, which seek profits from investments in companies with rapid growth potential. *The Small Business Administration (SBA) also sponsors a variety of loan programs, including small-business investment companies.* Finally, foreign firms and other nonbank lenders make funds available under various circumstances. Management advice is available from *advisory boards, management consultants, the SBA,* and the practice of *networking* (meeting regularly with people in related businesses to discuss problems and opportunities).

Learning Objective #5:

Franchising has become a popular form of small-business ownership because the *franchiser* (parent company) supplies financial, managerial, and marketing assistance to the *franchisee,* who buys the right to sell the franchiser's product. Franchising also enables small businesses to grow rapidly. Finally, the risks in franchising are lower than those in starting a new business from scratch. The costs of purchasing a franchise can be quite high, however, and the franchisee sacrifices independence and creativity. In addition, owning franchises provides no guarantee of success.

Critical Thinking Questions--*Answers*

1. First, one needs to commit to becoming a business owner because it will take a lot of hard work and dedication. The next step is to choose the good or service to be offered for sale. One should undertake market research to make sure there is sufficient demand for that good or service. Also, make sure the true nature of the business is understood. One may also want to establish a business plan. Make sure that business plan is succinct, yet thorough.

2. One should survey all of the advantages and disadvantages as discussed in the textbook, and weigh them in making a decision whether to sign the franchise contract.

Brain Teaser--*Answer*

1. Yes. Although taxes must be collected to pay for these programs, these programs typically more than pay for themselves through the additional tax revenues generated from the additional jobs and income these programs create.

Chapter 8
Managing Human Resources

LEARNING OBJECTIVES
After studying this chapter, you should be able to:

1. Define *human resource management*, discuss its strategic significance, and explain how managers plan for human resources.
2. Identify the issues involved in *staffing* a company, including *internal* and *external recruiting* and *selection*.
3. Discuss different ways in which organizations go about developing the capabilities of employees and managers.
4. Explain ways in which organizations evaluate employee performance.
5. Discuss the importance of *wages and salaries*, *incentives*, and *benefit programs* in attracting and keeping skilled workers.
6. Describe some of the key legal issues involved in hiring, compensating, and managing workers in today's workplace.
7. Discuss *workforce diversity*, the management of *knowledge workers*, and the use of *contingent and temporary workers* as important changes in the contemporary workplace.

TRUE-FALSE
Indicate whether the statement is generally true or false by placing a "T" or "F" in the space provided. If it is a false statement, correct it so that it becomes a true statement.

_____ 1. Human resource management is the set of organizational activities directed at attracting, developing, and maintaining an effective workforce.

_____ 2. Human resource management has become a major challenge for all businesses.

_____ 3. The first step in staffing business organizations is to train and develop employees.

_____ 4. After job analysis has been completed, the human resources manager develops a job description, and then a job specification.

_____ 5. The first stage in the hiring process is to interview each candidate for the job.

_____ 6. Interviewing is the session or procedure for orienting a new employee to the organization.

_____ 7. The most common method of work-based training is on-the-job training.

_____ 8. Many companies have developed performance appraisal systems to try to objectively evaluate employees according to set criteria.

_____ 9. Two methods of appraising performance of employees are the ranking and rating methods.

_____ 10. Basic compensation refers to the level of benefits provided to an employee.

_____ 11. Two general methods for compensating employees are through wages and salaries.

_____ 12. Wages (for hourly employees) and salaries (for nonhourly employees) are the most typical components of employee pay.

_____ 13. When an employee receives a "raise" that is an example of being compensated through a merit pay plan.

_____ 14. A commission is a group-based incentive system for distributing a portion of the company's profits to employees.

_____ 15. A benefit plan that allows an employee to choose from a variety of alternative benefits is called worker's compensation insurance.

_____ 16. The most popular types of benefits are health and retirement benefits.

_____ 17. The Equal Pay Act is a federal law forbidding discrimination on the basis of race, color, religious beliefs, sex, or national origin.

_____ 18. The practice of recruiting qualified employees belonging to racial, gender, or ethnic groups who are underrepresented in an organization is called the Fair Labor Standards plan.

_____ 19. Sexual harassment is the practice or instance of making unwelcome sexual advances in the workplace.

_____ 20. Businesses are realizing that diversity in their workforce reduces their competitive advantage.

_____ 21. In recent years the number of contingent workers employed has fallen dramatically.

MULTIPLE CHOICE

Circle the one best answer for each of the following questions.

1. Which of the following is *not* one of the functions of human resource management?
   a. Planning, recruiting, and selecting new employees
   b. Training and developing employees
   c. Managing employees
   d. Appraising and compensating employees

2. Which of the following statements is true?
   a. Keeping track of the labor market is quite easy.
   b. Effective human resource management is becoming more important in business.
   c. External recruiting is almost always more preferable to selecting a candidate to fill a position internally.
   d. The part-time labor force has shrunk in recent years.

3. Job analysis requires the human resource manager to
   a. develop a job description followed by a job specification.
   b. develop a job specification followed by a job description.
   c. continue to the next step which is to determine future human resource needs.
   d. continue to the next step which is to select an employee from a pool of candidates.

4. Which of the following correctly describes the steps involved in the human resource planning process?
   a. Develop a plan to match labor demand and supply, forecast internal and external supply of labor, forecast demand for labor, and then determine the job analysis.
   b. Develop a plan to match labor demand and supply, forecast internal and external supply of labor, determine the job analysis, and then forecast demand for labor.
   c. Determine the job analysis, forecast demand for labor, forecast internal and external supply of labor, and then develop a plan to match labor demand and supply.
   d. Forecast internal and external supply of labor, develop a plan to match labor demand and supply, determine the job analysis, and then forecast demand for labor.

5. Which of the following statements is true?
   a. When managers have determined that new employees are needed, they must then turn their attention to recruiting and hiring the right mix of people.
   b. Both internal and external staffing starts with effective recruiting.
   c. Once the recruiting process has attracted a pool of applicants, the next step is to select someone to hire.
   d. All of the above.

6. Which of the following would *not* be an appropriate question to ask of a candidate during an interview?
   a. Why do you wish to change employment?
   b. What are your expectations of this position?
   c. What is your religious affiliation?
   d. What are your long-term goals?

7. A training technique that ties training and development activities directly to task performance is
    a. an orientation program
    b. a work-based program
    c. an instructional-based program.
    d. management-development program.

8. Which of the following is true?
    a. A growing number of companies are helping their employees while they help themselves by offering college degree programs.
    b. The biggest problem with appraisal systems is finding a way to measure performance.
    c. Two general ways employees are compensated is through wages and salaries, and through benefits.
    d. All of the above are true.

9. Performance appraisals
    a. are the specific and formal evaluation of employees in order to determine the degree to which the employees are performing effectively.
    b. are important because they provide a benchmark to better assess the extent to which recruiting and selection processes are adequate.
    c. help managers assess the extent to which they are recruiting and selecting the best employees.
    d. All of the above.

10. Which of the following is *false* concerning compensation?
    a. Hourly employees earn wages; salaries are earned by nonhourly employees.
    b. Comparable worth is a concept of equal pay for jobs that are equal in value to the organization and require similar levels of education, training, and skills.
    c. Profit sharing is a payment to an employee equal to a certain percentage of sales made by that employee.
    d. A piece-rate incentive plan provides payment for each unit produced.

11. Accepting a lower base pay in exchange for bonuses based on meeting production or other goals is
    a. knowledge-based pay.
    b. performance-based compensation.
    c. a sales commission.
    d. a comparable worth pay scheme.

12. A company-sponsored program for providing retirees with income is
    a. a private pension plan
    b. a stock option plan
    c. an employee stock-ownership plan.
    d. a merit-pay plan.

13. Which of the following statements is true?
    a. A cafeteria benefit plan allows employees to choose the unique combination of benefits that suit their needs.
    b. Social security and worker's compensation are mandated protection plans offered all employees.
    c. Although no U.S. laws mandate paid time off, it has come to be expected by most employees.
    d. All of the above.

14. Which of the following statements is true?
   a.   Comparable worth is the principle that jobs that are worth the same should be compensated at the same level regardless of who performs them.
   b.   An affirmative action plan is a federal law requiring employees to provide unpaid leave for specific family and medical reasons.
   c.   The Civil Rights Act establishes minimum wage and overtime pay requirements.
   d.   In recent years the number of contingent workers has decreased dramatically.

JEOPARDY

You have 5 seconds to complete the question to each of the following answers.

	Staffing and Developing Human Resources	**Compensation**	**The Legal Environment of Human Resource Management**
$100	This lists the duties of a job and the conditions under which those duties are performed. What is_____ _____?	The two general methods for compensating employees. What are_____ _____?	Legally mandated nondiscrimination in employment on the basis of race, creed, sex, or national origin. What is_____ _____?
$200	When managers have determined that new employees are needed, they must then turn their attention to this. What is_____ _____?	The most popular type of benefit. What is_____ _____?	Federal law prohibiting discrimination against people over 40 on the basis of age. What is_____ _____?
$300	Work-based training, sometimes informal, conducted while an employee is in an actual work situation. What is_____ _____?	Payments to employees equal to a certain percentage of sales volume that they generate. What are_____ _____?	Agency created by Title VII to enforce discrimination laws. What is_____ _____?
$400	Work-based training in which employees are systematically moved from one job to another so that they can learn a wider array of tasks and skills. What is_____ _____?	Company-sponsored programs for providing retirees with income. What are_____ _____?	Practice of discriminating against well-represented groups by overhiring members of underrepresented groups. What is_____ _____?
$500	The overriding goal of this is to attract and keep good employees. What is_____ _____?	Benefit plan that sets limits on benefits per employee, each of whom may choose from a variety of alternative benefits. What is_____ _____?	Practice or instance of making unwelcome sexual advances in the workplace. What is_____ _____?

MATCH THE TERMS AND CONCEPTS TO THEIR DEFINITIONS

a. human resource management (HRM)
b. job analysis
c. job description
d. job specification
e. replacement chart
f. employee information system (or skills inventory)
g. recruiting
h. internal recruiting
i. external recruiting
j. validation
k. orientation
l. work-based program
m. on-the-job training
n. vestibule training
o. systematic job rotation and transfer
p. instructional-based program
q. lecture or discussion approach
r. computer-assisted training
s. performance appraisal
t. 360° feedback
u. simple ranking method
v. forced distribution method
w. graphic rating scale
x. critical incident method
y. compensation

z. wages
aa. salary
bb. pay survey
cc. job evaluation
dd. merit pay plan
ee. skill-based or knowledge-based pay
ff. piece-rate incentive plan
gg. individual incentive plan
hh. sales commission
ii. gainsharing program
jj. profit sharing
kk. benefits
ll. unemployment insurance
mm. social security
nn. worker's compensation insurance
oo. private pension plan
pp. wellness program
qq. cafeteria benefit plan
rr. equal employment opportunity
ss. illegal discrimination
tt. protected class
uu. Title VII of the Civil Rights Act of 1964
vv. Equal Pay Act of 1963
ww. comparable worth

xx. Age Discrimination Act of 1979
yy. Pregnancy Discrimination Act of 1979
zz. Civil Rights Act of 1991
aaa. Americans with Disabilities Act of 1990 (ADA)
bbb. Family and Medical Leave Act of 1993
ccc. Equal Employment Opportunity Commission (EEOC)
ddd. affirmative action program
eee. reverse discrimination
fff. Fair Labor Standards Act
ggg. Employee Retirement Income Security Act of 1974 (ERISA)
hhh. Occupational Safety and Health Act of 1970 (OSHA)
iii. sexual harassment
jjj. quid pro quo harassment
kkk. hostile work environment
lll. employment-at-will
mmm. workforce diversity
nnn. knowledge worker
ooo. contingent worker

_____ 1. Training designed to impart new knowledge and information.

_____ 2. Compensation in the form of money paid for discharging the responsibilities of a job.

_____ 3. Federal law regulating private pension plans.

_____ 4. Federal law prohibiting discrimination on the basis of disability and requiring employers to make reasonable accommodation for disabled applicants and employees.

_____ 5. Computerized system containing information on each employee's education, skills, work experiences, and career aspirations.

_____ 6. Prearranged company pensions provided to retired employees.

_____ 7. Training technique that ties training and development activities directly to task performance.

_____ 8. Set of individuals who by nature of one or more common characteristics are protected by law from discrimination on the basis of any of those characteristics.

_____ 9. Agency created by Title VII to enforce discrimination-related laws.

_____ 10. Range of workers' attitudes, values, and behaviors that differ by gender, race, and ethnicity.

_____ 11. Group-based incentive plan that gives rewards for productivity improvements.

_____ 12. Performance appraisal method that classifies employees into different performance categories based on a predetermined distribution.

_____ 13. Work-based training, sometimes informal, conducted while an employee is in actual work situation.

_____ 14. Principle that jobs which are worth the same should be compensated at the same level regardless of who performs them.

_____ 15. Formal evaluation of an employee's job performance in order to determine the degree to which the employee is performing effectively.

_____ 16. Federal law setting minimum-wage and overtime pay requirements.

_____ 17. Compensation in the form of money paid for time worked.

_____ 18. Employee who is of value because of the knowledge that he or she possesses.

_____ 19. Incentive-based pay plan that provides payment for each unit produced.

_____ 20. Instruction-based training in which knowledge and information are presented via computer.

_____ 21. Systematic evaluation of the duties, working conditions, tools, materials, and equipment related to the performance of a job.

_____ 22. Benefit plan that sets limits on benefits per employee, each of whom may choose from a variety of alternative benefits.

_____ 23. Practice of recruiting qualified employees belonging to racial, gender, or ethnic groups who are underrepresented in an organization.

_____ 24. Federal law forbidding employment discrimination on the basis of race, color, religious beliefs, sex, or national origin.

_____ 25. Performance rating method based on stated examples that reflect especially good or poor performance.

_____ 26. Worked-based training conducted in a simulated environment away from the work site.

_____ 27. Listing of each managerial position, who occupies it, how long that person will likely stay in the job, and who is qualified as a replacement.

_____ 28. Mandated coverage protecting employees who are laid off.

_____ 29. Form of sexual harassment in which sexual favors are requested in return for job-related benefits.

_____ 30. Performance-based pay plan basing part of compensation on employee merit.

_____ 31. Performance rating method using a numerical scale to rate performance along a set of dimensions.

_____ 32. Federal law requiring employers to provide unpaid leave for specified family and medical reasons.

_____ 33. Federal law forbidding discrimination against women who are pregnant.

_____ 34. Systematic analysis of jobs in an organization.

_____ 35. Performance appraisal system in which information is provided from all sources—supervisors, employees, peers, and so forth.

_____ 36. Practice of attracting people outside an organization to apply for jobs.

_____ 37. Legally mandated nondiscrimination in employment on the basis of race, creed, sex, or national origin.

_____ 38. Process of attracting qualified persons to apply for open jobs.

_____ 39. Group-based incentive plan in which employees are paid a share of company profits.

_____ 40. Performance appraisal method that ranks employees from best to worst.

_____ 41. Principle, increasingly modified by legislation and judicial decision, that organizations should be able to retain or dismiss employees at their discretion.

_____ 42. Set of organizational activities directed at attracting, developing, and maintaining an effective workforce.

_____ 43. Practice of considering present employees as candidates for job openings.

_____ 44. Legally required insurance covering workers who are injured or become ill on the job.

_____ 45. Set of rewards that organizations provide to individuals in return for their willingness to perform various jobs and tasks.

_____ 46. Federal law setting and enforcing guidelines for protecting workers from unsafe conditions and potential health hazards in the workplace.

_____ 47. Federal law requiring organizations to pay men and women the same pay for doing equal work.

_____ 48. Process of determining the predictive value of information.

_____ 49. Description of the skills, abilities, and other credentials required by a job.

_____ 50. Individual incentive plan rewarding employees with a percentage of sales volume that they generate.

_____ 51. Method used to obtain information about compensation paid to employees by other employers.

_____ 52. Form of sexual harassment, deriving from off-color jokes, lewd comments, and so forth, that makes the work environment uncomfortable for some employees.

_____ 53. Instructional-based training in which knowledge and information are descriptively presented.

_____ 54. Federal law prohibiting discrimination against people over 40 on the basis of age.

_____ 55. Process of introducing new employees to the organization so that they can more quickly become effective contributors.

_____ 56. Practice of discriminating against well-represented groups by over-hiring members of underrepresented groups.

_____ 57. Discrimination against protected classes that causes them to be unfairly differentiated from others.

_____ 58. Employee hired on something other than a full-time basis to supplement an organization's permanent work force.

_____ 59. Incentive-based pay plan that rewards individual performance on a real-time basis.

_____ 60. Work-based training in which employees are systematically moved from one job to another so that they can learn a wider array of tasks and skills.

_____ 61. Amendment that extends Title VII of the Civil Rights Act of 1964 and provides for compensatory and punitive damages.

_____ 62. Methods for determining the relative worth of jobs in order to set compensation levels.

_____ 63. Benefit in the form of programs designed to help employees from becoming sick.

_____ 64. Practice or instance of making unwelcome sexual advances in the workplace.

_____ 65. Performance-based pay plan rewarding employees for acquiring new skills or knowledge.

_____ 66. Compensation other than wages and salaries.

_____ 67. Mandated federal retirement program.

WORD SCRAMBLE

1. _____   2. _____   3. _____
    gasew   lasary   stifbene

LEARNING OBJECTIVES--POTENTIAL SHORT ANSWER OR ESSAY QUESTIONS

Learning Objective #1: **"Define *human resource management,* discuss its strategic significance, and explain how managers plan for human resources."**

Learning Objective #2: **"Identify the issues involved in *staffing* a company, including *internal* and *external recruiting* and *selection*."**

Learning Objective #3: **"Discuss different ways in which organizations go about developing the capabilities of employees and managers."**

Learning Objective #4: **"Explain ways in which organizations evaluate employee performance."**

Learning Objective #5: **"Discuss the importance of** *wages and salaries, incentives,* **and** *benefits programs* **in attracting and keeping skilled workers."**

Learning Objective #6: **"Describe some of the key legal issues involved in hiring, compensating, and managing workers in today's workplace."**

Learning Objective #7: **"Discuss** *workforce diversity,* **the management of** *knowledge workers,* **and the use of** *contingent and temporary workers* **as important changes in the contemporary workplace."**

CRITICAL THINKING QUESTIONS

1. Performance appraisals are almost always an anxious time for both employees and managers. Some experts argue that an effective way to reduce this anxiety is for managers and employees to get together ahead of time and define the specific criteria the employee will be judged by at appraisal time. How might this help to reduce the anxiety associated with performance appraisals?

2. What do you think are the benefits and costs of hiring someone to fill a new position from within the company? What about filling the job by hiring someone outside the company?

BRAIN TEASER

1. Why are many people opposed to comparable worth pay systems?

ANSWERS

True-False--*Answers*

1. True
2. True
3. False: The first step in staffing business organizations is to *plan, or to forecast future staffing needs.*
4. True
5. False: The first stage in the hiring process is to *select a small number of qualified candidates from all of the applications received.*
6. False: *Orientation* is the session or procedure for orienting a new employee to the organization.
7. True
8. True
9. True
10. False: Basic compensation refers to the *base* level of *wages or salary paid* to an employee.
11. False: Two general methods for compensating employees are through wages and salaries, *and through benefits (and services).*
12. True
13. True
14. False: *Profit sharing* is a group-based incentive system for distributing a portion of the company's profits to employees.
15. False: A benefit plan that allows an employee to choose from a variety of alternative benefits is called a *cafeteria benefit plan.*
16. True
17. False: The *Civil Rights* Act *of 1964* is a federal law forbidding discrimination on the basis of race, color, religious beliefs, sex, or national origin.
18. False: The practice of recruiting qualified employees belonging to racial, gender, or ethnic groups who are underrepresented in an organization is called *an affirmative action* plan.
19. True
20. False: Businesses are realizing that diversity in their workforce *increases* their competitive advantage.
21. False: In recent years the number of contingent workers employed has *risen* dramatically.

Multiple Choice--*Answers*

1. c	5. d	9. d	13. d
2. b	6. c	10. c	14. a
3. a	7. b	11. b	
4. c	8. d	12. a	

Jeopardy—*Answers*

	Staffing and Developing Human Resources	Compensation	The Legal Environment of Human Resource Management
$100	a job description	basic compensation (wages and salaries) and benefits	equal employment opportunity
$200	recruiting and hiring the right mix of people	health benefits	the Age Discrimination and Employment Act (ADEA)
$300	on-the-job training	sales commissions	the Equal Employment Opportunity Commission (EEOC)
$400	systematic job rotation and transfer	private pension plans	reverse discrimination

$500	training and development programs	a cafeteria benefit plan	sexual harassment

Match the Terms and Concepts to Their Definitions--*Answers*

1. p	9. ccc	17. z	25. x	33. yy	41. lll	49. d	57. ss	65. ee
2. aa	10. mmm	18. nnn	26. n	34. b	42. a	50. hh	58. ooo	66. kk
3. ggg	11. ii	19. ff	27. e	35. t	43. h	51. bb	59. gg	67. mm
4. aaa	12. v	20. r	28. ll	36. i	44. nn	52. kkk	60. o	
5. f	13. m	21. c	29. jjj	37. rr	45. y	53. q	61. zz	
6. oo	14. ww	22. qq	30. dd	38. g	46. hhh	54. xx	62. cc	
7. l	15. s	23. ddd	31. w	39. jj	47. vv	55. k	63. pp	
8. tt	16. fff	24. uu	32. bbb	40. u	48. j	56. eee	64. iii	

Word Scramble--*Answers*

1. wages   2. salary   3. benefits

Learning Objectives--Potential Short Answer or Essay Questions--*Answers*

Learning Objective #1:

Human resource management, or *HRM,* is the set of organizational activities directed at attracting, developing, and maintaining an effective workforce. HRM plays a key strategic role in organizational performance. Planning for human resource needs entails several steps. Conducting a *job analysis* enables managers to create detailed, accurate job descriptions and specifications. After analysis is complete, managers must *forecast* demand and supply for both the numbers and types of workers they will need. Then they consider steps to match supply with demand.

Learning Objective #2:

Recruiting is the process of attracting qualified persons to apply for jobs that an organization has open. *Internal recruiting* involves considering present employees for new jobs. This approach helps build morale and rewards an organization's best employees. *External recruiting* means attracting people from outside the organization to apply for openings. When organizations are actually selecting people for jobs, they generally use such selection techniques as *application blanks, tests, interviews,* and other techniques. Regardless of what selection techniques are used, they must be valid predictors of an individual's expected performance in the job.

Learning Objective #3:

If a company is to get the most out of its workers, it must develop both those workers and their skills. Nearly all employees undergo some initial *orientation* process that introduces them to the company and to their new jobs. Many employees are given the opportunity to acquire new skills through various *work-based* and/or *instructional-based programs*.

Learning Objective #4:

Performance appraisals help managers decide who needs training and who should be promoted. Appraisals also tell employees how well they are meeting expectations. Although a variety of alternatives are available for appraising performance, employee supervisors are most commonly used. No matter who does the evaluation, however, feedback to the employee is very important. Managers can select from a variety of ranking and rating methods for use in performance appraisal.

Learning Objective #5:

Wages and salaries, incentives, and *benefit packages* may all be parts of a company's *compensation program*. By paying its workers as well as or better than competitors, a business can attract and keep qualified personnel. Incentive programs can also motivate people to work more productively. *Indirect compensation* also plays a major role in effective and well-designed compensation systems.

Learning Objective #6:

In hiring, compensating, and managing workers, managers must obey a variety of federal laws. *Equal employment opportunity* and *equal pay* laws forbid discrimination other than action based on legitimate job requirements. The concept of *comparable worth* holds that different jobs requiring equal levels of training and skill should pay the same. Firms are also required to provide employees with safe working environments, as set down by the guidelines of the *Occupational Safety and Health Administration*. Managers must consider *employment-at-will* issues (that is, limitations on their rights to hire and fire at their own discretion). AIDS and *sexual harassment* are other key contemporary legal issues in business.

Learning Objective #7:

Workforce diversity refers to the range of workers' attitudes, values, beliefs, and behaviors that differ by gender, race, ethnicity, age, and physical ability. Today, many U.S. businesses are working to create workforces that reflect the growing diversity of the population as it enters the labor pool. Although many firms see the diverse workforce as a competitive advantage, not all are equally successful in or eager about implementing diversity programs.

Many firms today also face challenges in managing *knowledge workers*. The recent boom in high-technology companies has led to rapidly increasing salaries and high turnover among the workers who are best prepared to work in those companies. *Contingent workers* are temporary and part-time employees hired to supplement an organization's permanent work force. Their numbers have grown significantly since the early 1980s and are expected to rise further. The practice of hiring contingent workers is gaining in popularity because it gives managers more flexibility and because temps are usually not covered by employers' benefit programs.

Critical Thinking Questions--*Answers*

1. When managers and their employees work together in defining the specific criteria the employee will be judged by at performance appraisal time makes the measurement of performance at appraisal time easier. This is because the criteria by which performance will be measured would have been largely worked out in advance.

1. A benefit of hiring from within the firm is that the employee is already familiar with the organization and its culture. Another benefit is that it rewards hard work by reminding people that promotions are a realistic possibility. Some of the costs of hiring from within include the loss of an opportunity to "bring in new blood," and it may create some undesired animosity by those employees passed over.

The benefits and costs of hiring from outside the company are the converse of those described above. That is, hiring from outside provides an opportunity to bring in new ideas, and it precludes the necessity of having to choose from many current qualified employees. The costs include having to train and assimilate the new employee into the company.

Brain Teaser--*Answer*

1. Comparable worth pay systems are essentially comparable pay for comparable work. Comparable worth pay systems are opposed by some because of the difficulty in determining what is comparable. Who is going to determine what is comparable? Moreover, comparable worth reduces the ability of market forces (demand and supply forces) to operate and to determine wages. The fear is that this could give rise to some shortages or surpluses of certain types of workers. Nevertheless, everyone is in agreement that in some cases the "market forces" at play in real-world labor markets have given rise to inequities.

Chapter 9
Motivating, Satisfying, and Leading Employees

LEARNING OBJECTIVES
After studying this chapter, you should be able to:

1. Describe the nature and importance of *psychological contracts* in the workplace.
2. Discuss the importance of *job satisfaction* and *employee morale* and summarize their roles in human relations in the workplace.
3. Identify and summarize the most important *theories of employee motivation.*
4. Describe some of the strategies used by organizations to improve *job satisfaction* and *employee motivation.*
5. Discuss different managerial styles of *leadership* and their impact on human relations in the workplace.

TRUE-FALSE
Indicate whether the statement is generally true or false by placing a "T" or "F" in the space provided. If it is a false statement, correct it so that it becomes a true statement.

_____ 1. All organizations face the basic challenge of managing psychological contracts.

_____ 2. The key to increasing worker morale and productivity is to demonstrate to employees that their individual needs are different than the needs of the organization.

_____ 3. Evidence suggests that job satisfaction and employee morale may directly affect a company's performance.

_____ 4. In Frederick Taylor's view (the scientific management approach), people are motivated almost exclusively by money.

_____ 5. According to the Hawthorne effect, workers will be more productive if they believe they are receiving less special attention from managers.

_____ 6. Theory X argues that people are naturally responsible, growth oriented, self-motivated, and interested in being productive.

_____ 7. In attempting to motivate employees, Theory Y would emphasize management authority, and Theory X would emphasize employee growth and self-direction.

_____ 8. The most basic of needs according to Maslow's hierarchy are the self-actualization needs.

_____ 9. In Maslow's hierarchy of needs, the need for esteem can be met through job security and pension plans.

_____ 10. Hygiene factors such as working conditions, company policies, and job security have a negative effect on motivation only if they are deficient.

_____ 11. Motivators such as achievement, recognition, and responsibility are related negatively to increases in productivity.

_____ 12. The expectancy theory of motivation argues that people are motivated to work toward rewards that they want and that they believe they have a reasonable chance of obtaining.

_____ 13. The equity theory of motivation argues that people evaluate their treatment by employers relative to the treatment of others.

_____ 14. "Reinforcement" is used when a company pays piecework rewards.

_____ 15. "Management by objectives" is a set of procedures involving both managers and subordinates in setting goals and evaluating progress.

_____ 16. Goal setting is most effective as a means of increasing employee motivation when those goals are imposed from above.

_____ 17. Employee empowerment can be an effective motivational tool.

_____ 18. Job sharing is a method of increasing job satisfaction by allowing workers to adjust work schedules on a daily or weekly basis.

_____ 19. Job enrichment reduces specialization and makes work more meaningful by expanding each job's responsibilities.

_____ 20. The autocratic style of management is one in which managers generally ask for input from subordinates but retain final decision-making power.

_____ 21. Studies suggest that workers today are very interested in flexible working hours.

_____ 22. The challenges that make motivating workers difficult stem from changes in the economy, the work force, and organizational cultures.

MULTIPLE CHOICE

Circle the one best answer for each of the following questions.

1. Managers need to
    a. realize the importance of maintaining good relations with their employees.
    b. create a climate of openness and trust with their employees.
    c. realize that leadership, motivation, and communication are the major elements that contribute to good human relations.
    d. do all of the above.

2. Which of the following statements is true?
    a. Morale is the overall attitude that employees have toward their workplace.
    b. Job satisfaction is the degree of enjoyment that people derive from performing their jobs.
    c. Some of the most profitable companies are those with the greatest job satisfaction and highest employee morale.
    d. All of the above.

3. Frederick Taylor
    a. developed *scientific management*, a management approach that seeks to improve employee efficiency through the scientific study of work.
    b. believed workers are primarily motivated by a need to be loved and to feel a sense of belonging.
    c. believed paying workers more would reduce productivity.
    d. All of the above.

4. According to Maslow's hierarchy of needs,
    a. the higher levels of the hierarchy need to be satisfied before the lower-level needs can be addressed.
    b. the lowest level is self-actualization—the need to become everything one is capable of.
    c. the need for esteem relates to the feelings of self-worth and respect from others.
    d. the social needs are the most basic requirements for human life, and are seldom strong motivators for modern wage earners.

5. Employers providing job security and pension plans would best fulfill which of the following needs of workers?
    a. Physiological
    b. Safety (or security) needs
    c. Social needs
    d. Esteem needs

6. Employers giving employees the opportunity to expand their skills and take on additional responsibility would help satisfy which needs of workers?
    a. Security (or safety) needs
    b. Social needs
    c. Self-actualization needs
    d. Esteem needs

7. The Two-Factor Theory emphasized which two factors?
   a. Hygiene factors and motivators
   b. Social needs and physiological needs
   c. Money and job security
   d. Job enrichment and job sharing

8. According to the Two-Factor Theory,
   a. management may lessen dissatisfaction by improving hygiene factors that concern employees, but such improvements won't influence satisfaction.
   b. management can help employees feel more motivated by paying attention to motivators such as achievement, recognition, responsibility, and other personally rewarding factors.
   c. a skilled, well-paid employee may be motivated to perform better if motivators are supplied, but a young, unskilled or insecure employee who earns low wages will probably still need the support of strong hygiene factors to reduce dissatisfaction before the motivators can be effective.
   d. All of the above.

9. Theory X assumes
   a. employees are irresponsible.
   b. employees are not ambitious and dislike work.
   c. managers must use force, control, or threats to motivate workers.
   d. All of the above.

10. Which of the following is *not* associated with Theory Y?
    a. Employees like work.
    b. Employees are naturally committed to certain goals and are capable of creativity.
    c. Managers must use force, control, or threats to motivate workers.
    d. Employees seek out responsibility under the right circumstances.

11. Which of the following statements is true?
    a. The assumptions behind Theory X emphasize management authority.
    b. The assumptions behind Theory Y emphasize employee growth and self-direction.
    c. Managers who adopt the Expectancy Theory should focus on the increased job responsibilities workers strive for, and establish realistic steps to allow workers to achieve their goals.
    d. All of the above.

12. Which of the following statements is true?
    a. Management by objectives occurs when managers dictate goals to subordinates and evaluate workers based on their ability to realize these goals.
    b. The equity theory of motivation argues that people evaluate their treatment by employers relative to the treatment of others.
    c. Allowing workers a voice in company policy usually reduces morale because it increases the responsibility of workers.
    d. Flextime programs are a method of increasing job satisfaction by designing a more satisfactory fit between workers and their jobs.

13. Companies are trying to motivate their workers more by
    a. allowing employees to set clear and challenging personal goals that support organizational goals.
    b. using reinforcement.
    c. offering job rotation programs.
    d. All of the above.

14. Job enrichment is
    a. a method of increasing job satisfaction by adding one or more motivating factors to job activities.
    b. a scheduling system in which employees are allowed certain options regarding time arrival and departure.
    c. slicing a few hours off everybody's workweek and cutting pay to minimize layoffs.
    d. splitting a single full-time job between two employees for their convenience.

15. The management style in which managers generally issue orders and expect them to be obeyed without question is the
    a. autocratic management style of leadership.
    b. democratic management style of leadership.
    c. free-rein management style of leadership.
    d. oligarchic management style of leadership.

16. Leadership styles in the twenty-first century will most likely move in the direction of
    a. a less autocratic approach to decision-making.
    b. a greater awareness of diversity in the workforce.
    c. a more "network" mentality rather than a "hierarchical" one.
    d. All of the above.

JEOPARDY

You have 5 seconds to complete the question to each of the following answers.

	Motivation Theory	**Motivational Techniques**	**Managerial Styles and Leadership**
$100	The two-factor theory emphasizes these two elements of motivation. What are_____ _____?	The systematic use of rewards and punishments to change behavior. What is_____ _____?	The management style where managers dictate to workers and workers are expected to follow orders. What is_____ _____?
$200	This theory assumes employees dislike work and that managers must use threats to motivate them. What is_____ _____?	Scheduling system in which employees are allowed certain options regarding time of arrival and departure. What is_____ _____?	The management style where managers generally ask for input from subordinates but retain final decision-making power. What is_____ _____?
$300	This theory emphasizes the need for managers to treat all employees fairly. What is_____ _____?	Reducing work specialization and making work more meaningful by adding to the responsibilities of each job. What is_____ _____?	The management style where managers typically serve as advisers to subordinates who are allowed to make decisions. What is_____ _____?
$400	This theory assumes employees like work and seek out responsibility. What is_____	Working from home and communicating with the company's main office via computer and communication devices. What is_____	The management style usually most effective in the military. What is_____

	_____?	_____?	_____?
$500	Maslow's hierarchy of needs from the lowest to the highest. What is_____ _____?	Splitting a single full-time job between two employees for their convenience. What is_____ _____?	The management style most appropriate as a chairperson of a voluntary committee. What is_____ _____?

MATCH THE TERMS AND CONCEPTS TO THEIR DEFINITIONS

a. psychological contract
b. human relations
c. job satisfaction
d. morale
e. motivation
f. classical theory of motivation
g. Hawthorne effect
h. Theory X
i. Theory Y
j. hierarchy of human needs model

k. two-factory theory
l. expectancy theory
m. equity theory
n. reinforcement
o. management by objectives (MBO)
p. participative management and empowerment
q. job enrichment
r. job redesign
s. work sharing (or job sharing)

t. flextime programs
u. telecommuting
v. leadership
w. managerial style
x. autocratic style
y. democratic style
z. free-rein style
aa. contingency approach

_____ 1. Theory that behavior can be encouraged or discouraged by means of rewards or punishments.

_____ 2. Method of increasing job satisfaction by designing a more satisfactory fit between workers and their jobs.

_____ 3. Managerial style in which managers typically serve as advisers to subordinates who are allowed to make decisions.

_____ 4. Theory of motivation holding that people are naturally responsible, growth oriented, self-motivated, and interested in being productive.

_____ 5. Theory of motivation holding that people are motivated to work toward rewards that they want and that they believe they have a reasonable chance of obtaining.

_____ 6. Degree of enjoyment that people derive from performing their jobs.

_____ 7. Managerial style in which managers generally issue orders and expect them to be obeyed without question.

_____ 8. Method of increasing job satisfaction by giving employees a voice in the management of their jobs and the company.

_____ 9. Method of increasing job satisfaction by allowing workers to adjust work schedules on a daily or weekly basis.

_____ 10. Process of motivating others to work to meet specific objectives.

_____ 11. Interactions between employers and employees and their attitudes toward one another.

_____ 12. Managerial style in which managers generally ask for input from subordinates but retain final decision-making power.

_____ 13. Theory holding that workers are motivated solely by money.

_____ 14. Theory of motivation holding that people evaluate their treatment by employers relative to the treatment of others.

_____ 15. Set of expectations held by an employee concerning what he or she will contribute to an organization (referred to as *contributions*) and what the organization will in return provide the employee (referred to as *inducements*).

_____ 16. Approach to managerial style holding that the appropriate behavior in any situation is dependent (contingent) on the unique elements of that situation.

_____ 17. Method of increasing job satisfaction by adding one or more motivating factors to job activities.

_____ 18. Form of flextime that allows people to perform some or all of a job away from standard office settings.

_____ 19. Pattern of behavior that a manager exhibits in dealing with subordinates.

_____ 20. Overall attitude that employees have toward their workplace.

_____ 21. Theory of motivation describing five levels of human needs and arguing that basic needs must be fulfilled before people work to satisfy higher-level needs.

_____ 22. Method of increasing job satisfaction by allowing two or more people to share a single full-time job.

_____ 23. The set of forces that cause people to behave in certain ways.

_____ 24. Set of procedures involving both managers and subordinates in setting goals and evaluating progress.

_____ 25. Theory of motivation holding that job satisfaction depends on two types of factors, hygiene and motivation.

_____ 26. Tendency for productivity to increase when workers believe they are receiving special attention from management.

_____ 27. Theory of motivation holding that people are naturally irresponsible and uncooperative.

WORD SCRAMBLE

1. _____ _____   2. _____   3. _____
   krow   grashin   metfixel   roamel

LEARNING OBJECTIVES--POTENTIAL SHORT ANSWER OR ESSAY QUESTIONS

Learning Objective #1: "Describe the nature and importance of *psychological contracts* in the workplace."

Learning Objective #2: "Discuss the importance of *job satisfaction* and *employee morale* and summarize their roles in human relations in the workplace."

Learning Objective #3: "Identify and summarize the most important *theories of employee motivation*."

Learning Objective #4: "Describe some of the strategies used by organizations to improve *job satisfaction* and *employee motivation*."

Learning Objective #5: "Discuss different managerial styles of *leadership* and their impact on human relations in the workplace."

CRITICAL THINKING QUESTIONS

1. For each of the following, determine which of Maslow's hierarchy of needs management might be trying to meet.

   a. The company offers workers a wage sufficient to pay "the rent."

   b. The company offers workers health care benefits, sick leave pay, and a company-paid vacation as well as a company-paid life insurance package.

   c. Management encourages employees to play on the company softball or bowling team, to bring their families to the annual picnic, and to come to the annual Christmas party, etc.

   d. The company initiates an annual awards banquet that is also a "roast and toast" opportunity.

   e. The company will compensate employees for coursework obtained at an accredited college or university or offer a sabbatical for the same or similar reasons.

2. Within the context of this chapter, can you provide a historical explanation for one reason why unions were developed?

BRAIN TEASER

1. Some managers of production facilities in less developed foreign countries with less aggressive work ethics have found it challenging to motivate their workers. From what you have read in this chapter, what would you propose?

ANSWERS

True-False--*Answers*

1. True
2. False: The key to increasing worker morale and productivity is to demonstrate to employees that their individual needs *coincide with* than the needs of the organization.
3. True
4. True
5. False: According to the Hawthorne effect, workers will be more productive if they believe they are receiving *more* special attention from managers.
6. False: Theory *Y* argues that people are naturally responsible, growth oriented, self motivated, and interested in being productive.
7. False: In attempting to motivate employees, Theory *X* would emphasize management authority, and Theory *Y* would emphasize employee growth and self-direction.
8. False: The most basic of needs according to Maslow's hierarchy are the *physiological needs.*
9. False: In Maslow's hierarchy of needs, the need for esteem can be met *by motivational techniques of recognition such as a job title.*
10. True
11. False: Motivators such as achievement, recognition, and responsibility are related *positively* to increases in productivity.
12. True
13. True
14. True
15. True
16. False: Goal setting is most effective as a means of increasing employee motivation when *employees have input into the creation of clear and challenging--but achievable--goals.*
17. True
18. False: *Flextime* is a method of increasing job satisfaction by allowing workers to adjust work schedules on a daily or weekly basis.
19. True
20. False: The *democratic* style of management is one in which managers generally ask for input from subordinates but retain final decision-making power.
21. True
22. True

Multiple Choice--*Answers*

1. d	5. b	9. d	13. d
2. d	6. c	10. c	14. a
3. a	7. a	11. d	15. a
4. c	8. d	12. b	16. d

Jeopardy--*Answers*

	Motivation Theory	**Motivational Techniques**	**Managerial Styles and Leadership**
$100	hygiene factors and motivators	reinforcement	the autocratic management style
$200	Theory X	flextime	the democratic management style
$300	equity theory	job enrichment	the free-rein management style
$400	Theory Y	telecommuting	the autocratic management style

$500	physiological, safety, social, esteem, and self-actualization	work (or job) sharing	the free-rein management style

Match the Terms and Concepts to Their Definitions--*Answers*

1. n	6. c	11. b	16. aa	21. j	26. g
2. r	7. x	12. y	17. q	22. s	27. h
3. z	8. p	13. f	18. u	23. e	
4. i	9. t	14. m	19. w	24. o	
5. l	10. v	15. a	20. d	25. k	

Word Scramble--*Answers*

1. work sharing   2. flextime   3. morale

Learning Objectives--Potential Short Answer or Essay Questions--*Answers*

Learning Objective #1:

A *psychological contract* is the set of expectations held by an employee concerning what he or she will contribute to an organization (referred to as *contributions*) and what the organization will in return provide to the employee (referred to as *inducements*). Until the last decade or so, businesses generally offered their employees high levels of job security and employees were very loyal to their employers. More recently, however, new psychological contracts have been created in many sectors. Now, organizations offer less security but more benefits. In turn, employees are often willing to work longer hours but are also more willing to leave an employer for a better opportunity elsewhere.

Learning Objective #2:

Good *human relations*—the interactions between employers and employees and their attitudes toward one another—are important to business because they lead to high levels of *job satisfaction* (the degree of enjoyment that workers derive from their jobs) and *morale* (workers' overall attitudes toward their workplaces). Satisfied employees generally exhibit lower levels of absenteeism and turnover. They also have fewer grievances and engage in fewer negative behaviors.

Learning Objective #3:

Views of employee motivation have changed dramatically over the years. The *classical theory* holds that people are motivated solely by money. *Scientific management* tried to analyze jobs and increase production by finding better ways to perform tasks. The *Hawthorne studies* were the first to demonstrate the importance of making workers feel that their needs were being considered. The *human resources model* identifies two kinds of managers—*Theory X managers*, who believe that people are inherently uncooperative and must be constantly punished or rewarded, and *Theory Y managers*, who believe that people are naturally responsible and self-motivated to be productive.

Maslow's *hierarchy of needs model* proposes that people have several different needs (ranging from physiological to self-actualization), which they attempt to satisfy in their work. People must fulfill lower-level needs before seeking to fulfill higher-level needs. *Two-factor theory* suggests that if basic hygiene factors are not met, workers will be dissatisfied. Only by increasing more complex motivation factors can companies increase employees' performance.

Expectancy theory holds that people will work hard if they believe that their efforts will lead to desired rewards. *Equity theory* says that motivation depends on the way employees evaluate their treatment by an organization relative to its treatment of other workers.

Learning Objective #4:

Managers can use several strategies to increase employee satisfaction and motivation. The principle of *reinforcement*, or *behavior modification theory*, holds that reward and punishment can control behavior. *Rewards*, for example, are positive reinforcement when they are tied directly to desired or improved performance. *Punishment* (using unpleasant consequences to change undesirable behavior) is generally less effective.

Management by objectives (a system of collaborative goal setting) and *participative management and empowerment* (techniques for giving employees a voice in management decisions) can improve human relations by making an employee feel like part of a team. *Job enrichment, job redesign*, and *modified work schedules* (including *work-share programs, flextime*, and *alternative workplace strategies*) can enhance job satisfaction by adding motivation factors to jobs in which they are normally lacking.

Learning Objective #5:

Effective *leadership*—the process of motivating others to meet specific objectives—is an important determinant of employee satisfaction and motivation. Generally speaking, managers practice one of three basic managerial styles. *Autocratic managers* generally issue orders that they expect to be obeyed. *Democratic managers* generally seek subordinates' input into decisions. *Free-rein managers* are more likely to advise than to make decisions. The *contingency approach to leadership* views appropriate managerial behavior in any situation as dependent on the elements of that situation. Managers thus need to assess situations carefully, especially to determine the desire of subordinates to share input or exercise creativity. They must also be aware of the changing nature of both motivation and leadership as we move into the twenty-first century.

Critical Thinking Questions--*Answers*

1. a. Physiological needs
    b. Security (safety) needs
    c. Social needs
    d. Esteem (and social) needs
    e. Self-actualization needs

2. Generally, and historically speaking, unions were developed because management did a poor job of fulfilling workers' needs. Moreover, too many managers were operating under the assumptions of Theory X, which emphasizes management authority. Most workers have resented that kind of treatment.

Brain Teaser--*Answer*

1. There is no "correct" answer for this question. However, according to Maslow's theory, a satisfied need is not a motivator. Therefore, it may be helpful to try to get the employees to find new "needs" and to inform them of the things they can afford to buy (washing machines, better clothing, home electronics, etc.) if they simply work harder and receive the higher compensation as a consequence of their hard work. Evidence indicates that this has been somewhat successful in increasing some foreign workers' productivity. Nevertheless, assuming hygiene factors are met, then other motivators (working conditions, company policies, job security, etc.) need to be focused on. Those motivators need to be adapted to the foreign culture.

Chapter 10

Understanding Labor and Management Relations

LEARNING OBJECTIVES
After studying this chapter, you should be able to:

1. Explain why workers unionize.
2. Trace the evolution and discuss trends in *unionism* in the United States.
3. Describe the *major laws governing labor-management relations.*
4. Describe the union *certification* and *decertification processes.*
5. Identify the steps in the *collective bargaining process.*

TRUE-FALSE
Indicate whether the statement is generally true or false by placing a "T" or "F" in the space provided. If it is a false statement, correct it so that it becomes a true statement.

_____ 1. Unions were first created in response to their rather harsh treatment by management.

_____ 2. Industrial unions, which developed first, are composed of people who perform a particular type of skilled work, such as carpentry.

_____ 3. Most labor legislation was enacted in the 1930s and 1940s.

_____ 4. Since the mid-1950s, there has been an increase in the percentage of workers whom are members of labor unions.

_____ 5. In recent years, some companies have worked to create much more employee-friendly work environments and to treat all employees with respect and dignity, in part to reduce the desire for workers to want to unionize.

_____ 6. More and more unions are asking for—and often getting—voices in the management of the companies that employ them.

_____ 7. A national union is a union organized at the level of a single company, plant, or small geographic region.

_____ 8. A business agent is a full-time official who acts as a liaison between members of a large union and their supervisors.

_____ 9. The Norris-LaGuardia Act of 1932 established a minimum wage and outlawed child labor.

_____ 10. The Fair Labor Standards Act of 1938 mandated time-and-a-half pay for those who worked beyond the legally stipulated number of hours.

_____ 11. The Labor-Management Relations Act (Taft-Harley Act) protects the rights of workers to form unions, bargain collectively, and engage in strikes to achieve their goals.

_____ 12. The National Labor Relations Act (Wagner Act) defined certain union practices as unfair and illegal.

_____ 13. A union shop is a workplace in which workers must join a union within a specified period after being hired.

_____ 14. Right-to work laws make it illegal to require union membership as a condition of employment.

_____ 15. The Labor-Management Reporting and Disclosure Act (Landrum-Griffin Act) imposed regulations on internal union procedures, including elections of national leaders and filing of financial disclosure statements.

_____ 16. After defining the bargaining unit, the next step in unionizing is to request a certification election.

_____ 17. When the National Labor Relations Board (NLRB) holds a secret ballot election to determine unionization, if a simple majority of those voting approves the certification, the union then becomes the official bargaining agent of eligible employees.

_____ 18. Unions once established cannot be decertified.

_____ 19. Collective bargaining is an ongoing process involving both the drafting and the administering of the terms of a labor contract.

_____ 20. The items typically most important to union negotiators are compensation, benefits, and job security.

_____ 21. Bargaining items between unionized workers and management usually fall into two categories: mandatory items and permissive items.

_____ 22. A strike occurs when workers perform jobs at a slower pace than normal.

_____ 23. A boycott occurs when workers publicize their grievances at the entrance to an employer's facility.

_____ 24. If workers walk off their jobs, management can legally replace them with strikebreakers.

_____ 25. Voluntary arbitration is a method of resolving a labor dispute in which both parties are legally required to accept the judgement of a neutral party.

MULTIPLE CHOICE
Circle the one best answer for each of the following questions.

1. Which of the following is true concerning unions?
   a. An industrial union is made up of skilled craftspeople whose common interest is a specific skilled job.
   b. A craft union represents workers within an industry rather than skill or occupation.
   c. Labor unions were first created in response to the rather harsh conditions imposed on them by management.
   d. All of the above.

2. Which of the following is true about unions?
   a. Since the mid-1950s, labor unions in the United States have experienced increasing difficulties in attracting new members.
   b. Many of today's unions are less concerned in negotiating for higher wages and are more interested in other benefits like job security and improved pension programs.
   c. Despite declining membership and some loss of power, labor unions remain a major factor in the U.S. business world.
   d. All of the above.

3. Which of the following is a reason for the decline in union influence in recent years?
   a. Increased global competition has shifted to other countries many jobs that were traditionally unionized.
   b. In recent decades, there has been a more aggressive anti-unionization activity on the part of employers.
   c. The workforce today is composed of many more women and minorities that have much weaker traditions of union affiliation.
   d. All of the above.

4. The federal law protecting the rights of workers to form unions, bargain collectively, and engage in strikes to achieve their goals is the:
   a. Labor-Management Reporting and Disclosure Act (Landrum-Griffin Act).
   b. National Labor Relations Act (Wagner Act.)
   c. Labor-Management Relations Act (Taft-Hartley Act).
   d. Fair Labor Standards Act.

5. The federal law that addressed issues of minimum wages and maximum work hours was the
   a. Fair Labor Standards Act.
   b. National Labor Relations Act (Wagner Act.)
   c. Labor-Management Relations Act (Taft-Hartley Act).
   d. Labor-Management Reporting and Disclosure Act (Landrum-Griffin Act).

6. The Federal law defining certain union practices as unfair and illegal was the
   a. Fair Labor Standards Act.
   b. National Labor Relations Act (Wagner Act.)
   c. Labor-Management Relations Act (Taft-Hartley Act).
   d. Labor-Management Reporting and Disclosure Act (Landrum-Griffin Act).

7. A workplace in which workers must join a union within a specified period after being hired is
   a. a union shop.
   b. a closed shop.
   c. an agency shop.
   d. a yellow dog contract.

8. A workplace in which workers must pay union dues even if they do not join the union is
   a. a union shop.
   b. a closed shop.
   c. an agency shop.
   d. a yellow dog contract.

9. Right-to-work laws
   a. require workers to join the union as a condition of employment.
   b. make it illegal to require union membership as a condition of employment.
   c. require workers to hire only workers already belonging to the union.
   d. require workers to begin and continue employment without union affiliation.

10. After defining the bargaining unit, the next step in forming a union is to have
    a. at least 75% of the workers sign authorization cards; and then the management must recognize the union.
    b. at least 30% of the workers sign authorization cards; and then request the National Labor Relations Board to sponsor a certification election.
    c. at least 50% of the workers sign authorization cards; then management must recognize the union.
    d. workers request an election from the National Labor Relations Board; if at least 30% of the workers vote for authorization, then the union is certified and issues authorization cards to its members.

11. Which of the following is true of negotiations between a union and management?
    a. Permissive items are bargaining items that must be discussed in collective bargaining.
    b. Mediation is the process for resolving a labor contract dispute in which an impartial third party studies the issues and imposes a binding decision.
    c. A cost of living adjustment is a clause tying future raises to changes in consumer purchasing power.
    d. Very few unions negotiate for better pay and benefits.

12. Issues that may be subject to negotiation in the collective bargaining process include
    a. job security..
    b. compensation.
    c. benefits.
    d. All of the above.

13. Which of the following statements is true?
    a. A wage reopener clause allows wage rates to be re-negotiated during the life of a labor contract.
    b. A strikebreaker is a method of resolving a labor dispute in which a third party suggests, but does not impose, a settlement.
    c. Picketing is labor action in which workers refuse to buy the products of a targeted employer.
    d. A lockout is labor action in which employees temporarily walk off the job and refuse to work.

14. A wildcat strike is a
    a. strike that is unauthorized by the striker's union.
    b. strike in which one union strikes to support action initiated by another.
    c. labor action in which workers refuse to buy the products of a targeted employer.
    d. labor action in which workers perform jobs at a slower pace than normal.

15. Which of the following is an option for labor in the event that negotiations with management break down?
    a. Employ strikebreakers.
    b. Institute a lockout.
    c. Impose a boycott.
    d. Fire all strikers.

16. Which of the following is an option for management in the event that negotiations with labor break down?
    a. Go on strike.
    b. Seek a pact with other companies in the industry.
    c. Impose a slowdown.
    d. Implement a boycott.

17. Which of the following is true concerning labor-management relations?
    a. Employees and managers are becoming more cooperative and less adversarial.
    b. To enhance labor-management relations, management could offer better pay and working conditions, establish grievance procedures, comply with legislation that protects employee rights, and involve workers in the operation of the business.
    c. To enhance labor-management relations, labor could help management find ways to cut costs, accept more flexible compensation packages, and reduce cumbersome work rules.
    d. All of the above.

18. Compulsory arbitration is
    a. a method of resolving a labor dispute in which a third party suggests, but does not impose, a settlement.
    b. is a management tactic whereby workers are denied access to the employer's workplace.
    c. method of resolving a labor dispute in which both parties agree to submit to the judgement of a neutral party.
    d. method of resolving a labor dispute in which both parties are legally required to accept the judgement of a neutral party.

JEOPARDY

You have 5 seconds to complete the question to each of the following answers.

	Unions	Collective Bargaining	Options When Negotiations Break Down
$100	An organization of workers by industry rather than skill or occupation. What is_____ _____?	Designated group of employees who will be represented by a union What is_____ _____?	Labor action in which workers publicize their grievances at the entrance to an employer's facility. What is_____ _____?
$200	The recent trend in union membership. What is_____ _____?	Labor contract clause tying future raises to changes in consumer purchasing power. What is_____ _____?	Nonunion workers hired to replace striking workers. What is_____ _____?
$300	Union organized at the level of a single company, plant, or small geographic region. What is_____ _____?	A clause allowing wage rates to be renegotiated during the life of a labor contract. What is_____ _____?	Labor action in which workers refuse to buy the products of a targeted employer. What is_____ _____?
$400	Union employee who acts as liaison between union members and supervisors. What is_____ _____?	The three categories of issues that are typically most important to union negotiators. What is_____ _____?	Management tactic whereby workers are denied aces to the employer's workplace. What is_____ _____?
$500	The three steps in creating a union. What is_____ _____?	A bargaining item which both parties must negotiate if either wants to. What is_____ _____?	Method of resolving a labor dispute, in which a third party suggests, but does not impose a settlement. What is_____ _____?

MATCH THE TERMS AND CONCEPTS TO THEIR DEFINITIONS

a. labor union
b. labor relations
c. industrial unionism
d. Congress of Industrial Organization (CIO)
e. local union (local)
f. shop steward
g. business agent (or business representative)
h. Norris-LaGuardia Act
i. yellow-dog contract
j. National Labor Relations Act (Wagner Act)
k. National Labor Relations Board (NLRB)

l. Fair Labor Standards Act
m. Labor-Management Relations Act (Taft-Hartley Act)
n. closed shop
o. right-to-work laws
p. union shop
q. agency shop
r. Labor-Management Reporting and Disclosure Act (Landrum-Griffin Act)
s. bargaining unit
t. cost-of-living adjustment (COLA)
u. wage reopener clause
v. strike

w. economic strike
x. sympathy strike (or secondary strike)
y. wildcat strike
z. picketing
aa. boycott
bb. slowdown
cc. lockout
dd. strikebreaker
ee. mediation
ff. voluntary arbitration
gg. compulsory arbitration

_____ 1. Process of dealing with employees who are represented by a union.

_____ 2. Federal law (1935) protecting the rights of workers to form unions, bargain collectively, and engage in strikes to achieve their goals.

_____ 3. Workplace in which workers must join a union within a specified period after being hired.

_____ 4. Full-time official who acts as liaison between members of a large union and their supervisors.

_____ 5. Strike usually triggered by stalemate over one or more mandatory bargaining items.

_____ 6. Method of resolving a labor dispute in which a third party suggests, but does not impose, a settlement.

_____ 7. Labor action in which workers refuse to buy the products of a targeted employer.

_____ 8. Union organized at the level of a single company, plant, or small geographic region.

_____ 9. Federal law (1947) defining certain union practices as unfair and illegal.

_____ 10. Designated group of employees who will be represented by a union.

_____ 11. A group of individuals working together to achieve shared job-related goals, such as higher pay, shorter working hours, more job security, greater benefits, or better working conditions.

_____ 12. Management tactic whereby workers are denied access to the employer's workplace.

_____ 13. Federal law (1959) imposing regulations on internal union procedures, including elections of national leaders and filing of financial disclosure statements.

_____ 14. Federal agency established by the National Labor Relations Act to enforce its provisions.

_____ 15. Method of resolving a labor dispute in which both parties agree to submit to the judgment of a neutral party.

_____ 16. Strike that is unauthorized by the strikers' union.

_____ 17. Clause allowing wage rates to be renegotiated during the life of a labor contract.

_____ 18. Organizing of workers by industry rather than skill or occupation.

_____ 19. Illegal contract clause requiring workers to begin and continue employment without union affiliation.

_____ 20. Labor contract clause tying future raises to changes in consumer purchasing power.

_____ 21. Method of resolving a labor dispute in which both parties are legally required to accept the judgment of a neutral party.

_____ 22. Federal law (1938) setting minimum wage and maximum number of hours in the workweek.

_____ 23. Workplace in which an employer may hire only workers already belonging to a union.

_____ 24. Labor action in which workers publicize their grievances at the entrance to an employer's facility.

_____ 25. Federal law (1932) limiting the ability of courts to issue injunctions prohibiting certain union activities.

_____ 26. Statutes making it illegal to require union membership as a condition of employment.

_____ 27. Labor action in which employees temporarily walk off the job and refuse to work.

_____ 28. Strike in which one union strikes to support action initiated by another.

_____ 29. Group of industrial unions formed in 1938 that rapidly organized the auto, steel, mining, meatpacking, paper, textile, and electrical industries.

_____ 30. Workplace in which workers must pay union dues even if they do not join.

_____ 31. Labor action in which workers perform jobs at a slower than normal pace.

_____ 32. Union employee who acts as liaison between union members and supervisors.

_____ 33. Worker hired as permanent or temporary replacement for a striking employee.

WORD SCRAMBLE

1. _____   2. _____   3. _____   _____

    kirste   timedaion   onuni   pohs

LEARNING OBJECTIVES--POTENTIAL SHORT ANSWER OR ESSAY QUESTIONS

Learning Objective #1: "Explain why workers unionize."

Learning Objective #2: "Trace the evolution and discuss recent trends in *unionism* in the United States."

Learning Objective #3: "Describe the *major laws governing labor-management relations*."

Learning Objective #4: "Describe the union *certification* and *decertification processes*."

Learning Objective #5: "Identify the steps in the *collective bargaining process*."

CRITICAL THINKING QUESTIONS

1. What are three real-world examples of industrial unions? What are three real-world examples of craft unions?

2. What do you think could give rise to a resurgence in union membership in the United States? How likely do you think this is?

BRAIN TEASER

1. Can you think of some specific tactics used by craft unions that are not used by industrial unions in attempting to increase their members' wages?

ANSWERS

True-False—*Answers*

1. True
2. False: *Craft* unions, which developed first, are composed of people who perform a particular type of skilled work, such as carpentry.
3. True
4. False: Since the mid-1950s, there has been a *decrease* in the percentage of workers whom are members of labor unions.
5. True
6. True
7. False: A *local* union is a union organized at the level of a single company, plant, or small geographic region.
8. True
9. False: The *Fair Labor Standards Act of 1938* established a minimum wage and outlawed child labor.
10. True
11. False: The *National Labor Relations Act (Wagner Act)* protects the rights of workers to form unions, bargain collectively, and engage in strikes to achieve their goals.
12. False: The *Labor-Management Relations Act (Taft-Harley Act)* defined certain union practices as unfair and illegal.
13. True
14. True
15. True
16. False: After defining the bargaining unit, the next step in unionizing is to *get 30 percent of the eligible workers within the bargaining unit to sign authorization cards requesting* a certification election.
17. True
18. False: Unions once established *can* be decertified.
19. True
20. True
21. True
22. False: A *slowdown* occurs when workers perform jobs at a slower pace than normal.
23. False: *Picketing* occurs when workers publicize their grievances at the entrance to an employer's facility.
24. True
25. False: *Compulsory* arbitration is a method of resolving a labor dispute in which both parties are legally required to accept the judgement of a neutral party.

Multiple Choice--*Answers*

1. c	5. a	9. b	13. a	17. d
2. d	6. c	10. b	14. a	18. d
3. d	7. a	11. c	15. c	
4. b	8. c	12. d	16. b	

Jeopardy—*Answers*

	Types and Organizational Structure of Unions	Collective Bargaining	Options When Negotiations Break Down
$100	an industrial union	the bargaining unit	picketing
$200	decreasing membership	a cost-of-living adjustment	a strikebreaker
$300	a local union	a wage reopener clause	a boycott
$400	a shop steward	compensation, benefits, and job security	lockouts
$500	defining the bargaining unit, gaining authorization, and conducting an election	a mandatory item	mediation

Match the Terms and Concepts to Their Definitions--*Answers*

1. b	6. ee	11. a	16. y	21. gg	26. o	31. bb
2. j	7. aa	12. cc	17. u	22. l	27. v	32. f
3. p	8. e	13. r	18. c	23. n	28. x	33. dd
4. g	9. m	14. k	19. i	24. z	29. d	
5. w	10. s	15. ff	20. t	25. h	30. q	

Word Scramble--*Answers*

1. strike   2. mediation   3. union shop

Learning Objectives--Potential Short Answer or Essay Questions--*Answers*

Learning Objective #1:

The Industrial Revolution and the emergence of a factory based production system made many workers dependent on continuing factory employment. The treatment of labor as a raw material led to such abuses as minimal pay, long workdays and weeks, unsafe working conditions, and even child labor. Individuals had little recourse in rectifying problems. By organizing into labor unions, however, workers are able to act collectively to improve work conditions. Most importantly, acting as a group, they can engage in *collective bargaining* for higher wages, greater benefits, or better working conditions.

Learning Objective #2:

The earliest unions in the United States were local *craft unions* of specialized workers. Important early national unions included the *National Trades Union*, the *Knights of Labor, the American Federation of Labor (AFL)*, and the *Congress of Industrial Organizations (the CIO)*, the first U.S. *industrial union*. The last two merged in 1955 to form the *AFL-CIO*. Although their membership has slipped in recent years, unions remain an important force in U.S. business and political life and have gained better pay and working conditions for all workers, unionized and nonunionized.

Since the mid-1950s, labor unions in the United States have experienced increasing difficulties in attracting new members. Indeed, while millions of U.S. workers still belong to labor unions, union membership as a percentage of the total workforce has continued to decline at a very steady rate. Increasingly, unions recognize that they don't have as much power as they once held and that it is in their own best interests, as well as the best interests of the workers that they represent, to work with management instead of against it. Bargaining perspectives have also altered in recent years.

Learning Objective #3:

Several significant laws affect labor-management relations. The *Norris-LaGuardia Act* and the *National Labor Relations (Wagner) Act* limited the ability of employers to keep unions out of the workplace. The *Fair Labor Standards Act* established a minimum wage and outlawed child labor. But the *Taft-Hartley Act* and the *Landrum-Griffin Act* limited the power of unions and provided for the settlement of strikes in key industries. Other important laws include the Postal Reorganization Act of 1970, the Federal Service Labor-Management Relations Statute, the Civil Rights Act of 1964, and the Plant-Closing Notification Act.

Learning Objective #4:

Successful unionization requires first of all an interest among workers in forming a union. Those interested in forming the union begin by defining the *bargaining unit*. Organizers must then get 30 percent of the eligible workers in the bargaining unit to sign authorization cards requesting a *union certification election*. The *National Labor Relations Board* then sends representatives to the organization and holds a secret ballot election. If a majority of those voting approve the union certification, the union becomes the official bargaining agent of eligible employees. To decertify a union, 30 percent of eligible employees must sign decertification authorization cards. The NLRB will then conduct a *decertification election*. For the union to be decertified, a majority of those voting must favor the decertification.

Learning Objective #5:

Once certified, the union engages in collective bargaining with the organization. The initial step in collective bargaining is reaching agreement on a *labor contract*. Contract demands usually involve wages, job security, or management rights.

Both labor and management have several tactics that can be used against the other if negotiations break down. Unions may attempt a *strike* or a *boycott* of the firm or may engage in a *slowdown*. Companies may hire replacement workers (*strikebreakers*) or *lock out* all workers. In extreme cases, mediation or arbitration may be used to settle disputes. Once a contract has been agreed on, union and management representatives continue to interact to settle worker *grievances* and interpret the contract.

Critical Thinking Questions—*Answers*

1. Three real-world examples of industrial unions are the United Auto Workers (UAW), the United Mine Workers (UMW), and the Teamsters. Three real-world examples of craft unions are the local electricians union, the local bricklayers union, and the local painters union typically found on commercial construction sites.

2. A resurgence in union membership in the United States could be caused by the same general conditions which gave rise to their creation in the first place: low wages, poor working conditions, and a lack of benefits. How likely this is to happen in large part depends on how management treats workers in the future.

Brain Teaser---*Answer*

1. Industrial unions generally use the threat of a strike to try to restrict the supply of their labor to zero below the wage the union is striking for. Although, craft unions also try to restrict their supply in order to receive higher wages, they are often unable to effectively use the threat of a strike. Instead, they restrict the number of people able to practice their trade through long apprenticeship programs (e.g., the printers, plumbers, and electricians unions); licensing requirements where only a limited number of licenses will be granted (e.g., cosmetologists, barbers, and beauticians); stringent educational requirements (e.g. doctors and lawyers--the American Medical Association and the local Bar Association is essentially a union); or by issuing a limited number of membership cards where those cards, proving membership, are required to practice the trade or craft (e.g., bricklayers, carpenters, and other commercial construction trades). Anything that restricts the supply of workers who are able to practice the trade or craft, short of a strike, is generally the type of tactics used by craft unions that are not practiced by industrial unions.

Chapter 11

Understanding Marketing Processes and Consumer Behavior

LEARNING OBJECTIVES

After studying this chapter, you should be able to:

1. Define *marketing*.
2. Describe the five forces that constitute the *external marketing environment*.
3. Explain market *segmentation* and show how it is used in *target marketing*.
4. Explain the purpose and value of *marketing research*.
5. Describe the key factors that influence the *consumer buying process*.
6. Discuss the three categories of *organizational markets* and explain how *organizational buying behavior* differs from consumer buying behavior.

TRUE-FALSE

Indicate whether the statement is generally true or false by placing a "T" or "F" in the space provided. If it is a false statement, correct it so that it becomes a true statement.

___T___ 1. Marketing is the process of planning and executing the conception, pricing, promotion, and the distribution of ideas, goods, and services to create exchanges that satisfy individual and organizational objectives.

___F___ 2. Firms that sell their products to other manufacturers are engaged in consumer marketing.

___T___ 3. The political/legal environment of marketing includes the context within which people's values, beliefs, and ideas affect marketing decisions.

___F___ 4. The technological environment of marketing consists of the conditions, such as inflation, recession, and interest rates that influence consumer and organizational spending patterns.

___T___ 5. The competitive environment of marketing is the environment in which marketers must persuade buyers to purchase their products rather than their competitors'.

___F___ 6. Brand competition is competitive marketing of domestic products against foreign products.

___T___ 7. A marketing plan is a detailed and focused strategy for gearing marketing efforts to meet consumer needs and wants.

___T___ 8. Marketing managers must plan and set marketing goals.

_T_   9. Product differentiation is the creation of a product or product image that differs enough from existing products to attract consumers.

_F_   10. The components of the marketing mix are price, promotion, place and personality.

_F_   11. Marketing begins with a promotion strategy.

_T_   12. In the marketing mix, "place" refers to distribution.

_T_   13. A target market is a group of people that have similar wants and needs and that can be expected to show interest in the same products.

_T_   14. Market segmentation is the process of dividing a market into categories of customer types.

_F_   15. Market segmentation is designed to shut some customers out of the market.

_F_   16. Geographic segmentation is the classification of customers on the basis of their psychological makeup.

_T_   17. Product use segmentation is the categorization of customers based on the ways in which a product is used, the brand loyalty it enjoys, and the reasons for which it is purchased.

_F_   18. The first step in market research is to prepare a report.

_T_   19. The four basic methods of market research are observation, surveys, focus groups, and experimentation.

_T_   20. When making buying decisions, consumers first determine or respond to a problem or a need and then collect as much information as they think is necessary before making a purchase.

_F_   21. "Consumer" markets are markets in which customers buy goods or services for resale or for use in conducting their own operations.

_T_   22. One important difference between consumer and organizational buying behavior is that organizational buyers are usually better informed in the buying decision.

_T_   23. When marketing internationally, managers must take into account different social, political and economic environments found in foreign countries.

MULTIPLE CHOICE
Circle the one best answer for each of the following questions.

1. Marketing involves
   a. selling a product.
   b. selling services.
   c. selling ideas and causes.
   d. All of the above.

2. Which of the following statements is correct?
   a. Marketing plans and strategies are influenced by the external environment.
   b. Consumer goods are products purchased by companies to produce other products.
   c. A marketing manager has a big influence on the external marketing environment.
   d. All of the above.

3. Competition marketing that appeals to consumer perceptions of similar products is
   a. substitute product competition.
   b. brand competition.
   c. international competition.
   d. impossible.

4. The external marketing environment that includes the laws and regulations, both domestic and foreign, that may define or constrain business activities is known as the
   a. economic environment.
   b. social/cultural environment.
   c. political/legal environment.
   d. technological environment.

5. The external marketing environment that includes the context within which people's values, beliefs, and ideas affect marketing decisions is known as the
   a. competitive environment.
   b. social/cultural environment.
   c. political/legal environment.
   d. technological environment.

6. When marketers try to persuade buyers to purchase their products rather than their competitors' they are focusing on the
   a. competitive environment.
   b. social/cultural environment.
   c. economic environment.
   d. technological environment.

7. Which of the following is part of the marketing mix?
   a. Product and price.
   b. Place.
   c. Promotion.
   d. All of the above.

8. Distribution is that part of the marketing mix concerned with
   a. creating a product or product image that differs from existing products.
   b. selecting the most appropriate price at which to sell a product.
   c. getting products from producers to consumers.
   d. creation of a good, service, or idea designed to fill a consumer need.

9. The technique of communicating information about a product is the
   a. "promotion" component of the marketing mix.
   b. "product" component of the marketing mix.
   c. "place" component of the marketing mix.
   d. "price" component of the marketing mix.

10. The decisions about the channels through which a product is made available to consumers is part of the
    a. "promotion" component of the marketing mix.
    b. "product" component of the marketing mix.
    c. "place" component of the marketing mix.
    d. "price" component of the marketing mix.

11. The decision whether to undertake personal selling or to partake in public relations is part of the
    a. "promotion" component of the marketing mix.
    b. "product" component of the marketing mix.
    c. "place" component of the marketing mix.
    d. "price" component of the marketing mix.

12. The practice of building long-term, satisfying, relationships with customers and suppliers is called
    a. customer marketing.
    b. database marketing.
    c. relationship marketing.
    d. one-to-one marketing.

13. When markets are segmented according to characteristics of populations this is know as
    a. geographic segmentation.
    b. demographic segmentation.
    c. psychographic segmentation.
    d. product use segmentation.

14. Which of the following best describes the marketing research process?
    a. Study the current situation, select a research method, collect the data, analyze the data, and prepare a report.
    b. Select a research method, collect the data, analyze the data, study the current situation and prepare a report.
    c. Collect the data, analyze the data, select a research method, study the current situation, and prepare a report.
    d. Collect the data, analyze the data, prepare a report, select a research method, and study the current situation.

15. The market research technique that involves simply watching and recording consumer behavior is the
    a. observation technique of market research.
    b. survey technique of market research.
    c. focus group technique of market research.
    d. experimentation technique of market research.

16. Which of the following are factors that influence consumer behavior?
    a. Culture and social class.
    b. Lifestyle and personality.
    c. Self-image.
    d. All of the above.

17. Organizational or commercial markets fall into which of the following three categories?
    a. Product, resource and money markets.
    b. Industrial, reseller, and government/institutional markets.
    c. Primary, secondary and post-secondary markets.
    d. Goods, services and technology/idea markets.

18. Which of the following statements is true?
    a. The demand for industrial products is derived from the demand for the products these industries produce.
    b. An inelastic demand for a product means buyers are not relatively very responsive to the price.
    c. Organizational buyer's decisions are typically more sophisticated than the typical consumer's buying decision.
    d. All of the above.

JEOPARDY

You have 5 seconds to complete the questions to each of the following answers.

	The Marketing Environment and Market Segmentation	The Marketing Mix	Market Research, Consumer Behavior, and Organizational Markets
$100	This external marketing environment that includes laws and regulations. What is *Political/legal* *marketing environment* ?	The "Four Ps" of marketing. What is *product, price Promotion, place* ?	The study of consumer needs and wants and the ways in which sellers can best meet them. What is *marketing research* ?
$200	This is the context in which people's values, beliefs, and ideas, affect marketing decisions. What is *Social/cultural marketing environment* ?	Marketing begins with this. *Product component of the marketing mix* What is ?	Market research technique in which a group of people gathers to discuss an issue in depth. *Focus group* What is *marketing research technique* ?
$300	The environment in which marketers must persuade buyers to purchase their products as opposed to competitors'. What is *competitive marketing environment* ?	The most highly visible component of the marketing mix. *Promotion component of the marketing mix* What is ?	The buying process begins with this. *need, problem* What is ?
$400	A group of people that has similar wants and needs and that can be expected to show interest in the same products. What is *target market* ?	It is often a balancing act between setting this component of the marketing mix strategy high or low. What is *the pricing component of the marketing mix* ?	Another term for organizational markets. *commercial* What is *markets* ?
$500	Segmenting markets according to characteristics of populations. *demographic* What is *segmentation* ?	This is the component of the marketing mix concerned with getting the product to the customer at the right place and time. *place/distribution* What is *component of the marketing mix* ?	The three types of organizational markets. *industrial, reseller and gov't institutional* What is *markets* ?

MATCH THE TERMS AND CONCEPTS TO THEIR DEFINITIONS

a. marketing
b. consumer goods
c. industrial goods
d. services
e. relationship marketing
f. external environment
g. substitute product
h. brand competition
i. international competition
j   marketing mix
k. product
l. product differentiation

m. distribution
n. target market
o. market segmentation
p. geographic variables
q. demographic variables
r. psychographic variables
s. product use variables
t. consumer behavior
u. brand loyalty
v. rational motives
w. emotional motives
x. marketing plan

y. marketing research
z. secondary data
aa. primary data
bb. observation
cc. survey
dd. focus group
ee. experimentation
ff. industrial market
gg. reseller market
hh. institutional market
ii. derived demand
jj. inelastic demand

_w_ 1. Reasons for purchasing a product that are based on nonobjective factors.

_bb_ 2. Market research technique that involves simply watching and recording consumer behavior.

_r_ 3. Consumer characteristics, such as lifestyles, opinions, interests, and attitudes, that may be considered in developing a segmentation strategy.

_a_ 4. The process of planning and executing the conception, pricing, promotion, and distribution of ideas, goods, and services to create exchanges that satisfy individual and organizational objectives.

_h_ 5. Competitive marketing that appeals to consumer perceptions of similar products.

_e_ 6. Marketing strategy that emphasizes lasting relationships with customers and suppliers.

_p_ 7. Geographical units that may be considered in developing a segmentation strategy.

_gg_ 8. Organizational market consisting of intermediaries who buy and resell finished goods.

_y_ 9. The study of consumer needs and wants and the ways in which sellers can best meet them.

_ii_ 10. Demand for industrial products that results from demand for consumer products.

_l_ 11. Creation of a product or product image that differs enough from existing products to attract consumers.

_c_ 12. Products purchased by companies to produce other products.

_t_ 13. Various facets of the decision process by which customers come to purchase and consume products.

_q_ 14. Characteristics of populations that may be considered in developing a segmentation strategy.

_j_ 15. The combination of product, pricing, promotion, and distribution strategies used to market products.

_n_ 16. Group of people that has similar wants and needs and that can be expected to show interest in the same products.

_ee_ 17. Market research technique that attempts to compare the responses of the same or similar people under different circumstances.

_X_ 18. Detailed and focused strategy for gearing marketing efforts to meet consumer needs and wants.

_b_ 19. Products purchased by consumers for personal use.

_m_ 20. Part of the marketing mix concerned with getting products from producers to consumers.

_ff_ 21. Organizational market consisting of firms that buy goods that are either converted into products or used during production.

_v_ 22. Reasons for purchasing a product that are based on a logical evaluation of product attributes.

_cc_ 23. Market research technique using a questionnaire that is either mailed to individuals or used as the basis of interviews.

_d_ 24. Intangible products, such as time, expertise, or an activity, that can be purchased.

_s_ 25. Consumer characteristics based on the ways in which a product is used, the brand loyalty it enjoys, and the reasons for which it is purchased.

_dd_ 26. Market research technique in which a group of people is gathered, presented with an issue, and asked to discuss it in depth.

_f_ 27. Outside factors that influence marketing programs by posing opportunities or threats.

_o_ 28. Process of dividing a market into categories of customer types.

_hh_ 29. Organizational market consisting of such nongovernmental buyers of goods and services as hospitals, churches, museums, and charitable organizations.

_aa_ 30. Data developed through new research.

_g_ 31. Product that is dissimilar to those of competitors but that can fulfill the same need.

_y_ 32. Pattern of regular consumer purchasing based on satisfaction with a product.

_jj_ 33. Demand for industrial products that is not largely affected by price changes.

_i_ 34. Competitive marketing of domestic products against foreign products.

_z_ 35. Data readily available as a result of previous research.

_k_ 36. Good, service, or idea that is marketed to fill consumer needs and wants.

WORD SCRAMBLE

1. _____ _____ 2. _____ 3. _____
   ketmar   sementgation   veyrus   tionbutridis

LEARNING OBJECTIVES--POTENTIAL SHORT ANSWER OR ESSAY QUESTIONS

Learning Objective #1: "Define *marketing*."

Learning Objective #2: "Describe the five forces that constitute the *external marketing environment*."

Learning Objective #3: "Explain *market segmentation* and show how it is used in *target marketing*."

Learning Objective #4: "Explain the purpose and value of *market research*."

Learning Objective #5: "Describe the key factors that influence the *consumer buying process.*"

Learning Objective #6: "Discuss the three categories of *organizational markets* and explain how *organizational buying behavior* differs from consumer buying behavior."

CRITICAL THINKING QUESTIONS

1. How might a toy store use relationship marketing to improve customer loyalty?

2. Marketers often refer to the "Four Ps" of marketing. What are they?

BRAIN TEASER

1. Price discrimination occurs when a company sells a good or service at different prices to different people, where those price differences are not a reflection of cost differences. The purpose of price discrimination is to charge some customers a higher price, and therefore to increase company profits. What two conditions must exist in order for price discrimination to occur? What are some examples of price discrimination?

ANSWERS

True-False--*Answers*

1. True
2. False: Firms that sell their products to other manufacturers are engaged in *industrial* marketing.
3. False: The *social/cultural* environment of marketing includes the context within which people's values, beliefs, and ideas affect marketing decisions.
4. False: The *economic* environment of marketing consists of the conditions, such as inflation, recession, and interest rates that influence consumer and organizational spending patterns.
5. True
6. False: *International* competition is competitive marketing of domestic products against foreign products.
7. True
8. True
9. True
10. False: The components of the marketing mix are price, promotion, place and *product*.
11. False: Marketing begins with a *product—a good, service, or an idea designed to fill a consumer need.*
12. True
13. True
14. True
15. False: Market segmentation is designed to *divide the total market into smaller, relatively homogenous groups.*
16. False: *Psychographic* segmentation is the classification of customers on the basis of their psychological makeup.
17. True
18. False: The first step in market research is to *study the current situation..*
19. True
20. True
21. False: *Organizational (or commercial)* markets are markets in which customers buy goods or services for resale or for use in conducting their own operations.
22. True
23. True

Multiple Choice--*Answers*

1. d	5. b	9. a	13. b	17. b
2. a	6. a	10. c	14. a	18. d
3. b	7. d	11. a	15. a	
4. c	8. c	12. c	16. d	

Jeopardy—*Answers*

	The Marketing Environment and Market Segmentation	The Marketing Mix	Market Research, Consumer Behavior, and Organizational Markets
$100	the political/legal marketing environment	product, price, promotion, and place	marketing research
$200	the social/cultural marketing environment	product component of the marketing mix	a focus group marketing research technique
$300	competitive marketing environment	the promotion component of the marketing mix	a need or problem
$400	a target market	the pricing component of the marketing mix	commercial markets
$500	demographic segmentation	the place (distribution) component of the marketing mix	industrial markets, reseller markets, and government and institutional markets

Match the Terms and Concepts to Their Definitions--*Answers*

1. w	6. e	11. l	16. n	21. ff	26. dd	31. g	36. k
2. bb	7. p	12. c	17. ee	22. v	27. f	32. u	
3. r	8. gg	13. t	18. x	23. cc	28. o	33. jj	
4. a	9. y	14. q	19. b	24. d	29. hh	34. i	
5. h	10. ii	15. j	20. m	25. s	30. aa	35. z	

Word Scramble---*Answers*

1. market segmentation   2. survey   3. distribution

Learning Objectives--Potential Short Answer or Essay Questions--*Answers*

Learning Objective #1:
   According to the American Marketing Association, *marketing* is the process of planning and executing the conception, pricing, promotion, and distribution of ideas, goods, and services to create exchanges that satisfy individual and organizational objectives.

Learning Objective #2:
   The *external environment* consists of the outside forces that influence marketing strategy and decision making. The *political/legal environment* includes laws and regulations, both domestic and foreign, that may define or constrain business activities. The *social/cultural environment* is the context within which people's values, beliefs, and ideas affect marketing decisions. The *technological environment* includes the technological developments that affect existing and new products. The *economic environment* consists of the conditions, such as inflation, recession, and interest rates, that influence both consumer and organizational spending patterns. Finally, the *competitive environment* is the environment in which marketers must persuade buyers to purchase their products rather than their competitors'.

Learning Objective #3:

Market segmentation is the process of dividing markets into categories of customers. Businesses have learned that marketing is more successful when it is aimed toward specific *target markets*: groups of consumers with similar wants and needs. Markets may be segmented by *geographic, demographic, psychographic*, or *product use variables*.

Learning Objective #4:

Market research is the study of what buyers need and of the best ways to meet those needs. This process entails studying the firm's customers, evaluating possible changes in the marketing mix, and helping marketing managers make better decisions about marketing programs. *The marketing research process* involves the selection of a research method, the collection of data, the analysis of data, and the preparation of a report that may include recommendations for action. The four most common research methods are *observation, surveys, focus groups*, and *experimentation*.

Learning Objective #5:

A number of personal and psychological considerations, along with various social and cultural influences, affect consumer behavior. When making buying decisions, consumers first determine or respond to a problem or need and then collect as much information as they think necessary before making a purchase. *Postpurchase evaluations* are also important to marketers because they influence future buying patterns.

Learning Objective #6:

The *industrial market* includes firms that buy goods falling into one of two categories: goods to be converted into other products and goods that are used up during production. Farmers and manufacturers are members of the industrial market. Members of the *reseller market* (mostly wholesalers) are intermediaries who buy and resell finished goods. Besides governments and agencies at all levels, the *government and institutional market* includes such nongovernment organizations as hospitals, museums, and charities.

There are four main differences between consumer and organizational buying behavior. First, the nature of *demand* is different in organizational markets; it is often *derived* (resulting from related consumer demand) or inelastic (largely unaffected by price changes). Second, organizational buyers are typically professionals, specialists, or experts. Third, organizational buyers develop product specifications, evaluate alternatives more thoroughly, and make more systematic postpurchase evaluations. Finally, they often develop enduring buyer-seller relationships.

Critical Thinking Questions--*Answers*

1. A database can be collected on who buys what. The store could then send promotional materials inviting the customer to a special "invitation-only" sale of the items relevant for that aged child before the sale is advertised to the general public.

2. The "4 Ps" of marketing are Product, Price, Place, and Promotion.

Brain Teaser--*Answer*

1. The company must be able to segment its markets—to determine who is willing to pay a higher price. The second condition for price discrimination is that it must be difficult for the good or service to be resold (for obvious reasons). Examples of price discrimination exist in the pricing behavior of doctors (if you have health insurance coverage, you may be charged more than someone who does not), lawyers (how nervous are you?), electric companies (they charge higher prices to residential customers than commercial customers), movie theaters (the matinee showing is cheaper than the evening showing), car dealerships (how bad do you want that new car?), etc. Can you think of any more?

Chapter 12
Developing and Pricing Products

LEARNING OBJECTIVES
After studying this chapter, you should be able to:

1. Identify a *product* and distinguish between *consumer* and *industrial products*.
2. Trace the stages of the *product life cycle*.
3. Explain the importance of *branding*, *packaging*, and *labeling*.
4. Identify the various *pricing objectives* that govern *pricing decisions* and describe the *price-setting tools* used in making these decisions.
5. Discuss *pricing strategies* and *tactics* for both existing and new products.

TRUE-FALSE
Indicate whether the statement is generally true or false by placing a "T" or "F" in the space provided. If it is a false statement, correct it so that it becomes a true statement.

_____ 1. To succeed a product must include the right features and offer the right benefits.

_____ 2. The two general types of products are consumer products and industrial products.

_____ 3. An inexpensive product purchased and consumed rapidly and regularly is called a specialty good/service.

_____ 4. Industrial products are commonly divided into convenience goods, shopping goods and specialty goods.

_____ 5. Depending on how much they cost and how they will be used, industrial products can be divided into two categories: expense and capital items.

_____ 6. Among the strategies for increasing the likelihood of product success is "speed to market"—introducing new products to respond quickly to customer or market change.

_____ 7. Products move from the introductory phase through a maturity phase; then they pass into a growth phase and eventually decline.

_____ 8. The first two stages of product development involve generating and screening ideas to isolate those with the most potential.

_____ 9. A product's life cycle might be extended in foreign markets through product extension, product adaptation, and reintroduction.

_____ 10. A product mix is a series of similar products offered for sale by a firm.

_____ 11. The goal in developing brands is to increase brand loyalty.

_____ 12. Private brands are brand-name products purchased by, widely distributed by, and carrying the name of a manufacturer.

_____ 13. Packaging provides protection, makes products easier to display, and attracts attention.

_____ 14. Markup is the amount added to an item's cost to sell it at a profit.

_____ 15. A variable cost is any cost that does not change with the production level.

_____ 16. Breakeven analysis attempts to determine the quantity of a product that must be sold before a profit is made.

_____ 17. Penetration pricing is setting an initial high price to cover new product costs and generate a profit.

_____ 18. Price lining is setting a limited number of prices for certain categories of products.

_____ 19. Psychological pricing appeals to buyers' perceptions of relative prices.

_____ 20. Discounting is reducing prices to stimulate sales.

MULTIPLE CHOICE
Circle the one best answer for each of the following questions.

1. Which of the following is *not* part of the firm's marketing mix?
   a. Product
   b. Price
   c. Perception
   d. Promotion

2. Which of the following is not a consumer product category?
    a. A convenience good/service.
    b. An industrial good/service.
    c. A shopping good/service.
    d. A specialty good/service.

3. Which of the following statements is true?
    a. Consumer products are sold to other firms while industrial products are sold directly to consumers.
    b. Buyers will pay less for common, rapidly consumed convenience goods than for less frequently purchased shopping and specialty goods.
    c. In industrial markets, capital items such as buildings and equipment are generally less expensive and more rapidly consumed than expense items.
    d. All of the above.

4. A group of similar products intended for a similar group of buyers who will use them in similar ways is called
    a. an expense item.
    b. a capital item.
    c. a product line.
    d. a product mix.

5. The stage of a product's life-cycle where the product begins to earn its highest profits, and the product's sales begin to slow is the
    a. introduction stage.
    b. growth stage.
    c. maturity stage.
    d. decline stage.

6. The four stages of the product life cycle begin with
    a. the introduction of the product, then its growth, its maturity, and finally its decline.
    b. the introduction of the product, then its maturity, growth, and finally its decline.
    c. the introduction of the product, then its growth, its decline, and finally its maturity.
    d. its growth, its maturity, its decline, and then its reintroduction.

7. Which of the following correctly describes the stages of product development?
    a. Screening of ideas, business analysis, prototype development, product testing, and then commercialization.
    b. Prototype development, product testing, screening of ideas, business analysis, and then commercialization.
    c. Business analysis, screening of ideas, prototype development, product testing, and then commercialization.
    d. Product testing, business analysis, prototype development, screening of ideas, and then commercialization.

8. Which of the following statements is true?
   a. Product extension is marketing an existing product globally instead of just domestically.
   b. Product adaptation is modifying a product to give it greater appeal in other countries.
   c. Reintroduction is the process of reviving for new markets products that are obsolete in older ones.
   d. All of the above.

9. Which of the following statements is true?
   a. Licensed brands are products that are widely produced and widely distributed by the same manufacturer.
   b. Private brands are items for whose names sellers have bought the rights from organizations or individuals.
   c. National brands are developed by wholesalers or retailers and commissioned from manufacturers.
   d. Labeling information is often heavily regulated.

10. Break-even analysis
    a. attempts to find that volume of production for which variable costs equal fixed costs.
    b. attempts to determine the quantity of a product that must be sold before a profit can be earned.
    c. determines the amount of markup required in order to earn a profit.
    d. All of the above.

11. Which of the following statements is true?
    a. Price skimming is charging a high price for a new product during the introductory stage and lowering the price later.
    b. Penetration pricing is introducing a new product at a low price in hopes of building sales volume quickly.
    c. A price leader is a dominant firm that establishes product prices that other companies follow.
    d. All of the above.

12. Odd-even pricing is
    a. a price reduction offered as an incentive to purchase.
    b. setting a limited number of prices for certain categories of products.
    c. a psychological pricing tactic based on the premise that customers prefer prices not stated in even dollar amounts.
    d. setting an initial low price to establish a new product in the market.

13. Setting an initial high price to cover new product costs and generate a profit is know as
    a. penetration pricing
    b. discounting
    c. price lining
    d. price skimming

JEOPARDY

You have 5 seconds to complete the question to each of the following answers.

	Products, New Product Development, and Product Life-Cycle	Branding, Packaging and Labeling	Pricing Strategies and Decisions
$100	The two general types of products. What is_____?	Part of a product packaging that identifies its name, manufacturer, and contents. What is_____?	Amount added to an item's cost to sell it at a profit. What is_____?
$200	The number of steps in the new product development process. What is_____?	Brand-name product that a wholesaler or retailer has commissioned from a manufacturer. What is_____?	Setting a limited number of prices for certain categories of products. What is_____?
$300	The four stages of the product life cycle. What is_____?	Use of an established brand name by purchasing it from the organization or individual whom owns it. What is_____?	Charging a high price for a new product during the introductory stage and lowering the price later. What is_____?
$400	The stage of a product's life cycle where, if the product attracts and satisfies enough customers, it shows a profit. What is_____?	Brand-name product produced by, widely distributed by, and carrying the name of a manufacturer. What is_____?	Introducing a new product at a low price in hopes of building sales volume quickly. What is_____?
$500	The stage of a product's life cycle where profits fall as sales are lost to new products in their introductory stage. What is_____?	The purposes of packaging. What is_____?	Method of calculating the minimum volume of sales needed at a given price to cover all costs. What is_____?

MATCH THE TERMS AND CONCEPTS TO THEIR DEFINITIONS

a.   feature
b.   convenience good/service
c.   shopping good/service
d.   specialty good/service
e.   expense item
f.   capital item
g.   product mix
h.   product line
i.   speed to market
j.   product life cycle (PLC)
k.   product adaptation

l.   reintroduction
m.   branding
n.   national brand
o.   licensed brand
p.   private brand (or private label)
q.   packaging
r.   pricing
s.   pricing objectives
t.   market share
u.   markup
v.   variable cost

w.   fixed cost
x.   breakeven analysis
y.   breakeven point
z.   price leader
aa. price skimming
bb. penetration pricing
cc. psychological pricing
dd. odd-even pricing
ee. discount

_____ 1. Expensive, long-lasting, infrequently purchased industrial product such as a building.

_____ 2. Brand-name product for whose name the seller has purchased the right from an organization or individual.

_____ 3. Product modified to have greater appeal in foreign markets.

_____ 4. Assessment of the quantity of a product that must be sold before the seller makes a profit.

_____ 5. Setting an initial low price to establish a new product in the market.

_____ 6. Inexpensive product purchased and consumed rapidly and regularly.

_____ 7. Price reduction offered as an incentive to purchase.

_____ 8. Brand-name product that a wholesaler or retailer has commissioned from a manufacturer.

_____ 9. Amount added to an item's cost to sell it at a profit.

_____ 10. Series of stages in a product's profit-producing life.

_____ 11. Tangible quality that a company builds into a product.

_____ 12. Industrial product purchased and consumed rapidly and regularly for daily operations.

_____ 13. Dominant firm that establishes product prices that other companies follow.

_____ 14. Process of using symbols to communicate the qualities of a product made by a particular producer.

_____ 15. Group of similar products intended for a similar group of buyers who will use them in similar ways.

_____ 16. Cost unaffected by the quantity of a product produced or sold.

_____ 17. Group of products that a firm makes available for sale.

_____ 18. Process of determining what a company will receive in exchange for its products.

_____ 19. Quantity of a product that must be sold before the seller covers variable and fixed costs and makes a profit.

_____ 20. Psychological pricing tactic based on the premise that customers prefer prices not stated in even dollar amounts.

_____ 21. Brand-name product produced by, widely distributed by, and carrying the name of a manufacturer.

_____ 22. Moderately expensive, infrequently purchased product.

_____ 23. Strategy of introducing new products to respond quickly to customer or market changes.

_____ 24. Physical container in which a product is sold, advertised, or protected.

_____ 25. Expensive, rarely purchased product.

_____ 26. Pricing tactic that takes advantage of the fact that consumers do not always respond rationally to stated prices.

_____ 27. Cost that changes with the quantity of a product produced or sold.

_____ 28. As a percentage, total of market sales for a specific company or product.

_____ 29. Setting an initial high price to cover new product costs and generate a profit.

_____ 30. Goals that producers hope to attain in pricing products for sale.

_____ 31. Process of reviving for new markets products that are obsolete in older ones.

WORD SCRAMBLE

1. _____ _____   2. _____   3. _____
   ductrop   nile   pukmar   countsid

LEARNING OBJECTIVES--POTENTIAL SHORT ANSWER OR ESSAY QUESTIONS

Learning Objective #1: **"Identify a *product* and distinguish between *consumer* and *industrial products*."**

Learning Objective #2: "Trace the stages of the *product life cycle*."

Learning Objective #3: **"Explain the importance of** *branding, packaging*, **and** *labeling***."**

Learning Objective #4: **"Identify the various** *pricing objectives* **that govern** *pricing decisions* **and describe the** *price-setting tools* **used in making these decisions."**

Learning Objective #5: **"Discuss** *pricing strategies* **and** *tactics* **for both existing and new products."**

CRITICAL THINKING QUESTIONS

1. What can be done to extend the life of a mature product?

2. What is the break-even volume of sales needed for a firm that sells its product at $4 per unit and has fixed costs of $20,000 and variable costs per unit of $3?

BRAIN TEASER

1. Sometimes we hear about "predatory" pricing. What is that?

ANSWERS

True-False--*Answers*

1. True
2. True
3. False: An inexpensive product purchased and consumed rapidly and regularly is called a *convenience* good/service.
4. False: *Consumer* products are commonly divided into convenience goods, shopping goods and specialty goods.
5. True
6. True
7. False: Products move from the introductory phase through a *growth* phase; then they pass into a *maturity* phase and eventually decline.
8. True
9. True
10. False: A product *line* is a series of similar related products offered for sale by a firm.
11. True
12. False: *National* brands are brand-name products purchased by, widely distributed by, and carrying the name of a manufacturer.
13. True
14. True
15. False: A *fixed* cost is any cost that does not change with the production level.
16. True
17. False: *Price skimming* is setting an initial high price to cover new product costs and generate a profit.
18. True
19. True
20. True

Multiple Choice--*Answers*

1. c	5. c	9. d	13. d
2. b	6. a	10. b	
3. b	7. a	11. d	
4. c	8. d	12. c	

Jeopardy—*Answers*

	Products, New Product Development, and Product Life-Cycle	Branding, Packaging and Labeling	Pricing Strategies and Decisions
$100	consumer and industrial products	a label	markup
$200	seven	a private brand (or private label)	price lining
$300	introduction, growth, maturity, and decline	a licensed brand	price skimming
$400	the growth stage	a national brand	penetration pricing
$500	the decline stage	to provide protection, to make products easier to display, and to attract attention	break-even analysis

Match the Terms and Concepts to Their Definitions--*Answers*

1. f	6. b	11. a	16. w	21. n	26. cc	31. l
2. o	7. ee	12. e	17. g	22. c	27. v	
3. k	8. p	13. z	18. r	23. i	28. t	
4. x	9. u	14. m	19. y	24. q	29. aa	
5. bb	10. j	15. h	20. dd	25. d	30. s	

Word Scramble--*Answers*

1. product line   2. markup   3. discount

Learning Objectives--Potential Short Answer or Essay Questions--*Answers*

Learning Objective #1:

Products are a firm's reason for being. Product *features*—the tangible and intangible qualities that a company builds into its products—offer benefits to buyers whose purchases are the main source of most companies' profits. In developing products, firms must decide whether to produce *consumer goods* for direct sale to individual consumers or *industrial goods* for sale to other firms. Marketers must recognize that buyers will pay less for common, rapidly consumed *convenience goods* than for less frequently purchased *shopping* and *specialty goods*. In industrial markets, *expense items* are generally less expensive and more rapidly consumed than such *capital items* as buildings and equipment.

Learning Objective #2:

New products have a life cycle that corresponds to the following stages: *introduction* (the product reaches the marketplace and receives extensive promotion); *growth* (if it attracts and satisfies enough customers, it shows a profit); *maturity* (although it begins to earn its highest profits, the product's sales begin to slow); and *decline* (profits fall as sales are lost to new products in the introduction stage).

The fact that 9 of 10 new products will fail reflects the current *product mortality rate*. Among the strategies for increasing the likelihood of product success is *speed to market*—introducing new products to respond quickly to customer or market changes. In foreign markets, there are also three strategies for lengthening a product's life cycle: *product extension* (marketing an existing product globally instead of just domestically); *product adaptation* (modifying a product to give it greater appeal in other countries); and *reintroduction* (reviving for new markets a product that is becoming obsolete in old ones).

Learning Objective #3:

Each product is given an identity by its brand and the way it is packaged and labeled. The goal in developing *brands*—symbols to distinguish products and signal their uniform quality—is to increase *brand loyalty* (the preference that consumers have for a product with a particular brand name). *National brands* are products that are produced and widely distributed by the same manufacturer. *Licensed brands* are items for whose names sellers have bought the rights from organizations or individuals. *Private brands* (or *private labels*) are developed by wholesalers or retailers and commissioned from manufacturers.

Packaging provides an attractive container and advertises a product's features and benefits. It also reduces the risk of damage, spoilage, or theft. *Labeling* is the part of a product's packaging that usually identifies the producer's name, the manufacturer, and the contents. Labeling information is often heavily regulated.

Learning Objective #4:

A firm's *pricing decisions* reflect the *pricing objectives* set by its management. Although these objectives vary, they all reflect the goals that a seller hopes to reach in selling a product. They include *profit maximizing* (pricing to sell the number of units that will generate the highest possible total profits) and *meeting market share goals* (ensuring continuous sales by maintaining a strong percentage of the total sales for a specific product type). Other considerations include the need to survive in a competitive marketplace, social and ethical concerns, and even a firm's image.

Price-setting tools are chosen to meet a seller's pricing objectives. *Cost-oriented pricing* recognizes the need to cover the variable costs of producing a product (costs that change with the number of units produced or sold). In determining the price level at which profits will be generated, *breakeven analysis* also considers *fixed costs* (costs, such as facilities and salaries, that are unaffected by the number of items produced or sold).

Learning Objective #5:

Either a *price-skimming strategy* (pricing very high) or *a penetration-pricing strategy* (pricing very low) may be effective for new products. Depending on the other elements in the marketing mix, existing products may be priced at, above, or below prevailing prices for similar products. Guided by a firm's pricing strategies, managers set prices using tactics such as *price lining* (offering items in certain categories at a set number of prices), *psychological pricing* (appealing to buyers' perceptions of relative prices), and *discounting* (reducing prices to stimulate sales).

The electronic marketplace has introduced two competing pricing systems—dynamic versus fixed. *Dynamic pricing* is feasible because the flow of information on the Net notifies millions of buyers around the world of instantaneous changes in product availability. Sellers can also alter prices privately, on a customer-to customer basis, to attract sales that might be lost under traditional fixed-price structures.

Critical Thinking Questions--*Answers*

1. Generally, a company can extend the life of a mature product by broadening its appeal or making minor improvements. In addition, some companies have extended the life of their mature products by aggressively introducing their products in less developed nations.
2. Break-even point = $20,000/($4 - $3) = 20,000 units.

Brain Teaser--*Answer*

1. Predatory pricing is often used to refer to a company which prices its product below its own costs (or below "fair" market value) in order to drive their competitors out of business (on the assumption they can sustain losses longer than their competitors can).

Chapter 13
Promoting Products

LEARNING OBJECTIVES
After studying this chapter, you should be able to:

1. Identify the important objectives of *promotion* and discuss the considerations entailed in selecting a *promotional mix*.
2. Discuss the most important *advertising strategies* and describe the key *advertising media*.
3. Outline the tasks involved in *personal selling* and list the steps in the *personal selling process*.
4. Describe the various types of *sales promotions*.
5. Describe the development of *international promotional strategies*.
6. Show how small businesses use promotional activities.

TRUE-FALSE
Indicate whether the statement is generally true or false by placing a "T" or "F" in the space provided. If it is a false statement, correct it so that it becomes a true statement.

_____ 1. Two general values to be gained from any promotional activity are communicating information and creating more satisfying customers.

_____ 2. The ultimate goal of any promotion is to reduce costs of production.

_____ 3. Positioning a product means establishing an identifiable product image in the minds of consumers.

_____ 4. Some of the more important promotional tools are personal selling, advertising, sales promotions, and public relations.

_____ 5. A push promotional strategy is designed to appeal directly to consumers who will demand a product from retailers.

_____ 6. Comparative advertising tries to influence consumers to buy one company's products instead of those of its rivals.

_____ 7. Advertising media include the Internet, newspapers, television, direct mail, radio, magazines, and outdoor advertising.

_____ 8. Radio accounts for the largest percent of advertising expenditures.

_____ 9. Personal selling tasks include order processing, creative selling, and missionary selling.

_____ 10. Retail selling is selling products to businesses, either for manufacturing other products, or for resale.

_____ 11. The seven steps in the personal selling process are prospecting, and qualifying, approaching, presenting a demonstration, handling objections, closing, and following up.

_____ 12. Closing is the step in the personal selling process in which salespeople identify potential customers.

_____ 13. Missionary selling is the promotion of a firm and its products rather than to try to close sales.

_____ 14. Coupons, point-of-purchase displays, premiums, and trade shows are all types of advertising.

_____ 15. Personal selling is the most expensive form of promotion per contact.

_____ 16. Advertising is specifically designed to try to encourage favorable reviews of products in newspapers and magazines and on radio and television.

_____ 17. Because consumers and investors support companies with good reputations, smart companies use public relations to build and protect their reputations.

MULTIPLE CHOICE
Circle the one best answer for each of the following questions.

1. Which of the following is *not* part of the promotional mix?
   a. Personal selling
   b. Pricing
   c. Advertising
   d. Public relations

2. Promotion seeks to accomplish which of the following things with customers?
   a. Make them aware and knowledgeable of products.
   b. Persuade them to like products.
   c. Persuade them to purchase products.
   d. All of the above.

3. Marketers may use promotion to
   a. communicate information.
   b. position products.
   c. add value and to control sales volume.
   d. All of the above.

4. Which of the following statements is true?
    a. In the push strategy, the producer "pushes" an item to distributors, who in turn promote the product to end-users.
    b. The "pull" approach depends on stimulating enough consumer demand to "pull" a product through wholesalers and retailers.
    c. Consumer products are more likely to rely on pull strategies; organizational products are more often pushed.
    d. All of the above.

5. In deciding on the appropriate promotional mix, marketers consider all of the following *except*
    a. the proper distribution channel.
    b. the promotional mix budget.
    c. the good or service being offered.
    d. characteristics of the target audience.

6. Which of the following statements is true?
    a. Firms rarely use a combination of push and pull strategies to increase the impact of their promotional efforts.
    b. Reminder advertising is intended to remind existing customers of a product's availability and benefits.
    c. Persuasive advertising directly compares two or more products.
    d. All of the above.

7. Which of the following forms of advertising would likely be most appropriate in the introductory stage of a product's life cycle?
    a. Comparative advertising.
    b. Persuasive advertising.
    c. Informative advertising.
    d. Reminder advertising.

8. Which of the following statements is true?
    a. The media mix is the combination of advertising media chosen to carry a message about a product.
    b. Institutional advertising promotes a cause, viewpoint, or candidate.
    c. Brand advertising promotes and firm's long-term image.
    d. All of the above.

9. Advertising promoting a specific brand is
    a. advocacy advertising.
    b. institutional advertising.
    c. brand advertising.
    d. comparative advertising.

10. Which of the following is *not* part of an advertising campaign?
    a. Identifying the target audience and establishing the advertising budget.
    b. Defining the objectives of the advertising messages, and creating the messages.
    c. Selecting the appropriate media and evaluating advertising effectiveness.
    d. Closing a sale and ensuring after-sale service.

11. Which of the following is *not* one of the seven steps in the personal-selling process?
    a. Approaching the prospect.
    b. Making the presentation.
    c. Delivering the product.
    d. Handling objections.

12. The step in the personal selling process in which salespeople determine whether prospects have the authority and ability to pay is
    a. prospecting.
    b. qualifying.
    c. order processing.
    d. closing.

13. The personal selling task in which salespeople receive orders and see to their handling and delivery is called
    a. closing.
    b. creative selling.
    c. order processing.
    d. missionary selling.

14. Personal selling
    a. involves direct, person-to-person communication, either face-to-face or by phone.
    b. has the disadvantage of being relatively expensive.
    c. has the advantage of allowing for immediate interaction between buyers and sellers, and enables sellers to adjust their message to the specific needs and interests of their individual customers.
    d. All of the above.

15. A sales promotion technique in which offers of free or reduced-price items are used to stimulate purchases is called a
    a. premium.
    b. trade show.
    c. point-of-purchase display.
    d. coupon.

16. Which of the following is true?
    a. The global perspective to international advertising directs its marketing to local or regional markets.
    b. Publicity is a promotional tool in which information about a company or product is transmitted by general mass media.
    c. Rarely do large companies undertake public relations.
    d. All of the above.

17. Which of the following needs to be considered when developing international promotional strategies?
    a. Product variations.
    b. Language differences.
    c. Cultural and image differences.
    d. All of the above.

18. Small businesses
    a. can advertise effectively and economically on the Internet.
    b. can engage in personal selling activities in local, national, and international markets.
    c. rely more heavily on premiums and special sales over coupons and contests, because coupons and contests are more expensive and harder to manage.
    d. All of the above.

JEOPARDY
You have 5 seconds to complete the questions to each of the following answers.

	The Promotional Mix and Personal Selling	Advertising	Sales Promotions and Public Relations
$100	Four important promotional tools. What is_____ ?	Advertising strategy that tries to influence consumers to buy one company's products instead of those of its rivals. What is_____ ?	A certificate issued entitling the buyer to a reduced price. What is_____ ?
$200	Four promotional objectives What is_____ ?	Advertising strategy that tries to keep a product's name in the minds of consumers. What is_____ ?	Product displays located in certain areas to stimulate purchase. What is_____ ?
$300	When a salesperson tries to persuade buyers to purchase products by providing information about their benefits. What is_____ ?	Advertising medium in which messages are mailed directly to consumers' homes or places of business. What is_____ ?	When members of an industry gather to display, demonstrate, and sell products. What is_____ ?
$400	When a salesperson promotes a firm or a product rather than trying to close a sale. What is_____ ?	Advertising promoting a cause, viewpoint, or candidate. What is_____ ?	An offer of free or reduced-price items used to stimulate purchases. What is_____ ?
$500	The seven steps in the personal-selling process. What is_____ ?	Advertising promoting a firm's long-term image. What is_____ ?	The overriding objective of public relations by a firm. What is_____ ?

MATCH THE TERMS AND CONCEPTS TO THEIR DEFINITIONS

a. promotion
b. positioning
c. pull strategy
d. push strategy
e. promotional mix
f. advertising
g. persuasive advertising
h. comparative advertising
i. reminder advertising
j   advertising media
k. direct mail
l. media mix

m. brand advertising
n. advocacy advertising
o. institutional advertising
p. advertising campaign
q. advertising agency
r. personal selling
s. retail selling
t. industrial selling
u. order processing
v. creative selling
w. missionary selling
x. prospecting

y. qualifying
z. closing
aa. sales promotion
bb. coupon
cc. point-of-purchase (POP) display
dd. premium
ee. trade show
ff. publicity
gg. public relations
hh. global perspective

_____   1. Sales promotion technique in which offers of free or reduced-price items are used to stimulate purchases.

_____ 2. Company-influenced publicity directed at building good will between an organization and potential customers.

_____ 3. Advertising promoting a specific brand.

_____ 4. Advertising strategy that tries to keep a product's name in the consumer's mind.

_____ 5. Personal selling situation in which products are sold for buyers' personal or household use.

_____ 6. Personal selling tasks in which salespeople promote their firms and products rather than try to close sales.

_____ 7. Step in the personal selling process in which salespeople ask prospective customers to buy products.

_____ 8. Advertising strategy that tries to influence consumers to buy one company's products instead of those of its rivals.

_____ 9. Process of establishing an identifiable product image in the minds of consumers.

_____ 10. Promotional tool in which information about a company or product is transmitted by general mass media.

_____ 11. Short-term promotional activity designed to stimulate consumer buying or cooperation from distributors and sales agents.

_____ 12. Aspect of the marketing mix concerned with the most effective techniques for selling a product.

_____ 13. Sales promotion technique in which product displays are located in certain areas to stimulate purchase.

_____ 14. Combination of tools used to promote a product.

_____ 15. Advertising promoting a cause, viewpoint, or candidate.

_____ 16. Advertising strategy that directly compares two or more products.

_____ 17. Personal selling task in which salespeople try to persuade buyers to purchase products by providing information about their benefits.

_____ 18. Arrangement of ads in selected media to reach targeted audiences.

_____ 19. Sales promotion technique in which various members of an industry gather to display, demonstrate, and sell products.

_____ 20. Promotional tool consisting of paid, nonpersonal communication used by an identified sponsor to inform an audience about a product.

_____ 21. Promotional strategy designed to encourage wholesalers or retailers to market products to consumers.

_____ 22. Personal selling task in which salespeople receive orders and see to their handling and delivery.

_____ 23. Step in the personal selling process in which salespeople determine whether prospects have the authority and ability to pay.

_____ 24. Company's approach to directing its marketing toward worldwide rather than local or regional markets.

_____ 25. Advertising medium in which messages are mailed directly to consumers' homes or places of business.

_____ 26. Promotional strategy designed to appeal directly to consumers who will demand a product from retailers.

_____ 27. Sales promotion technique in which a certificate is issued entitling the buyer to a reduced price.

_____ 28. Independent company that provides some or all of a client firm's advertising needs.

_____ 29. Combination of advertising media chosen to carry message about a product.

_____ 30. Variety of communication devices for carrying a seller's message to potential customers.

_____ 31. Step in the personal selling process in which salespeople identify potential customers.

_____ 32. Personal selling situation in which products are sold to businesses, either for manufacturing other products or for resale.

_____ 33. Advertising promoting a firm's long-term image.

_____ 34. Promotional tool in which a salesperson communicates one-on-one with potential customers.

WORD SCRAMBLE

1. _____   2. _____   _____   3. _____   _____
   stingidaver   lasse   romontopi   clipub   snaletior

LEARNING OBJECTIVES--POTENTIAL SHORT ANSWER OR ESSAY QUESTIONS

Learning Objective #1: "**Identify the important objectives of *promotion* and discuss the considerations entailed in selecting a *promotional mix*.**"

Learning Objective #2: **"Discuss the most important *advertising strategies* and describe the key *advertising media.*"**

Learning Objective #3: **"Outline the tasks involved in *personal selling* and list the steps in the *personal selling process.*"**

Learning Objective #4: **"Describe the various types of *sales promotions.*"**

Learning Objective #5: **"Describe the development of *international promotional strategies.*"**

Learning Objective #6: "Show how small businesses use promotional activities."

CRITICAL THINKING QUESTIONS

1. What are the advantages and disadvantages of using each of the following advertising medium?

    a. Newspapers

    b. Television

    c. Direct mail

    d. Radio

    e. Magazines

    f. Outdoor advertising

    g. Internet advertising

    h. Virtual advertising

2. Suppose a firm has developed a new product. The company is so excited about its new product that it states, "this good will sell itself!" Does this mean that a promotional strategy is not important? Generally, what kind of marketing strategy would you recommend for this good?

BRAIN TEASER

1. Advertising agencies often argue that "advertising doesn't cost; it pays!" What do they mean? Is that possible? Generally, what is the recommended amount of advertising dollars that should be spent by a company in promoting its good or service?

ANSWERS

True-False--*Answers*

1. True
2. False: The ultimate goal of any promotion is to *increase sales*.
3. True
4. True
5. False: A *pull* promotional strategy is designed to appeal directly to consumers who will demand a product from retailers.
6. False: *Persuasive* advertising tries to influence consumers to buy one company's products instead of those of its rivals.
7. True
8. False: *Newspapers* account for the largest percent of advertising expenditures.
9. True
10. False: *Industrial* selling is selling products to businesses, either for manufacturing other products or for resale.
11. True
12. False: *Prospecting* is the step in the personal selling process in which salespeople identify potential customers.
13. True
14. False: Coupons, point-of-purchase displays, premiums and trade shows are all types of *sales promotions*.
15. True
16. False: *Publicity* is specifically designed to try to encourage favorable reviews of products in newspapers and magazines and on radio and television.
17. True

Multiple Choice--*Answers*

1. b	5. a	9. c	13. c	17. d
2. d	6. b	10. d	14. d	18. d
3. d	7. c	11. c	15. a	
4. d	8. a	12. b	16. b	

Jeopardy—*Answers*

	The Promotional Mix and Personal Selling	Advertising	Sales Promotions and Public Relations
$100	personal selling, advertising, sales promotions, and public relations.	persuasive advertising	a coupon
$200	communicating information, positioning products, adding value, and controlling sales volume	reminder advertising	point-of-purchase displays
$300	creative selling	direct mail	a trade show
$400	missionary selling	advocacy advertising	a premium
$500	prospecting and qualifying, approaching, making the presentation, handling objections, closing, and following up	institutional advertising	to enhance a company's reputation with consumers and investors

Match the Terms and Concepts to Their Definitions--*Answers*

1. dd	6. w	11. aa	16. h	21. d	26. c	31. x
2. gg	7. z	12. a	17. v	22. u	27. bb	32. t
3. m	8. g	13. cc	18. p	23. y	28. q	33. o
4. i	9. b	14. e	19. ee	24. hh	29. l	34. r
5. s	10. ff	15. n	20. f	25. k	30. j	

Word Scramble--*Answers*

1. advertising   2. sales promotion   3. public relations

Learning Objectives--Potential Short Answer or Essay Questions--*Answers*

Learning Objective #1:

Although the ultimate goal of a *promotion* is to increase sales, other goals include *communicating information, positioning a product, adding value*, and *controlling sales volume*. In deciding on the appropriate *promotional mix*, marketers must consider the good or service being offered, characteristics of the target audience and the buyer's decision process, and the promotional mix budget.

Learning Objective #2:

Advertising strategies often depend on the *product life cycle stage*. In the introductory stage, *informative advertising* helps to build awareness. As a product passes through the growth and maturity stages, *persuasive advertising, comparative advertising*, and *reminder advertising* are often used. *Advertising media* include the Internet, newspapers, television, direct mail, radio, magazines, and outdoor advertising, as well as other channels such as *Yellow Pages*, special events, and door-to-door selling. The combination of media that a company chooses is called its *media mix*.

Learning Objective #3:

Personal selling tasks include *order processing, creative selling* (activities that help persuade buyers), and *missionary selling* (activities that *promote firms and products rather than simply close sales). The personal* selling process consists of six steps: *prospecting and qualifying* (identifying potential customers with the authority to buy), *approaching* (the first moments of contact), *presenting and demonstrating* (presenting the promotional message that explains the product), *handling objections, closing* (asking for the sale), and *following up* (processing the order and ensuring after-sale service).

Learning Objective #4:

Coupons provide savings off the regular price of a product. *Point-of-purchase (POP) displays* are intended to grab attention and help customers find products in stores. Purchasing incentives include *samples* (which let customers try products without buying them) and *premiums* (rewards for buying products). At *trade shows*, sellers rent booths to display products to customers who already have an interest in buying. *Contests* are intended to increase sales by stimulating buyers' interest in products.

Learning Objective #5:

Many firms began exploring the possibilities of international sales when domestic sales flattened out in the mid-twentieth century. Because advertising is the best tool for stimulating product awareness on a country-by-country basis, it has played a key role in the growth of international marketing. Whereas some firms prefer a *decentralized approach* (separate marketing management for different countries), others have adopted a *global perspective* (coordinating marketing programs directed at one worldwide audience). Because the global perspective requires products designed for multinational markets, companies such as Coca-Cola, McDonald's, and many others have developed *global brands*. In promoting these products, global advertising must overcome such challenges as product variations, language differences, cultural receptiveness, and image differences.

Learning Objective #6:

Small business can advertise effectively and economically on the Internet. They can also engage in personal selling activities in local, national, and international markets. Because coupons and contests are more expensive and harder to manage, small business owners are likely to rely more heavily on premiums and special sales.

Critical Thinking Questions—*Answers*

1. a. The main advantage of newspaper advertising is flexible, rapid coverage, However, newspapers are generally thrown out after one day, and they do not usually allow advertisers to target audiences very well.

    b. Television has the advantage of exercising a broad range of consumer's senses, it reaches a large audience that also allows for some targeting. However, television advertising is very expensive. Also, because of the brevity of TV ads, a company's message may get confused with so many other commercials, and the brevity does not allow enough time to educate viewers about complex products.

    c. Direct mail allows a company to select its audience and to personalize its message. However, it can involve the largest advance cost.

    d. Radio allows for target marketing, but radio ads are over quickly and only provide audio presentations.

    e. Magazines provide for ready market segmentation and allow for detailed information. They also last longer than most print media. Magazine advertising has its drawbacks. Publishers usually require that ads are submitted well in advance and there is no guarantee where the ad will appear in the magazine.

    f. Outdoor advertising is inexpensive and faces little competition for customers' attention. However, outdoor ads can present only limited amounts of information, and sellers have little control over audiences.

    g. Internet advertising allows for targeting customers but may not be read by anyone. However, it does allow advertisers to measure the success of each ad by counting the number of "hits" to an Internet location.

    h. The verdict on virtual advertising is still out because it is so new. However, its use has many advertisers excited.

2. If a good "sells itself," then this means it will likely be very popular with consumers. Therefore, sales are likely to pick up over a relatively short period of time, as consumers become familiar with its existence. However, this does not mean that a promotional strategy is not important. Generally, the company would want to undertake informative advertising that would expose the product to as many customers as possible so that it can "sell itself."

Brain Teaser—*Answer*

1. Advertising, if properly undertaken, can increase sales revenues more than it increases a company's cost. Advertising can increase a firm's profits. A firm should continue to undertake advertising (through whatever medium) for as long as it generates more sales revenues than it costs the company.

Chapter 14
Distributing Products

LEARNING OBJECTIVES
After studying this chapter, you should be able to:

1. Identify the different *channels of distribution* and explain different *distribution strategies*.
2. Explain the differences between *merchant wholesalers* and *agents/brokers*.
3. Identify the different types of *retailing* and *retail stores*.
4. Describe the major activities in the *physical distribution process*.
5. Compare the five basic forms of *transportation* and identify the types of firms that provide them.

TRUE-FALSE
Indicate whether the statement is generally true or false by placing a "T" or "F" in the space provided. If it is a false statement, correct it so that it becomes a true statement.

_____ 1. Intermediaries (or middlemen) are generally classified as either being wholesalers and retailers.

_____ 2. Retailers sell products to other businesses that then resell them to final consumers, while wholesalers sell products directly to consumers.

_____ 3. A distribution channel is the path that a product follows from producer to end-user.

_____ 4. The distribution of consumer products can travel through direct channels, through a retailer, wholesaler, or sales agent or broker.

_____ 5. A sales agent/broker is an independent intermediary who usually represents many manufacturers and sells to wholesalers or retailers.

_____ 6. Generally, nondirect distribution channels mean a higher price for end users: The more members in the channel—the more intermediaries—the higher the final price.

_____ 7. Intermediaries can actually save time and money for some consumers.

_____ 8. An exclusive distribution strategy is one in which a company uses only wholesalers and retailers who give special attention to specific products.

_____ 9. Wholesalers may extend credit, as well as store, repackage, and deliver products to other members of the distribution channel.

_____ 10. Unlike agents and brokers, wholesalers never take legal possession of products.

_____ 11. In e-commerce, e-agents assist Internet users in finding products and best prices.

_____ 12. Bargain retailers include department stores, supermarkets, hypermarkets, and specialty stores.

_____ 13. Interactive marketing is a nonstore retailing that uses a Web site to provide real-time sales and customer service.

_____ 14. A mail-order firm is an example of a retail outlet.

_____ 15. Physical distribution includes all the activities needed to move products from manufacturers to consumers.

_____ 16. Warehousing costs do not include the costs of inventory control and material handling.

_____ 17. Telephone and fiber optic cable lines are the major transportation modes used in the distribution process.

_____ 18. The distribution strategy's overarching goal is to get the product desired by consumers when and where it is desired.

MULTIPLE CHOICE
Circle the one best answer for each of the following questions.

1. Whether a firm relies on independent intermediaries or uses its own distribution networks and sales forces, hinges on
    a. the company's target markets.
    b. the nature of its product.
    c. the cost of maintaining distribution and sales networks.
    d. All of the above.

2. Which of the following describes a type of distribution channel?
    a. Producer to consumer.
    b. Producer to retailer to consumer.
    c. Producer to wholesaler to retailer to consumer.
    d. All of the above.

3. The distribution of consumer products can either be through a
    a. direct channel.
    b. retailer.
    c. wholesaler, sales agent or broker.
    d. All of the above.

4. Choosing one distribution channel over another depends on
    a. the number of outlets where the product is available.
    b. the cost of distribution.
    c. the need for control over the product as it moves through the channel to the final consumer.
    d. All of the above.

5. The distribution of products for businesses can either be through a
    a. direct channel.
    b. retailer.
    c. wholesaler, sales agent or broker.
    d. All of the above.

6. A distribution strategy by which a product is distributed through as many channels as possible is
    a. an intensive distribution.
    b. an exclusive distribution.
    c. a selective distribution.
    d. a restrictive distribution.

7. An exclusive distribution strategy
    a. is designed to move products from the consumer to the producer.
    b. tries to distribute a product through as many channels as possible.
    c. grants exclusive rights to distribute or sell a product to a limited number of wholesalers or retailers in a given geographic area.
    d. uses only wholesalers and retailers who give special attention to specific products.

8. Wholesalers
    a. function as sales and merchandising arms of manufacturers who do not have their own sales forces.
    b. may provide advertising and display merchandising services.
    c. may provide storage and delivery services.
    d. All of the above.

9. Independent wholesalers that do not take title to the goods they distribute, but may or may not take possession of those goods, are called:
    a. rack jobbers.
    b. agents and brokers.
    c. full-service merchant wholesalers.
    d. limited-service merchant wholesalers.

10. Which of the following statements is true?
    a. A warehouse club (wholesale club) is a bargain retailer offering large discounts on brand-name merchandise to customers who have paid annual membership fees.
    b. Retailers can be described according to two classifications: product line retailers and bargain retailers.
    c. A specialty store is a very large product line retailer carrying a wide variety of unrelated products.
    d. All of the above.

11. Which of the following is a type of nonstore retailer?
    a. Electronic storefronts.
    b. Discount stores.
    c. Specialty stores.
    d. Supermarkets.

12. A warehouse providing short-term storage of goods for which demand is both constant and high is a
    a. public warehouse.
    b. private warehouse.
    c. distribution center.
    d. storage warehouse.

13. Which of the following statements is true?
    a. Inventory control is concerned with transporting, arranging, and retrieving supplies.
    b. Material handling is concerned with maintaining adequate, but not excessive, supplies.
    c. In addition to storage, insurance, and wage-related costs, the cost of warehousing goods also includes inventory control and material handling.
    d. All of the above.

14 Modes of transportation in the distribution process differ
    a. in cost and availability.
    b. in reliability and speed.
    c. in the number of points served.
    d. All of the above.

15 Which of the following statements is true about modes of transportation?
    a. Air transportation is the fastest and least expensive.
    b. Water transportation is the slowest and most expensive.
    c. Since transport companies were deregulated in 1980, they have become more cost-efficient and competitive by developing such innovations as intermodal transportation and containerization.
    d. All of the above.

JEOPARDY

You have 5 seconds to complete the questions to each of the following answers.

	Channels of Distribution	Wholesaling and Retailing	Managing Physical Distribution
$100	The total number of different types of distribution channels. What is_____ _____?	These wholesalers differ in the number and types of distribution functions they offer. What is_____ _____?	The major modes of transportation. What is_____ _____?
$200	The first four distribution channels discussed in the textbook serve these end-users. What is_____ _____?	The difference between wholesalers and agents/brokers. What is_____ _____?	The three major activities in the physical distribution process. What is_____ _____?
$300	The fifth distribution channel discussed in the textbook includes this. What is_____ _____?	The two classifications of retailers. What is_____ _____?	Warehouse operation that tracks inventory on hand and ensures an adequate supply at all times. What is_____ _____?
$400	Channels 6 through 8 serve these end-users What is_____ _____?	These include department stores, supermarkets, hypermarkets, and specialty stores. What is_____ _____?	Warehouse operation involving the transportation, arrangement, and orderly retrieval of goods in inventory. What is_____ _____?
$500	The three different types of distribution strategies. What is_____ _____?	This type of retailing may use direct mail catalogs, vending machines, video marketing, telemarketing, electronic shopping, and direct selling. What is_____ _____?	The overall objective of the physical distribution process. What is_____ _____?

MATCH THE TERMS AND CONCEPTS TO THEIR DEFINITIONS

a. electronic storefront
b. e-intermediary
c. shopping agent (e-agent)
d. syndicated selling
e. cybermall
f. multilevel marketing
g. distribution mix
h. intermediary
i. wholesaler
j   retailer
k. distribution channel
l. direct channel
m. sales agent/broker
n. industrial distribution
o. sales office
p. intensive distribution
q. exclusive distribution
r. selective distribution
s. channel conflict
t. channel captain
u. vertical marketing system (VMS)
v. merchant wholesaler

w. full-service merchant wholesaler
x. limited-function merchant wholesaler
y. drop shipper
z. rack jobber
aa. department store
bb. supermarket
cc. hypermarket
dd. scrambled merchandising
ee. specialty store
ff. bargain retailer
gg. discount house
hh. off-price store
ii. catalog showroom
jj. factory outlet
kk. warehouse club (or wholesale club)
ll. convenience store
mm. direct-response retailing
nn. mail order (or catalog marketing)
oo. video marketing

pp. telemarketing
qq. electronic shopping
rr. direct selling
ss. wheel of retailing
tt. physical distribution
uu. warehousing
vv. private warehouse
ww. public warehouse
xx. storage warehouse
yy. distribution center
zz. inventory control
aaa. material handling
bbb. intermodal transportation
ccc. common carrier
ddd. freight forwarder
eee. contract carrier
fff. private carrier
ggg. order processing
hhh. order cycle time
iii. hub

_____ 1. Large product line retailer characterized by organization into specialized departments.

_____ 2. Internet distribution channel member who assists in moving products through to customers or who collects information about various sellers to be presented in convenient format for Internet customers.

_____ 3. Intermediary who sells products directly to consumers.

_____ 4. In customer service operations, the filling of orders as they are received.

_____ 5. Nonstore retailing by direct interaction with customers to inform them of products and to receive sales orders.

_____ 6. Independently owned and operated warehouse that stores goods for many firms.

_____ 7. Strategy by which a manufacturer grants exclusive rights to distribute or sell a product to a limited number of wholesalers or retailers in a given geographic area.

_____ 8. Distribution channel consisting of self-employed distributors who receive commissions for selling products to customers and for recruiting new distributors.

_____ 9. Combined use of several different modes of transportation.

_____ 10. Merchant wholesaler who provides credit, marketing, and merchandising services in addition to traditional buying and selling services.

_____ 11. Bargain retailer that generates large sales volume by offering goods at substantial price reductions.

_____ 12. Distribution channel in which a product travels from producer to consumer without intermediaries.

_____ 13. Nonstore retailing in which information about the seller's products and services is connected to consumers' computers, allowing consumers to receive the information and purchase the products in the home.

_____ 14. Warehouse providing short-term storage of goods for which demand is both constant and high.

_____ 15. Central distribution outlet that controls all or most of a firm's distribution activities.

_____ 16. Limited-function merchant wholesaler who receives customer orders, negotiates with producers, takes title to goods, and arranges for shipment to customers.

_____ 17. E-intermediary (middleman) in the Internet distribution channel who assists users in finding products and prices but who does not take possession of products.

_____ 18. Network of channel members involved in the flow of manufactured goods to industrial customers.

_____ 19. Physical distribution operation concerned with the storage of goods.

_____ 20. Bargain retailer offering large discounts on brand-name merchandise to customers who have paid annual membership fees.

_____ 21. Very large product line retailer carrying a wide variety of unrelated products.

_____ 22. E-commerce practice whereby a Web site offers other Websites commissions for referring customers.

_____ 23. Conflict arising when the members of a distribution channel disagree over the roles they should play or the rewards they should receive.

_____ 24. Nonstore retailing to consumers via standard and cable television.

_____ 25. Transporting company that leases bulk space from other carriers to be resold to firms making smaller shipments.

_____ 26. Small retail store carrying one product line or category of related products.

_____ 27. Unified distribution channel composed of separate businesses centrally controlled by a single member.

_____ 28. Manufacturer or retailer that maintains its own transportation system.

_____ 29. Individual or firm that helps to distribute a product.

_____ 30. Concept of retail evolution holding that low-service, low-price stores add services and raise prices until they lose price-sensitive customers and are replaced by new firms that enter the market to fill the need for low-price stores.

_____ 31. Bargain retailer in which customers place orders for catalog items to be picked up at on-premises warehouses.

_____ 32. Commercial Web site in which customers gather information about products, buying opportunities, placing orders, and paying for purchases.

_____ 33. Limited-function merchant wholesaler who sets up and maintains display racks in retail stores.

_____ 34. Independent transporting company that usually owns the vehicles in which it transports products.

_____ 35. Independent intermediary who usually represents many manufacturers and sells to wholesalers or retailers.

_____ 36. Strategy by which a company uses only wholesalers and retailers who give special attention to specific products.

_____ 37. Form of nonstore retailing typified by door-to-door sales.

_____ 38. Retail practice of carrying any product that is expected to sell well regardless of a store's original product offering.

_____ 39. Independent wholesaler who takes legal possession of goods produced by a variety of manufacturers and then resells them to other businesses.

_____ 40. Warehouse operation involving the transportation, arrangement, and orderly retrieval of goods in inventory.

_____ 41. In customer service operations, total time elapsed between placement and receipt of orders.

_____ 42. Form of nonstore retailing in which customers place orders for catalog merchandise received through the mail.

_____ 43. Bargain retailer that buys excess inventories from high-quality manufacturers and sells them at discounted prices.

_____ 44. Collection of virtual storefronts (business Web sites) representing a variety of products and product lines on the Internet.

_____ 45. Strategy by which a product is distributed through as many channels as possible.

_____ 46. Retailer carrying a wide range of products at bargain prices.

_____ 47. Merchant wholesaler who provides a limited range of services.

_____ 48. Transporting company, such as a truck line or railroad, that transports goods for any shipper.

_____ 49. Large product line retailer offering a variety of food and food-related items in specialized departments.

_____ 50. Combination of distribution channels by which a firm gets its products to end users.

_____ 51. Channel member who is most powerful in determining the roles and rewards of other members.

_____ 52. Office maintained by a manufacturer as a contact point with its customers.

_____ 53. Activities needed to move a product efficiently from manufacturer to consumer.

_____ 54. Warehouse owned by, and providing storage for, a single company.

_____ 55. Network of interdependent companies through which a product passes from producer to end user.

_____ 56. Nonstore retailing in which the telephone is used to sell directly to consumers.

_____ 57. Warehouse operation that tracks inventory on hand and ensures that an adequate supply is in stock at all times.

_____ 58. Intermediary who sells products to other businesses for resale to final consumers.

_____ 59. Bargain retailer owned by the manufacturer whose products it sells.

_____ 60. Warehouse providing storage for extended periods of time.

_____ 61. Retail store offering easy accessibility, extended hours, and fast service.

WORD SCRAMBLE

1. _____   _____ 2. _____   _____ 3. _____
   sluvexcie   buttridision   plahysic   tribdistuion   selaitrer

LEARNING OBJECTIVES--POTENTIAL SHORT ANSWER OR ESSAY QUESTIONS

Learning Objective #1: "Identify the different *channels of distribution* and explain different *distribution strategies*."

Learning Objective #2: **"Explain the differences between *merchant wholesalers* and *agents/brokers*."**

Learning Objective #3: **"Identify the different types of *retailing* and *retail stores*."**

Learning Objective #4: **"Describe the major activities in the *physical distribution process*."**

Learning Objective #5: "Compare the five basic forms of *transportation* and identify the types of firms that provide them."

CRITICAL THINKING QUESTIONS

1. For each of the following determine the channel number as discussed in the textbook (see Figure 14.1 on page 381).
   a. This channel involves direct sales to consumers.

   b. This channel involves selling to consumers through a wholesaler and a retailer.

   c. This channel involves selling to a consumer through a retailer only.

   d. This channel involves selling to a consumer through an agent/broker, a wholesaler and a retailer.

   e. This channel includes only an agent between the producer and the customer.

   f. This channel includes retail superstores that get products from producers or wholesalers (or both) for re-selling to business customers.

   g. This channel entails selling to business users through wholesalers.

   h. This channel involves a direct sale to an industrial user.

2. For each of the following, determine what might be the most appropriate distribution channel (refer to the channel number as discussed in the textbook, Figure 14.1 on page 381). Assume the product is sold to consumers.
   a. There are a large number of transactions necessary in getting the product to the consumer.

   b. The value of each transaction in the distribution channel is high.

   c. The market is growing very rapidly.

   d. Customers are clustered in a limited geographic area.

   e. The product is complex, innovative, and specialized.

BRAIN TEASER

1. Why do companies need to modify their marketing channel distribution strategies periodically?

ANSWERS

True-False--*Answers*
1. True
2. False: *Wholesalers* sell products to other businesses that then resell them to final consumers, while *retailers* sell products directly to consumers.
3. True
4. True
5. True
6. True
7. True
8. False: *A selective* distribution strategy is one in which a company uses only wholesalers and retailers who give special attention to specific products.
9. True
10. False: Unlike *wholesalers*, *agents and brokers* never take legal possession of products.
11. True
12. False: *Product line retailers* include department stores, supermarkets, hypermarkets, and specialty stores.
13. True
14. False: A mail-order firm is an example of a *nonstore retailer*.
15. True
16. False: Warehousing costs *do* include the costs of inventory control and material handling.
17. False: *Trucks, railroads, planes, water carriers, and pipelines* are the major transportation modes used in the distribution process.
18. True

Multiple Choice--*Answers*

1. d	5. d	9. c	13. c
2. d	6. a	10. b	14. d
3. d	7. c	11. a	15. c
4. d	8. d	12. c	16. d

Jeopardy—*Answers*

	Channels of Distribution	Wholesaling and Retailing	Managing Physical Distribution
$100	eight	full-service and limited-function wholesalers	trucks, railroads, ships, airplanes, and pipelines.
$200	consumers	unlike wholesalers, agents and brokers never take legal possession of products	customer service, warehousing, and transportation of products
$300	only an agent between the producer and the consumer	product-line and bargain retailers	inventory control
$400	business users	product-line retailers	material handling
$500	intensive, exclusive and selective distribution	nonstore retailing	to get the product to the consumer at the right place and at the right time

Match the Terms and Concepts to Their Definitions--*Answers*

1. aa	8. f	15. iii	22. d	29. h	36. r	43. hh	50. g	57. zz
2. b	9. bbb	16. y	23. s	30. ss	37. rr	44. e	51. t	58. i
3. j	10. w	17. c	24. oo	31. ii	38. dd	45. p	52. o	59. jj
4. ggg	11. gg	18. n	25. ddd	32. a	39. v	46. ff	53. tt	60. xx
5. mm	12. l	19. uu	26. ee	33. z	40. aaa	47. x	54. vv	61. ll
6. ww	13. qq	20. kk	27. u	34. eee	41. hhh	48. ccc	55. k	
7. q	14. yy	21. cc	28. fff	35. m	42. nn	49. bb	56. pp	

Word Scramble--*Answers*

1. exclusive distribution   2. physical distribution   3. retailers

Learning Objectives--Potential Short Answer or Essay Questions--*Answers*

Learning Objective #1:

In selecting a *distribution mix*, a firm may use all or any of eight *distribution channels*. The first four are aimed at getting products to consumers, the fifth is for consumers or business customers, and the last three are aimed at getting products to business customers. Channel 1 involves direct sales to consumers. Channel 2 includes a *retailer*. Channel 3 involves both a retailer and a *wholesaler*, and Channel 4 includes an *agent* or *broker* who enters the system before the wholesaler and retailer. Channel 5 includes only an agent between the producer and the customer. Channel 6, which is used extensively for e-commerce, involves a direct sale to an industrial user. Channel 7, which is used infrequently, entails selling to business users through wholesalers. Channel 8 includes retail superstores that get products from producers or wholesalers (or both) for re-selling to business customers. *Distribution strategies* include *intensive, exclusive,* and *selective distribution,* which differ in the number of products and channel members involved and in the amount of service performed in the channel.

Learning Objective #2:

Wholesalers act as distribution *intermediaries*. They may extend credit as well as store, repackage, and deliver products to other members of the channel. *Full-service* and *limited-function merchant wholesalers* differ in the number and types of distribution functions they offer. Unlike wholesalers, *agents* and *brokers* never take legal possession of products. Rather, they function as sales and merchandising arms of manufacturers who do not have their own sales forces. They may also provide such services as advertising and display merchandising. In e-commerce, *e-agents* assist Internet users in finding products and best prices.

Learning Objective #3:

Retailers can be described according to two classifications: *product line retailers* and *bargain retailers*. Product line retailers include *department stores, supermarkets, hypermarkets*, and *specialty stores*. Bargain retailers include *discount houses, off-price stores, catalog showrooms, factory outlets, warehouse clubs*, and *convenience stores*. These retailers differ in terms of size, goods and services offered, and pricing. Some retailing also takes place without stores.

Nonstore retailing may use *direct mail catalogs, vending machines, video marketing, telemarketing, electronic shopping*, and *direct selling*. Internet retail shopping includes *electronic storefronts* where customers can examine a store's products, receive information about sellers and their products, place orders, and make payments electronically. Customers can also visit *cybermalls*— a collection of virtual storefronts representing a variety of product lines on the Internet.

Learning Objective #4:

Physical distribution includes all the activities needed to move products from manufacturers to consumers, including *customer service, warehousing*, and *transportation* of products. Warehouses may be *public* or *private* and may function either as long-term *storage warehouses* or as *distribution centers*. In addition to storage, insurance, and wage-related costs, the cost of warehousing goods also includes *inventory control* (maintaining adequate but not excessive supplies) and *material handling* (transporting, arranging, and retrieving supplies).

Learning Objective #5:

Trucks, railroads, planes, water carriers (boats and barges), and pipelines are the major *transportation modes* used in the distribution process. They differ in cost, availability, reliability, speed, and number of points served. Air is the fastest but most expensive mode; water carriers are the slowest but least expensive. Since transport companies were deregulated in 1980, they have become more cost-efficient and competitive by developing such innovations as *intermodal transportation* and *containerization*. Transportation in any form may be supplied by *common carriers, freight forwarders, contract carriers*, or *private carriers*.

Critical Thinking Questions--*Answers*

1. a. Channel 1.
   b. Channel 3.
   c. Channel 2.
   d. Channel 4.
   e. Channel 5.
   f. Channel 8.
   g. Channel 7.
   h. Channel 6.

2. a. Possibly channel 4 to take advantage of the services of a longer distribution channel.
   b. Possibly channel 1 to avoid the high cost of each transaction.
   c. Possibly channel 3 to allow wholesalers the opportunity to manage a growing inventory.
   d. Possibly channel 1 or 2 because of the limited geography.
   e. Possibly channel 4 to allow the expertise of the various distribution channels to inform customers.

Brain Teaser--*Answer*

1. In short, companies need to modify their marketing channel distribution strategies periodically to remain competitive. We live in a rapidly changing, dynamic, and increasingly competitive market environment. Battles over how products will be distributed are inevitable. Firms must remain flexible and willing to change distribution channels (and the companies they are doing business with) if they wish to survive the competition. Unfortunately, some businesses will be hurt by this change.

Chapter 15

Producing Goods and Services

LEARNING OBJECTIVES

After studying this chapter, you should be able to:

1. Explain the meaning of the term *production* or *operations* and describe the four kinds of *utility* it provides.
2. Describe and explain the three classifications of *operations processes*.
3. Identify the characteristics that distinguish *service operations* from *goods production* and explain the main differences in the *service focus*.
4. Describe the factors involved in *operations planning*.
5. Explain some of the activities involved in *operations control*, including *materials management* and the use of certain *operation control tools*.

TRUE-FALSE

Indicate whether the statement is generally true or false by placing a "T" or "F" in the space provided. If it is a false statement, correct it so that it becomes a true statement.

_____ 1. Production (or operations) management refers to the systematic direction and control of the processes that transform resources into finished services and goods for consumers.

_____ 2. The four kinds of utility products create for customers are time, place, ownership, and space utility.

_____ 3. Time utility refers to consumer satisfaction derived from a product being available where it is most convenient for the customer.

_____ 4. All goods manufacturing processes can be classified as being either analytical or synthetic processes.

_____ 5. An analytical goods manufacturing process combines raw materials to produce a finished product.

_____ 6. Service operations are classified according to the extent of customer contact.

_____ 7. A high-contact service operations process is one in which the customer need not be part of the system to receive the service.

_____ 8. The creation of both goods and services involves resources, transformations, and finished products.

_____ 9. Service providers typically focus on the customer-service link, often acknowledging the customer as part of the operations process.

_____ 10. Operations planning involves the analysis of six key factors: forecasts, capacity planning, location planning, layout planning, quality planning, and methods planning.

_____ 11. Capacity planning for goods means ensuring that manufacturing capacity is slightly below the normal demand for its product.

_____ 12. Location planning for low-contact services focuses on locating the service near customers, who are part of the system.

_____ 13. Service flow analysis and process flow charts are helpful for identifying all operations activities and eliminating wasteful steps from production.

_____ 14. A process layout is a spatial arrangement of production facilities designed to move families of products through similar flow paths.

_____ 15. A master production plan shows which products will be produced, when production will occur, and what resources will be used during specified time periods.

_____ 16. Follow-up is an essential and ongoing facet of operations control.

_____ 17. Just-in-time production systems are concerned with the planning, organizing, and controlling of the flow of materials.

_____ 18. Just-in-time systems are more susceptible to disruptions in the flow of raw materials, but allow for disruptions to get resolved more quickly.

_____ 19. Material requirements planning (MRP) uses computer-controlled schedules for moving inventories through each stage of production.

_____ 20. The five main areas in material management are transportation, warehousing, purchasing, supplier selection, and inventory control.

MULTIPLE CHOICE

Circle the one best answer for each of the following questions.

1. Which of the following statements is true?
    a. Production and employment in the services sector of our economy has been rising more rapidly than the goods sector.
    b. Resources are those things used in the production of goods and services.
    c. Utility is a product's ability to satisfy a human want.
    d. All of the above.

2. Which of the following is a resource?
    a. Knowledge.
    b. Raw materials and equipment.
    c. Labor.
    d. All of the above.

3. Which of the following is *not* one of the kinds of utility goods and services provided to customers?
    a. Form.
    b. Leisure.
    P. Place.
    d. Time.

4. The satisfaction derived by having a product available where it is most convenient for customers is
    a. Time utility.
    b. Form utility.
    c. Place utility.
    d. Ownership utility.

5. Which of the following is true about operations processes?
    a. A synthetic process is a production process in which resources are broken down into components to create finished products.
    b. An analytic process occurs when resources are combined to create finished products.
    c. A high-contact service system exists when the customer is part of the system during service delivery.
    d. All of the above.

6. The production of services, as opposed to goods, are
    a. largely intangible.
    b. more likely to be customized.
    c. more unstorable.
    d. All of the above.

7. The spatial arrangement of production activities designed to move resources through a smooth, fixed sequence of steps is
    a. product layout.
    b. forecasting.
    c. location planning.
    d. quality planning.

8. Capacity planning
    a. is a facet of a long-range production plan that predicts future demand.
    b. for goods means ensuring that a manufacturing firm's capacity slightly exceeds the normal demand for its product.
    c. in low-contact services means managers must plan capacity to meet peak demand.
    d. All of the above.

9. The spatial arrangement of production activities designed to move resources through a smooth, fixed sequence of steps is
    a. product layout.
    b. process layout.
    c. cellular layout.
    d. quality planning.

10. Planning, organizing, and controlling the flow of materials from design through distribution of finished goods is
    a. purchasing.
    b. follow-up.
    c. materials management.
    d. warehousing.

11. Within a business, acquiring the raw materials and services that a manufacturer needs is the function of
    a. the transportation department.
    b. the purchasing department.
    c. the warehousing department.
    d. the inventory control department.

12. Management of the production process designed to manufacture goods or supply services that meet specific standards is
    a. bill of materials control.
    b. supplier selection control.
    c. quality control.
    d. inventory control.

13. A system for determining the right quantity of various items to have on hand and keeping track of their location, use, and condition is called
    a. supply-chain management.
    b. inventory control.
    c. purchasing.
    d. lead time.

14. Just-in-time (JIT) systems attempt to reduce waste and improve quality by
    a. ordering supplies only when they are needed.
    b. holding a sufficient buffer stock of inventory to handle unforeseen circumstances.
    c. increasing finished-goods inventory to ensure that only non-defects will be shipped to customers.
    d. All of the above.

JEOPARDY

You have 5 seconds to complete the question to each of the following answers.

	Operations Processes	**Operations Planning**	**Operations Control**
$100	Production process in which resources are broken down into components to create finished products. What is_____ _____?	This planning analyzes how much of a product a firm must be able to produce. What is_____ _____?	The planning, organizing, and controlling of the flow of materials. What is_____ _____?
$200	Production process in which resources are combined to create finished products. What is_____ _____?	In this planning, systems are developed so that products meet the firm's standards. What is_____ _____?	The operations control tool concerned with storing raw materials and finished goods. What is_____ _____?
$300	A service production process in which the customer is part of the system during service delivery. What is_____ _____?	This key issue in designing operations is concerned with the arrangement of production work centers and other elements. What is_____ _____?	The operations control tool that is concerned with acquiring raw materials and manufacturing services needed. What is_____ _____?
$400	Products of a production process that are largely intangible, customized, and unstorable. What is_____ _____?	The three layout alternatives. What is_____ _____?	This brings together all materials and parts needed at each production stage at the precise moment they are required. What is_____ _____?
$500	These providers of products typically focus on the customer-service link. What is_____ _____?	The method for analyzing a service by showing the flow of processes that constitute it. What is_____ _____?	Production method in which a bill of materials is used to ensure the right amounts of materials are delivered to the right place at the right time. What is_____ _____?

MATCH THE TERMS AND CONCEPTS TO THEIR DEFINITIONS

a. service operations
b. goods production
c. utility
d. operations (or production) production management
e. operations (or production) managers
f. analytic process
g. synthetic process
h. high-contact system
i. low-contact system
j. forecast

k. capacity
l. process layout
m. product layout
n. assembly line
o. U-shaped production line
p. cellular layout
q. fixed-position layout
r. service flow analysis
s. master production schedule
t. operations control
u. follow-up
v. materials management

w. standardization
x. supplier selection
y. inventory control
z. just-in-time (JIT)
aa. material requirements (MRP)
bb. bill of materials
cc. manufacturing resource planning (MRP II)
dd. quality control

_____ 1. Production process in which resources are broken down into components to create finished products.

_____ 2. Spatial arrangement of production activities designed to move resources through a smooth, fixed sequence of steps.

_____ 3. Production method in which a bill of materials is used to ensure that the right amounts of materials are delivered to the right place at the right time.

_____ 4. Schedule showing which products will be produced, when production will take place, and what resources will be used.

_____ 5. Produces tangible products, such as radios, newspapers, buses, and textbooks.

_____ 6. Advanced version of MRP that ties together all parts of an organization into its production activities.

_____ 7. Planning, organizing, and controlling the flow of materials from design through distribution of finished goods.

_____ 8. Production layout in which machines and workers are placed in a narrow *U* shape rather than a straight line.

_____ 9. Level of customer contact in which the customer need not be a part of the system to receive the service.

_____ 10. In materials management, receiving, storing, handling, and counting of all raw materials, partly finished goods, and finished goods.

_____ 11. Product layout that brings production activities (labor, materials, and equipment) to the location where the work is done.

_____ 12. Systematic direction and control of the processes that transform resources into finished products.

_____ 13. Amount of a product that a company can produce under normal working conditions.

_____ 14. Spatial arrangement of production facilities designed to move families of products through similar flow paths.

_____ 15. Production method that brings together all materials and parts needed at each production stage at the precise moment they are required.

_____ 16. Process of monitoring production performance by comparing results with plans.

_____ 17. Method for analyzing a service by showing the flow of processes that constitute it.

_____ 18. A product's ability to satisfy a human want.

_____ 19. Level of customer contact in which the customer is part of the system during service delivery.

_____ 20. Product layout in which a product moves step-by-step through a plant on conveyor belts or other equipment until it is completed.

_____ 21. Production control tool that specifies the necessary ingredients of a product, the order in which they should be combined, and how many of each are needed to make one batch.

_____ 22. Produces tangible and intangible services, such as entertainment, transportation, and education.

_____ 23. Use of standard and uniform components in the production process.

_____ 24. Facet of a long-range production plan that predicts future demand.

_____ 25. Managers responsible for production, inventory, and quality control.

_____ 26. Management of the production process designed to manufacture goods or supply services that meet specific quality standards.

_____ 27. Production control activity for ensuring that production decisions are being implemented.

_____ 28. Spatial arrangement of production activities that groups equipment and people according to function.

_____ 29. Production process in which resources are combined to create finished products.

_____ 30. Process of finding and selecting suppliers from whom to buy.

WORD SCRAMBLE

1. _____   _____
   donroptuci   sramagem

2. _____   _____
   atpersonio   mentageman

3. _____   _____
   layquit   trolcon

LEARNING OBJECTIVES--POTENTIAL SHORT ANSWER OR ESSAY QUESTIONS

Learning Objective #1: **"Explain the meaning of the term** *production* **or** *operations* **and describe the four kinds of** *utility* **it provides."**

Learning Objective #2: **"Describe and explain the three classifications of** *operations processes*.**"**

Learning Objective #3: **"Identify the characteristics that distinguish** *service operations* **from** *goods production* **and explain the main differences in the** *service focus*.**"**

Learning Objective #4: "Describe the factors involved in *operations planning*."

Learning Objective #5: "Explain some of the activities involved in *operations control*, including *materials management* and the use of certain *operations control tools*."

CRITICAL THINKING QUESTIONS

1. For each of the following goods manufacturing processes, determine whether the production process is synthetic or analytic?
    a. Meats found in the meat department at your local grocery store.

    b. Automobiles.

    c. Household cleaning solutions.

    d. Paper.

2. For each of the following service manufacturing processes, determine whether the production process is high-contact or low-contact?
    a. Haircuts.

    b. Automotive repair shops.

    c. Dry cleaners.

    d. Medical care.

BRAIN TEASER

1. Which type of process layout plan characterizes your college or university in its production of educational services?

ANSWERS

True-False—*Answers*

1. True
2. False: The four kinds of utility products create for customers are time, place, ownership, and *form* utility.
3. False: Time utility refers to consumer satisfaction derived from a product being available *when* it is most convenient for the customer.
4. True
5. False: *A synthetic* goods manufacturing process combines raw materials to produce a finished product.
6. True
7. False: A *low*-contact service operations process is one in which the customer need not be part of the system to receive the service.
8. True
9. True
10. True
11. False: Capacity planning for goods means ensuring that manufacturing capacity is slightly *above* the normal demand for its product.
12. False: Location planning for *high*-contact services focuses on locating the service near customers who are part of the system.
13. True
14. False: A *cellular* layout is a spatial arrangement of production facilities designed to move families of products through similar flow paths.
15. True
16. True
17. False: *Materials management* is concerned with the planning, organizing, and controlling of the flow of materials.
18. True
19. True
20. True

Multiple Choice--*Answers*

1. d	5. c	9. a	13. b
2. d	6. d	10. c	14. a
3. b	7. a	11. b	
4. c	8. b	12. c	

Jeopardy---*Answers*

	Operations Processes	Operations Planning	Operations Control
$100	an analytic process	capacity planning	materials management
$200	a synthetic process	quality methods planning	warehousing
$300	a high-contact system	layout planning	purchasing
$400	services production processes	product, process and cellular configurations	just-in-time production systems
$500	service providers	service flow analysis	material requirements planning (MRP)

Match the Terms and Concepts to Their Definitions--*Answers*

1. f	6. cc	11. q	16. t	21. bb	26. dd
2. m	7. v	12. d	17. r	22. a	27. u
3. aa	8. o	13. k	18. c	23. w	28. l
4. s	9. i	14. p	19. h	24. j	29. g
5. b	10. y	15. z	20. n	25. e	30. x

Word Scramble---*Answers*

1. production managers   2. operations management   3. quality control

Learning Objectives--Potential Short Answer or Essay Questions--*Answers*

Learning Objective #1:

Production (or *operations*) refers to the processes and activities for transforming resources into finished services and goods for customers. Resources include knowledge, physical materials, equipment, and labor that are systematically combined in a production facility to create four kinds of *utility* for customers: *time utility* (which makes products available when customers want them),*place utility* (which makes products available where they are convenient for customers), possession or *ownership utility* (by which customers benefit from possessing and using the product), and *form utility* (which results from the creation of the product).

Learning Objective #2:

Operations managers in manufacturing use one of two classifications to describe operations processes. Criteria include the *type of technology* used (chemical, fabrication, assembly, transport, or clerical) to transform raw materials into finished goods and whether products are submitted to *analytic or synthetic processes* (that is, whether the process breaks down resources into components or combines raw materials into finished products). Service operations are classified according to the *extent of customer contact*, as either high-contact systems (the customer is part of the system) or low-contact (customers are not in contact while the service is provided).

Learning Objective #3:

Although the creation of both goods and services involves resources, transformations, and finished products, service operations differ from goods manufacturing in several important ways. In service production, the raw materials are not, say, glass or steel, but rather people who choose among sellers because they have unsatisfied needs or possessions in need of care or alteration. Therefore, whereas services are typically performed, goods are physically produced. In addition, services are largely *intangible*, more likely than physical goods to be *customized* to meet the purchaser's needs, and more *unstorable* than most products. Service businesses therefore focus explicitly on these characteristics of their products. Because services are intangible, for instance, providers work to ensure that customers receive value in the form of pleasure, satisfaction, or a feeling of safety. Often, they also focus on both the transformation process and the final product (say, making the loan interview a pleasant experience as well as providing the loan itself). Finally, service providers typically focus on the *customer-service link*, often acknowledging the customer as part of the operations process.

Learning Objective #4:

Operations planning involves the analysis of six key factors. *Forecasts* of future demand for both new and existing products provide information for developing production plans. In *capacity planning*, the firm analyzes how much of a product it must be able to produce. In high-contact services, managers must plan capacity to meet peak demand. Capacity planning for goods means ensuring that manufacturing capacity slightly exceeds the normal demand for its product. *Location planning* for goods and for low-contact services involves analyzing proposed facility sites in terms of proximity to raw materials and markets, availability of labor, and energy and transportation costs. Location planning for high-contact services, in contrast, involves locating the service near customers, who are part of the system. *Layout planning* involves designing a facility so that customer needs are supplied for high-contact services so as to enhance production efficiency. Layout alternatives include product, process, and cellular configurations. In *quality planning*, systems are developed to ensure that products meet a firm's quality standards. Finally, in *methods planning*, specific production steps and methods for performing them are identified. *Service flow analysis* and *process flow charts* are helpful for identifying all operations activities and eliminating wasteful steps from production.

Learning Objective #5:

Operations control requires production managers to monitor production performance, by comparing results with detailed plans and schedules, and then to take corrective action as needed. *Materials management* is the planning, organizing, and controlling of the flow of materials. It focuses on the control of *transportation* (transporting resources to the manufacturer and products to customers), *warehousing* (storing both incoming raw materials and finished goods), *purchasing* (acquiring the raw materials and services that a manufacturer needs), *supplier selection*, and *inventory control*. To control operations processes, managers use various methods. For example, *worker training* programs can assist in quality control, the management of the operations process so as to ensure that services and goods meet specific quality standards. *Just-in-time (JIT) production systems* bring together all materials and parts needed at each production stage at the precise moment they are required. JIT reduces manufacturing inventory costs and reveals production problems that need improvement. *Material requirements planning (MRP)* is another method for ensuring that the right amounts of materials are delivered to the right place at the right time for manufacturing. It uses computer-controlled schedules for moving inventories through each stage of production.

Critical Thinking Questions---*Answers*

1. a. Analytic because the whole steers, pigs, chickens and fish are broken down into component parts to create the package finished products.
    b. Synthetic because raw materials are combined to create the finished car.
    c. Synthetic because various chemicals are combined to create household cleaning solutions.
    d. Analytic because trees are broken down into component parts and paper is only one product that comes from harvesting trees.

2. a. High-contact because the customer is part of the system during system delivery.
    b. Low-contact because customers need not be part of the system to receive the service.
    c. Low-contact because customers need not be part of the system to receive the service.
    d. High-contact because the customer is part of the system during system delivery.

Brain Teaser--*Answer*

1. Colleges and universities utilize a process layout where different tasks are carried out in separate departments---classrooms, labs, recreation facilities, living quarters, etc. Each area contains specialized equipment and personnel. Also note that the delivery of higher education is a high-contact service production system, and should be arranged to meet customer (student) needs and expectations.

Chapter 16

Managing Quality and Productivity

LEARNING OBJECTIVES

After studying this chapter, you should be able to:

1. Describe the connection between *productivity* and *quality*.
2. Explain the decline and recovery in U.S. productivity that has occurred in the last 25 or 30 years.
3. Explain *total* and *partial measures of productivity* and show how they are used to keep track of national, industrywide, and companywide productivity.
4. Identify the activities involved in *total quality management* and describe six tools that companies can use to achieve it.
5. Identify two trends in productivity and quality management and discuss three ways in which companies can compete by improving productivity and quality.

TRUE-FALSE

Indicate whether the statement is generally true or false by placing a "T" or "F" in the space provided. If it is a false statement, correct it so that it becomes a true statement.

_____ 1. Quality is a measure of economic performance: It compares how much is produced with the resources used to produce it.

_____ 2. Productivity is a product's fitness for use plus its success in offering features that consumers want.

_____ 3. Profitable competition in today's intensely globally competitive market environment requires high levels of both productivity and quality.

_____ 4. Although the United States is the most productive country in the world, by the early 1970s other nations had begun catching up with U.S. productivity.

_____ 5. Because services account for 60 percent of national income in the United States, it is imperative that productivity in this area increase if the U.S. is to experience continued increases in its standard of living.

_____ 6. In the 1990s, the United States regained much of its competitive advantage in world markets by becoming more customer-oriented and focusing on quality improvement.

_____ 7. Quality measures are ratios of outputs (goods and services produced) and inputs (the resources needed to produce outputs).

_____ 8. Total factor productivity focuses on certain key input factors while ignoring others.

_____ 9. Labor productivity is the most common national productivity measure.

_____ 10. Capital productivity focuses on money and investment as input factors.

_____ 11. Total quality management (TQM) is the planning, organizing, directing, and controlling of the activities needed to get high-quality goods and services into the marketplace.

_____ 12. Planning for quality begins after products are designed or redesigned.

_____ 13. Performance quality is the consistency of a product's quality from unit to unit.

_____ 14. Quality ownership is the principle of total quality management that holds that quality belongs to each person who creates it while performing a job.

_____ 15. Statistical process control (SPC) is a process of evaluating all work activities, materials flows, and paperwork to determine the value they add for customers.

_____ 16. Two specific types of statistical process control methods are process variation studies and the use of control charts.

_____ 17. Quality/cost studies are useful because they not only identify a firm's current costs but also reveal areas with the largest cost-savings potential.

_____ 18. "Getting closer to the consumer" is a total quality management tool that provides a better understanding of what consumers want so that firms can satisfy them more effectively.

_____ 19. ISO 2000 is a process that involves the fundamental redesign of business operations in the interest of gaining improvements in quality, cost, and service.

_____ 20. To increase quality and productivity, businesses must invest in innovation and technology.

_____ 21. Contrary to popular belief, studies indicate that the quality of work life has little to do with a worker's productivity and a firm's ability to produce high-quality products.

_____ 22. Continuous quality improvement requires a firm to focus on short-term profit maximization.

MULTIPLE CHOICE

Circle the one best answer for each of the following questions.

1. Which of the following statements is true concerning productivity?
   a. Increases in productivity mean we are able to produce more with fewer resources.
   b. An increase in productivity within a nation increases the average absolute standard of living.
   c. The growth rate of productivity is the annual increase in a nation's output over the previous year.
   d. All of the above.

2. Which of the following statements is true concerning quality?
   a. Quality is a product's fitness for use plus its success in offering features that consumers want.
   b. Quality has little to do with productivity.
   c. There is little need to focus on productivity if quality increases.
   d. All of the above.

3. Which of the following statements is true?
   a. The U.S. growth rate of productivity increased from about 1979 through the early 1990s.
   b. Over the last decade, productivity in the service sector of the U.S. economy has been increasing while the manufacturing sector has been decreasing.
   c. High productivity for a company gives it a competitive edge because its costs are lower than those of other companies.
   d. All of the above.

4. Which of the following statements is true concerning productivity and quality in the United States?
   a. The U.S. has become more competitive in the last decade because of a greater emphasis on producing high quality products and by becoming more customer-oriented.
   b. Certain industries and companies remain less competitive than others.
   c. The U.S. has earned a more competitive position in the global economy in recent years because of its recognition of the connection between customers, quality, productivity, and profits.
   d. All of the above.

5. Materials productivity
   a. is the most common national productivity measure.
   b. focuses on the productivity of materials and is especially important in non-labor intensive industries.
   c. focuses on money and investment as input factors.
   d. All of the above.

6. Which of the following statements is true?
   a. Labor unions must consider productivity when negotiating contracts.
   b. Investors and suppliers consider industry productivity when making loans, buying securities, and planning production.
   c. Government bodies use productivity as a means of authorizing programs and projecting tax revenues.
   d. All of the above.

7. Which of the following is *not* part of Total Quality Management (TQM)?
   a. Planning for quality.
   b. Organizing for quality.
   c. Advertising quality.
   d. Directing quality.

8. The total quality management approach requires
   a. performance quality, quality reliability, and quality ownership.
   b. the belief that producing high-quality goods and services is an effort that must be undertaken by all parts of the organization.
   c. managers to motivate employees throughout the company to achieve quality goals.
   d. All of the above.

9. Methods for gathering data to analyze variations in production activities to see when adjustments are needed is
   a. statistical process control (SPC).
   b. value-added analysis.
   c. benchmarking.
   d. undertaking quality/cost studies.

10. The process by which a company implements the best practices from its own past performance and those of other companies to improve its own products is
    a. undertaking a quality/cost study.
    b. benchmarking.
    c. undertaking statistical process control (SPC).
    d. assembling a quality improvement team.

11. Which of the following statements is *false*?
    a. A control chart is used to plot test samples on a diagram to determine when a process is beginning to depart from normal operating conditions.
    b. Process variation is variation in products arising from changes in production inputs.
    c. Internal failures are reducible costs incurred after defective products have left a plant.
    d. Quality improvement teams may increase worker morale and create a sense of quality ownership.

12. Rent trends in productivity and quality assurance include
    a. the emergence of international quality standards.
    b. the radical redesign of business processes to improve quality.
    c. an emphasis on the need for quality improvement programs to show monetary benefits.
    d. All of the above.

13. ISO 9000
    a. is a certification program attesting to the fact that a factory, a laboratory, or an office has met the rigorous quality management requirements set by the International Organization for Standardization.
    b. allows firms to demonstrate that they follow documented procedures for testing products, training workers, keeping records, and fixing product defects.
    c. certification has become the passkey to doing business is Western Europe.
    d. All of the above.

14. The reengineering process entails
    a. identifying a business activity that will be changed and evaluating information and human resources to see if they can meet the requirements for change.
    b. diagnosing the current process to identify its strengths and weaknesses.
    c. creating a new process design and implementing the new design.
    d. All of the above.

JEOPARDY

You have 5 seconds to complete the question to each of the following answers.

	Productivity and Quality	**Total Quality Management**	**Productivity and Quality Trends**
$100	A measure of a product's fitness for use plus its success in offering features that consumers want. What is_____ _____?	The sum of all of the activities involved in getting high-quality products into the marketplace. What is_____ _____?	A certification program attesting that an organization has met certain international quality management standards. What is_____ _____?
$200	A measure of outputs in relation to inputs. What is_____ _____?	The process of evaluating all work activities, material flows, and paperwork to determine the value they add for customers. What is_____ _____?	A quality improvement process that entails rethinking an organization's approach to productivity and quality. What is_____ _____?
$300	The most common measure of national productivity which focuses on labor as an input. What is_____ _____?	The method for gathering data to analyze variations in production activities to see when adjustments are needed. What is_____ _____?	One ingredient for improving productivity and quality that has to do with innovation and technology. What is_____ _____?
$400	The impact on the standard of living for a nation if productivity increases. What is_____ _____?	The method of identifying current costs and areas with the greatest cost-saving potential. What is_____ _____?	One ingredient for improving productivity and quality that has to do with the firm's perspective on its goals. What is_____ _____?
$500	A factor that accounts for the growth in productivity and greater quality production in the U.S. in recent years. What is_____ _____?	The TQM tool in which groups of employees work together to improve quality. What is_____ _____?	One ingredient for improving productivity and quality that has to do with the quality of work life. What is_____ _____?

MATCH THE TERMS AND CONCEPTS TO THEIR DEFINITIONS

a. quality
b. level of productivity
c. growth rate of productivity
d. total factor productivity ratio
e. partial productivity ratio
f. materials productivity
g. labor productivity
h. total quality management (TMQ) or (quality assurance)

i. performance quality
j. quality reliability
k. quality ownership
l. value-added analysis
m. statistical process control (SPC)
n. process variation
o. internal failures
p. external failures

q. quality improvement (QI) team
r. benchmarking
s. reengineering
t. continuous improvement
u. employee empowerment

_____ 1. Productivity measure that considers only certain input resources.

_____ 2. Variation in products arising from changes in production inputs.

_____ 3. Process of evaluating all work activities, materials flows, and paperwork to determine the value they add for customers.

_____ 4. A product's fitness for use; its success in offering features that consumers want.

_____ 5. Concept that all employees are valuable contributors to a firm's business and should be entrusted with decisions regarding their work.

_____ 6. The sum of all activities involved in getting high-quality products into the marketplace.

_____ 7. Productivity measure that considers all types of input resources (labor, capital, materials, energy, and purchased business services).

_____ 8. Quality improvement process that entails rethinking an organization's approach to productivity and quality.

_____ 9. Dollar value of goods and services relative to the resources used to produce them.

_____ 10. Process by which a company implements the best practices from its own past performance and those of other companies to improve its own products.

_____ 11. Consistency of a product's quality from unit to unit.

_____ 12. Reducible costs incurred after defective products have left a plant.

_____ 13. An ongoing commitment to improving products and processes in the pursuit of ever-increasing customer satisfaction.

_____ 14. Partial productivity ratio calculated by dividing total output by total material inputs.

_____ 15. Annual increase in a nation's output over the previous year.

_____ 16. Partial productivity ratio calculated by dividing total output by total labor inputs.

_____ 17. TQM tool in which groups of employees work together to improve quality.

_____ 18. Principle of total quality management that holds that quality belongs to each person who creates it while performing a job.

_____ 19. The performance features offered by a product.

_____ 20. Methods for gathering data to analyze variations in production activities to see when adjustments are needed.

_____ 21. Reducible costs incurred during production and before bad products leave a plant.

WORD SCRAMBLE

1. _____   2. _____   3. _____

    bringmakchen   ereneginringe   talquiy

LEARNING OBJECTIVES--POTENTIAL SHORT ANSWER OR ESSAY QUESTIONS

Learning Objective #1: "Describe the connection between *productivity* and *quality*."

Learning Objective #2: "Explain the decline and recovery in U.S. productivity that has occurred over the last 25 or 30 years."

Learning Objective #3: "Explain *total* and *partial measures of productivity* and how they are used to keep track of national, industrywide, and companywide productivity."

Learning Objective #4: "Identify the activities involved in *total quality management* and describe six tools that companies can use to achieve it."

Learning Objective #5: "Identify two trends in productivity and quality management and discuss three ways in which companies can compete by improving productivity and quality."

CRITICAL THINKING QUESTIONS

1. What are the six steps in the reengineering process?

2. In trying to offer more satisfactory services, many companies have discovered five criteria that customers use to judge service quality. What are those five criteria?

BRAIN TEASER

1. What would a point outside the upper or lower control limits on a statistical process control chart imply about the production process being observed? What should management do to enhance the quality of their product over time?

ANSWERS

True-False--*Answers*

1. False: *Productivity* is a measure of economic performance: It compares how much is produced with the resources used to produce it.
2. False: *Quality* is a product's fitness for use plus its success in offering features that consumers want.
3. True
4. True
5. True
6. True
7. False: *Productivity measures* are ratios of outputs (goods and services produced) and inputs (the resources needed to produce outputs).
8. False: *Partial* factor productivity focuses on certain key input factors while ignoring others.
9. True
10. True
11. True
12. False: Planning for quality begins *before* products are designed or redesigned.
13. False: *Quality reliability* is the consistency of a product's quality from unit to unit.
14. True
15. False: *Value-added analysis* is a process of evaluating all work activities, materials flows, and paperwork to determine the value they add for customers.
16. True
17. True
18. True
19. False: ISO 2000 is a process that involves the fundamental redesign of business operations in the interest of gaining improvements in quality, cost, and service.
20. True
21. False: Studies indicate that *increasing* the quality of work life *will increase* worker's productivity and a firm's ability to produce high-quality products.
22. False: Continuous quality improvement requires a firm to *adopt a long-run perspective.*

Multiple Choice--*Answers*

1. d	5. b	9. a	13. d
2. a	6. d	10. b	14. d
3. c	7. c	11. c	
4. d	8. d	12. d	

Jeopardy---*Answers*

	Productivity and Quality	Total Quality Management	Productivity and Quality Trends
$100	quality	total quality management (TQM) (or quality assurance)	ISO 9000
$200	productivity	value-added analysis	business process reengineering
$300	labor productivity	statistical process control (SPC)	the need to be innovative and to invest in technology
$400	to increase the standard of living for a nation	a quality/cost study	the need to adopt a long-term perspective.
$500	a focus on becoming more customer-oriented, and undertaking quality improvement practices	a quality improvement team	the need to enhance the quality of work life for employees

Match the Terms and Concepts to Their Definitions--*Answers*

1. e	6. h	11. j	16. g	21. o
2. n	7. d	12. p	17. q	
3. l	8. s	13. t	18. k	
4. a	9. b	14. f	19. i	
5. u	10. r	15. c	20. m	

Word Scramble---*Answers*

1. benchmarking   2. reengineering   3. quality

Learning Objectives--Potential Short Answer or Essay Questions--*Answers*

Learning Objective #1:
   Productivity is a measure of economic performance: It compares how much is produced with the resources used to produce it. *Quality* is a product's fitness for use. However, an emphasis solely on productivity or solely on quality is not enough. Profitable competition in today's business world demands high levels of both productivity and quality.

Learning Objective #2:
   Although the United States is the most productive country in the world, by the early 1970s other nations had begun catching up with U.S. productivity. In particular, the U.S. *growth rate of productivity* slowed from about 1979 into the early 1990s. Moreover, even though U.S. manufacturing productivity is increasing, the service sector is bringing down overall productivity growth. Because services now account for 60 percent of national income, productivity in this area must improve. Finally, certain industries and companies remain less productive than others.

On the other hand, in the years just before 1994, U.S. firms began regaining significant market share in such industries as airplanes, computers, construction equipment, and transistors. Abandoning a long-standing focus on lower wage rates in other countries, U.S. companies focused instead on revitalizing productivity by becoming more customer-oriented. In addition, quality improvement practices were widely implemented. Recovery has resulted from a recognition of the connection among customers, quality, productivity, and profits.

Learning Objective #3:

Productivity measures are ratios of *outputs* (goods and services produced) and *inputs* (the resources needed to produce outputs). *Total factor productivity* includes all types of input resources: materials, labor, capital, energy, and purchased business services. In contrast, *partial productivity measures* focus on certain key input factors while ignoring others. Thus *materials productivity* focuses on the productivity of materials and is especially important in non–labor-intensive industries. *Labor productivity*, the most common national productivity measure, focuses on labor as an input. The United States also measures *capital productivity*, which focuses on money and investment as input factors.

Learning Objective #4:

Total quality management (TQM) is the planning, organizing, directing, and controlling of all the activities needed to get high-quality goods and services into the marketplace. Managers must set goals for and implement the processes needed to achieve high quality and reliability levels. *Value-added analysis* evaluates all work activities, materials flows, and paperwork to determine what value they add for customers. *Statistical process control methods*, such as *process variation studies* and *control charts*, can help keep quality consistently high. *Quality/cost studies*, which identify potential savings, can help firms improve quality. *Quality improvement teams* also can improve operations by more fully involving employees in decision making. *Benchmarking*—studying the firm's own performance and the best practices of other companies to gather information for improving a company's own goods and services—has become an increasingly common TQM tool. Finally, *getting closer to the customer* provides a better understanding of what customers want so that firms can satisfy them more effectively.

Learning Objective #5:

Recent trends include *ISO 9000*, a certification program (originating in Europe) attesting that an organization has met certain international quality management standards. *Process reengineering* involves the fundamental redesign of business operations in the interest of gaining improvements in quality, cost, and service. The reengineering process consists of six steps, starting with the company's vision statement and ending with the implementation of the reengineered process.

Productivity and quality can be competitive tools only if firms attend to all aspects of their operations. To increase quality and productivity, businesses must invest in innovation and technology. They must also adopt a long-run perspective for continuous improvement. In addition, they should realize that placing greater emphasis on the quality of work life can also help firms compete. Satisfied, motivated employees are especially important in increasing productivity in the fast-growing service sector.

Critical Thinking Questions---*Answers*

1. The six steps are: (1) state the case for action; (2) identify the process for reengineering; (3) evaluate information and human resource requirements for reengineering; (4) understand the current process; (5) create a new process; and (6) implement the reengineered process. (See page 456 in the textbook.)

2. The five criteria to judge service criteria are reliability, responsiveness, assurance, empathy, and tangibles. (See page 460 in the textbook.)

Brain Teaser--*Answer*

1. Any point outside the upper or lower control limits would imply that the process is out of control. Although variation in any process is to be expected, variation outside the control limits is unacceptable. Whenever management observes this, it must try to determine what caused the unacceptable variation and correct it, thus enhancing quality over time.

Chapter 17

Information Systems and Communication Technology

LEARNING OBJECTIVES

After studying this chapter, you should be able to:

1. Explain why businesses must manage *information* and show how computer systems and communication technologies have revolutionized *information management*.
2. Identify and briefly describe three elements of *data communication networks*—the Internet, the World Wide Web, and intranets.
3. Describe five *new options for organizational design* that have emerged from the rapid growth of information technologies.
4. Discuss different information-systems *applications systems* that are available for users at various organizational levels.
5. Identify and briefly describe the *main elements of an information system*.

TRUE-FALSE

Indicate whether the statement is generally true or false by placing a "T" or "F" in the space provided. If it is a false statement, correct it so that it becomes a true statement.

_____ 1   The management of a firm's information system is a core activity because all of a firm's business activities are linked to it.

_____ 2   Data is meaningful, useful interpretation of information.

_____ 3   An internet service provider (ISP) is a commercial firm that maintains a permanent connection to the internet and sells temporary connections to subscribers.

_____ 4   The World Wide Web is a system with universally accepted standards for storing, formatting, retrieving, and displaying information.

_____ 5   The internet is the world's largest computer network.

_____ 6.   The rapid growth of information technologies has had little impact on the structure of business organizations.

_____ 7.   The rapid growth of information technologies has resulted in leaner organizations characterized by geographic separation of the workplace and company headquarters.

_____ 8. The rapid growth of information technologies has resulted in less collaboration among internal units of a company and outside firms.

_____ 9. Each business function—marketing, human resources, accounting, production, and finance—has the same information requirements.

_____ 10. Transaction processing systems (TPS) are applications for basic day-to-day business transactions.

_____ 11. Information-systems employees who run a company's computer equipment are referred to as robotics.

_____ 12. Computer-aided design (CAD) is computer-based electronic technology that assists in designing products by simulating a real product and displaying it in three-dimensional graphics.

_____ 13. Information systems for knowledge workers and office applications include personal productivity tools such as word processing, document imaging, desktop publishing, computer-aided design, and simulation modeling.

_____ 14. Artificial intelligence is a quick reference, easy-access program to assist upper-level managers.

_____ 15. Artificial intelligence (AI) and expert systems are designed to imitate human behavior and provide computerized assistance in performing certain business activities.

_____ 16. Software is the physical devices and components, including the computer, in the information system.

_____ 17. Control is an important part of the information system because it ensures not only that the system operates correctly, but also that data and information are transmitted through secure channels to people who really need them.

_____ 18. The database is the organized collection of all the data files in the information system.

_____ 19. Information systems include knowledge workers like systems analysts and programmers.

_____ 20. Telecommunication components of an information system include multimedia technology that incorporates sound, animation, video, and photography along with ordinary graphics and text.

MULTIPLE CHOICE
Circle the one best answer for each of the following questions.

1. Information systems
    a. are designed to determine what information will be needed.
    b. must gather the data required and provide the technology to convert data into desired information.
    c. must control the flow of information so that it goes only to people who need it.
    d. All of the above.

2. A computer system that allows people to communicate simultaneously from different locations via software or telephone is
    a. electronic mail (email).
    b. electronic conferencing.
    c. a fax.
    d. groupware.

3. A software and hardware system that prevents outsiders from accessing a company's internal network is called
    a. a firewall.
    b. a search engine.
    c. a browser.
    d. a web server.

4. Software supporting the graphics and linking capabilities necessary to navigate the World Wide Web is
    a. a search engine.
    b. a firewall.
    c. a browser.
    d. an extranet.

5. As a result of growth in information technologies, companies are
    a. leading to organizations with more employees and more complicated organizational structures.
    b. offering customers less variety and slower delivery cycles.
    c. changing the very nature of the management process.
    d. more likely to hire more employees to work at one central location.

6. Top-level managers are most likely to use which of the following general types of information systems?
    a. Strategic information systems.
    b. Management information systems.
    c. Knowledge information systems.
    d. Operational information systems.

7. Mid-level managers are most likely to use which of the following general types of information systems?
    a. Strategic information systems.
    b. Management information systems.
    c. Knowledge information systems.
    d. Operational information systems.

8. An information systems application that is useful for routine transactions, such as taking reservations and meeting payrolls that follow predetermined steps, is
   a. a computer-aided design.
   b. a transaction processing system (TPS).
   c. an executive support system (ESS).
   d. artificial intelligence.

9. An interactive computer-based system that locates and presents information needed to support decision-making is called
   a. a management information system (MIS).
   b. an executive support system (ESS).
   c. a decision-support system (DDS).
   d. a transactions processing system (TPS)

10. Which of the following statements is true?
    a. Management information systems (MISs) support an organization's managers by providing daily reports, schedules, plans, and budgets.
    b. Middle managers, the largest MIS user group, need networked information to plan upcoming activities and to track current activities.
    c. Decision-support systems (DISs) are interactive applications that assist the decision-making process of middle- and top-managers.
    d. All of the above.

11. Which of the following is software?
    a. An input device such as a keyboard.
    b. A central processing unit (CPU).
    c. Applications programs such as word processing, spreadsheets, or Web browsers.
    d. Output device such as a video monitor or printer.

12. Which of the following is part of an information network system?
    a. Hardware and software.
    b. Control and database.
    c. People and telecommunications.
    d. All of the above.

13. Part of the computer system where data processing takes place is called
    a. an application program.
    b. the central processing unit (CPU).
    c. the graphical user interface (GUI).
    d. an input device.

14. Which of the following statements is true?
    a. Databases consist of fields, records, and files.
    b. Most business application programs fall into one of four categories—word processing, spreadsheets, database management, and graphics.
    c. An electronic spreadsheet is an applications program with row-and-column format that allows users to store, manipulate, and compare numeric data.
    d. All of the above.

15. Which of the following statements is true?
    a. A client-server network is an information-technology system consisting of clients (users) that are electronically linked to share network resources provided by a server.
    b. Networked systems classified according to geographic scope may be either local or wide area networks.
    c. A local area network (LAN) is a network of computers and workstations, usually within a company, that are linked together by cable.
    d. All of the above.

JEOPARDY

You have 5 seconds to complete the question to each of the following answers.

	Data Communication Networks	Information-Systems Applications	Elements of an Information System
$100	Global network (such as the Internet) that permits users to send electronic messages and information quickly and economically What is_____?	Applications for basic day-to-day business transactions. What is_____?	The physical devices and components of an information system. What is_____?
$200	The largest public communication network that is a gigantic network of networks linking millions of computers. What is_____?	This supports an organization's middle managers by providing networked information to plan upcoming events and to track current activities. What is_____?	Programs that instruct a computer in what to do. What is_____?
$300	A communication system with universally accepted standards for storing, formatting, retrieving, and displaying information. What is_____?	These systems are interactive applications that assist the decision-making processes for middle- and top-managers. What is_____?	Centralized, organized collection of relevant data. What is_____?
$400	Private networks that any company can develop to transmit information throughout the firm. What is_____?	A computer-system application that imitates human behavior. What is_____?	This ensures that the information system is operating according to specific procedures and within specific guidelines. What is_____?
$500	Software and hardware system that prevents outsiders from accessing a company's internal network. What is_____?	Quick-reference information-system application designed specially for instant access by upper-level managers. What is_____?	A connected network of communication appliances that may be linked to mass media. What is_____?

MATCH THE TERMS AND CONCEPTS TO THEIR DEFINITIONS

a. information management
b. electronic information technologies (EIT)
c. groupware
d. Internet service provider (ISP)
e. mass customization
f. knowledge workers
g. transaction process systems (TPS)
h. system operations personnel
i. computer-aided design (CAD)
j decision support system (DSS)
k. executive support system (ESS)
l. artificial intelligence (AI)
m. computer network
n. client-server network
o. information managers
p. data
q. information
r. information system (IS)
s. computer system
t. hardware
u. input device
v. central processing unit (CPU)
w. main memory
x. program
y. output device
z. random access memory (RAM)

aa. secondary storage
bb. hard disk
cc. diskette
dd. CD-ROM
ee. read-only memory (ROM)
ff. software
gg. system program
hh. language program
ii. application program
jj. graphical user interface (GUI)
kk. icon
ll. firewall
mm. database
nn. batch processing
oo. online processing
pp. word-processing program
qq. electronic spreadsheet
rr. database management program
ss. computer graphics program
tt. presentation graphics software
uu. desktop publishing
vv. microcomputer (or personal computer)
ww. minicomputer
xx. mainframe
yy. supercomputer
zz. system architecture
aaa. centralized system

bbb. decentralized system
ccc. computer network
ddd. wide area network (WAN)
eee. local area network (LAN)
fff. modem
ggg. fiber optic cable
hhh. server
iii. client PC
jjj. microprocessor chip
kkk. artificial intelligence (AI)
lll. expert system
mmm. fax machine
nnn. voice mail
ooo. electronic mail (e-mail)
ppp. executive information system (EIS)
qqq. operations information system
rrr. data communication network
sss. Internet
ttt. World Wide Web
uuu. Browser
vvv. Intranet
zzz. multimedia communication system

_____ 1. Information-systems employees who run a company's computer equipment.

_____ 2. Applications that enable users to create visual presentations that can include animation and sound.

_____ 3. Part of the computer CPU that houses the memory of programs it needs to operate.

_____ 4. Machine that can transmit copies of documents (text and graphics) over telephone lines.

_____ 5. Private network of internal Web sites and other sources of information available to a company's employees.

_____ 6. Method of entering data and processing them immediately.

_____ 7. All the computer and information technology devices which, by working together, drive the flow of digital information throughout a system.

_____ 8. Commercial firm that maintains a permanent connection to the Net and sells temporary connections to subscribers.

_____ 9. Computer whose capacity and speed enable it to serve many users simultaneously.

_____ 10. Secondary storage device permanently installed in a computer.

_____ 11. System program (such as FORTRAN) that allows users to give computers their own instructions.

_____ 12. Information-systems applications, based on telecommunications technologies, that use networks of appliances or devices to communicate information by electronic means.

_____ 13. Easy-access information cluster specially designed for upper-level managers.

_____ 14. Subsystem of computers providing access to the Internet and offering multimedia and linking capabilities.

_____ 15. Applications program for creating, storing, searching, and manipulating an organized collection of data.

_____ 16. Form of computer system architecture in which processing is done in many locations by means of separate computers, databases, and personnel.

_____ 17. Interactive computer-based system that locates and presents information needed to support decision making.

_____ 18. Any computer attached to a network server.

_____ 19. Electronic system designed to turn data into information.

_____ 20. Software supporting the graphics and linking capabilities necessary to navigate the World Wide Web.

_____ 21. Centralized, organized collection of related data.

_____ 22. Raw facts and figures.

_____ 23. Internal operations for arranging a firm's information resources to support business performance and outcomes.

_____ 24. Secondary storage device that can hold instructions to be read by the computer but accepts no written instructions.

_____ 25. Computer system that electronically transmits letters, reports, and other information between computers.

_____ 26. Network of computers and workstations, usually within a company, that are linked together by cable.

_____ 27. Information-technology system consisting of clients (users) that are electronically linked to share network resources provided by a server, such as a host computer.

_____ 28. Process of combining word-processing and graphics capability to produce virtually typeset-quality text from personal computers.

_____ 29. Global data communication network serving millions of computers with information on a wide array of topics and providing communication flows among certain private networks.

_____ 30. Method of collecting data over a period of time and then processing them as a group or batch.

_____ 31. Employees who use information and knowledge as raw materials and who rely on information technology to design new products or business systems.

_____ 32. Computer-system application that imitates human behavior by performing physical tasks using thought processes, sensing, and learning.

_____ 33. Part of the computer system that enters data into it.

_____ 34. Network of computers and workstations located far from one another and linked by telephone wires or by satellite.

_____ 35. Quick-reference information-system application designed specially for instant access by upper-level managers.

_____ 36. Connected network of communication appliances (such as faxes or TVs) that may be linked to forms of mass media (such as print publications or TV programming).

_____ 37. Applications program with a row-and-column format that allows users to store, manipulate, and compare numeric data.

_____ 38. Construction and programming of computers to imitate human thought processes.

_____ 39. Short-term memory that is active while the computer is performing its functions.

_____ 40. Global network (such as the Internet) that permits users to send electronic messages and information quickly and economically.

_____ 41. Small image in a GUI that enables users to select applications or functions.

_____ 42. Physical components of a computer system.

_____ 43. Computer-based electronic technology that assists in designing products by simulating a real product and displaying it in three-dimensional graphics.

_____ 44. Applications program that converts numeric and character data into pictorial information such as graphs and charts.

_____ 45. Flexible production process that generates customized products in high volumes at low cost.

_____ 46. Form of computer system architecture in which all processing is done in one location through a centralized computer, database, and staff.

_____ 47. Computer whose capacity, speed, and cost fall between those of microcomputers and mainframes.

_____ 48. Meaningful, useful interpretation of data.

_____ 49. Any medium (such as disks) for storing data or information outside the computer's CPU.

_____   50. Glass-fiber cables that carry data in the form of light pulses.

_____   51. Managers responsible for designing and implementing systems to gather, organize, and distribute information.

_____   52. Applications program that allows computers to store, edit, and print letters and numbers for documents created by users.

_____   53. Software that connects members of a group for shared e-mail distribution, electronic meetings, appointments, and group writing.

_____   54. Information-processing applications for routine, day-to-day business activities involving well-defined processing steps.

_____   55. Form of artificial intelligence that attempts to imitate the behavior of human experts in a particular field.

_____   56. Portable, easily removed secondary storage device.

_____   57. System for transforming raw data into information that can be used in decision making.

_____   58. Group of interconnected computer systems able to exchange information with one another from different locations.

_____   59. Software and hardware system that prevents outsiders from accessing a company's internal network.

_____   60. Software (such as Lotus 1-2-3) that processes data according to a user's special needs.

_____   61. Computer system used to manage production and manufacturing operations.

_____   62. Part of a computer system that presents results, either visually or in printed form.

_____   63. Device that provides a computer-to-computer link over telephone wires.

_____   64. Largest, fastest, most expensive form of computer.

_____   65. Part of the computer system where data processing takes place.

_____   66. Computer-based system for receiving and delivering incoming telephone calls.

_____   67. Programs that instruct a computer in what to do.

_____   68. Location of a computer system's elements (data-entry and data-processing operations, database, data output, and computer staff).

_____   69. Set of instructions used by a computer to perform specified activities.

_____   70. Any user-shared component (such as a minicomputer) at the center of a local area network.

_____   71. Software that tells the computer what resources to use and how to use them.

_____   72. Software that provides a visual display to help users select applications.

_____ 73. Single silicon chip containing a computer's central processing unit.

_____ 74. Smallest, slowest, least expensive form of computer.

_____ 75. Secondary storage device that can store sound and video data but accepts no new written data.

WORD SCRAMBLE

1. _____   2. _____   3. _____
    wardhare   woupgrare   omteropcrmicu

LEARNING OBJECTIVES--POTENTIAL SHORT ANSWER OR ESSAY QUESTIONS

Learning Objective #1: **"Explain why businesses must manage *information* and show how computer systems and communication technologies have revolutionized *information management*."**

Learning Objective #2: **"Identify and briefly describe three elements of *data communication networks*—the Internet, the World Wide Web, and intranets."**

Learning Objective #3: **"Describe five *new options for organizational design* that have emerged from the rapid growth of information technologies."**

Learning Objective #4: **"Discuss different information-systems *applications* that are available for users at various organizational levels."**

Learning Objective #5: **"Identify and briefly describe the *main elements of an information system.*"**

CRITICAL THINKING QUESTIONS

1. Which layer of management principally uses operational information systems? Management information systems?

2. What have been the four most commonly used applications of business computing?

BRAIN TEASER

1. Will there likely be a larger market for the sale of consumer or industrial products on the Internet?

ANSWERS

True-False--*Answers*

1. True
2. False: *Information* is meaningful, useful interpretation of *data*.
3. True
4. True
5. True
6. False: The rapid growth of information technologies has *changed* the structure of business organizations.
7. True
8. False: The rapid growth of information technologies has resulted in *more* collaboration among internal units of a company and outside firms.
9. False: Each business function—marketing, human resources, accounting, production, and finance—has *different* information requirements.
10. True
11. False: Information-systems employees who run a company's computer equipment are referred to as *system operations personnel*.
12. True
13. True
14. False: *An executive support system (ESS)* is a quick reference, easy-access program to assist upper-level managers.
15. True
16. False: *Hardware* is the physical devices and components, including the computer, in the information system.
17. True
18. True
19. True
20. True

Multiple Choice--*Answers*

1. d	5. c	9. c	13. b
2. b	6. a	10. d	14. d
3. a	7. b	11. c	15. d
4. c	8. b	12. d	

Jeopardy—*Answers*

	Data Communication Networks	Information-Systems Applications	Elements of an Information System
$100	a global communication network	transactions processing systems (TPSs)	hardware
$200	the Internet	a management information systems (MIS)	software
$300	the World Wide Web	decision-support systems (DSSs)	a database
$400	an Intranet	artificial intelligence	control
$500	a firewall	an executive support system (ESS)	a multimedia communication system

Match the Terms and Concepts to Their Definitions—*Answers*

1. h	10. bb	19. s	28. uu	37. qq	46. aaa	55. lll	64. yy	73. jjj
2. tt	11. hh	20. uuu	29. sss	38. kkk	47. ww	56. cc	65. v	74. vv
3. w	12. b	21. mm	30. nn	39. z	48. q	57. r	66. nnn	75. dd
4. mmm	13. ppp	22. p	31. f	40. rrr	49. aa	58. ccc	67. ff	
5. vvv	14. ttt	23. a	32. l	41. kk	50. ggg	59. ll	68. zz	
6. oo	15. rr	24. ee	33. u	42. t	51. o	60. ii	69. x	
7. m	16. bbb	25. ooo	34. ddd	43. i	52. pp	61. qqq	70. hhh	
8. d	17. j	26. eee	35. k	44. ss	53. c	62. y	71. gg	
9. xx	18. iii	27. n	36. www	45. e	54. g	63. fff	72. jj	

Word Scramble---*Answers*

1. hardware   2. groupware   3. microcomputer

Learning Objectives--Potential Short Answer or Essay Questions--*Answers*

Learning Objective #1:

Because businesses are faced with an overwhelming amount of *data* and *information* about customers, competitors, and their own operations, the ability to manage this input can mean the difference between success and failure. The management of its information system is a core activity because all of a firm's business activities are linked to it. New digital technologies have taken an integral place among an organization's resources for conducting everyday business.

Learning Objective #2:

Data communication networks, both public and private, carry streams of digital data (electronic messages) back and forth quickly and economically via *telecommunication systems*. The largest public communications network, the *Internet*, is a gigantic network of networks linking millions of computers offering information on business around the world. The Net is the most important e-mail system in the world. Individuals can subscribe to the Net via an Internet *service provider (ISP)*. The *World Wide Web* is a system with universally accepted standards for storing, formatting, retrieving, and displaying information. It provides the common language that enables users around the world to "surf" the Net using a common format. *Intranets* are private networks that any company can develop to extend Net technology internally—that is, for transmitting information throughout the firm. Intranets are accessible only to employees, with access to outsiders prevented by hardware and software security systems called *firewalls*.

Learning Objective #3:

Information networks are leading to *leaner* organizations—businesses with fewer employees and simpler organizational structures—because networked firms can maintain electronic, rather than human, information linkages among employees and customers. Operations are *more flexible* because electronic networks allow businesses to offer greater product variety and faster delivery cycles. Aided by intranets and the Internet, *greater collaboration* is possible, both among internal units and with outside firms. *Geographic separation* of the workplace and company headquarters is more common because electronic linkages are replacing the need for physical proximity between the company and its workstations. *Improved management processes* are feasible because managers have rapid access to more information about the current status of company activities and easier access to electronic tools for planning and decision-making.

Learning Objective #4:

Transaction processing systems (TPS) are applications for basic day-to-day business transactions. They are useful for routine transactions, such as taking reservations and meeting payrolls, that follow predetermined steps. Systems for *knowledge workers and office applications* include personal productivity tools such as *word processing, document imaging, desktop publishing, computer-aided design*, and *simulation modeling. Management information systems (MISs)* support an organization's managers by providing daily reports, schedules, plans, and budgets. Middle managers, the largest MIS user group, need networked information to plan upcoming activities and to track current activities. *Decision support systems (DSSs)* are interactive applications that assist the decision-making processes of middle- and top-level managers. *Executive support systems (ESSs)* are quick-reference, easy-access programs to assist upper-level managers. *Artificial intelligence (AI)* and *expert systems* are designed to imitate human behavior and provide computer-based assistance in performing certain business activities.

Learning Objective #5:

Hardware is the physical devices and components, including the computer, in the *information system (IS)*. It consists of an input device (such as a keyboard), a central processing unit (CPU), a main memory, disks for data storage, and output devices (such as video monitors and printers). *Software* includes the computer's operating system, application programs (such as word processing, spreadsheets, and Web browsers), and a graphical user interface (GUI) that helps users select among the computer's many possible applications.

Control is important to ensure not only that the system operates correctly, but also that data and information are transmitted through secure channels to people who really need them. Control is aided by the use of electronic security measures, such as firewalls, that bar entry to the system by unauthorized outsiders. The *database* is the organized collection of all the data files in the system. *People* are also part of the information system. IS *knowledge workers* include systems analysts who design the systems and programmers who write software instructions that tell computers what to do. System users, too, are integral to the system. *Telecommunication* components include multimedia technology that incorporates sound, animation, video, and photography along with ordinary graphics and text. Electronic discussion groups, videoconferencing, and other forms of interactive dialog are possible with communication devices (such as global positioning systems and personal digital assistants) and communication channels (such as satellite communications).

Critical Thinking Questions--*Answers*

1. Operational information systems, because they typically support daily operations and decision making, are principally used by lower-level managers and supervisors. On the other hand, management information systems, because they assist in managerial decision making, are typically used by middle-level management.

2. The four most commonly used applications of business computing are word processing, spreadsheets, database management, and communications.

Brain Teaser--*Answer*

1. There will likely be a larger market for the sale of consumer products on the Internet because consumer products are typically less sophisticated. On the other hand, industrial products are typically more sophisticated and, as such, personal selling is generally more effective.

Chapter 18
Understanding Principles of Accounting

LEARNING OBJECTIVES
After studying this chapter, you should be able to:

1. Explain the role of accountants and distinguish between the kinds of work done by *public* and *private* accountants.
2. Discuss the *CPA Vision Project* and explain how the CPA profession is changing.
3. Explain how the following concepts are used in *recordkeeping: the accounting equation* and *double-entry accounting.*
4. Describe the three basic *financial statements* and show how they reflect the activity and financial condition of a business.
5. Explain how computing key *financial ratios* can help in analyzing the financial strengths of a business.
6. Explain some of the special issues facing accountants at firms that do international business.

TRUE-FALSE
Indicate whether the statement is generally true or false by placing a "T" or "F" in the space provided. If it is a false statement, correct it so that it becomes a true statement.

_____ 1. Accounting is important to business because it helps managers plan and control a company's operation; and it helps outsiders evaluate a business.

_____ 2. Bookkeeping is the same as accounting.

_____ 3. Managerial accounting is the area of accounting concerned with preparing financial information for users outside the organization.

_____ 4. Certified public accountants (CPAs) are professionally licensed by the state and offer services to the public.

_____ 5. Generally accepted accounting principles (GAAP) are professionally approved standards and practices used by the accountants in the preparation of financial reports.

_____ 6. The internal auditor is the highest-ranking accountant in a company.

_____ 7. Private accountants are independent of the businesses, organizations, and individuals they serve.

_____ 8. The CPA Vision Project developed recommendations for change, including a set of core services that the accounting profession should offer clients, and a set of core competencies that CPAs should possess.

_____ 9. Assets equal Liabilities minus Owner's Equity is the basic accounting equation.

_____ 10. Owner's equity is any economic resource expected to benefit a firm or an individual who owns it.

_____ 11. Owner's equity consists of two sources of capital: the amount that the owners originally invested; and the profits earned by and reinvested in the company.

_____ 12. Double-entry bookkeeping is a system of recording financial transactions to keep the accounting equation in balance.

_____ 13. Three broad categories of financial statements are balance sheets, income statements, and statements of cash flow.

_____ 14. The income statement provides a snapshot of the business at a particular time, whereas the balance sheet reflects the results of operations over a period of time.

_____ 15. Profit equals revenues minus expenses.

_____ 16. Retained earnings are earnings not distributed to its owners in the form of dividends.

_____ 17. Net income (or net profit) equals gross profit minus operating expenses and income taxes.

_____ 18. The statement of cash flows indicates a firm's cash receipts and cash payments that presents information on its sources and uses of cash.

_____ 19. The liquidity, current, quick (or acid-test), and debt-to-equity ratios all measure solvency (a firm's ability to pay its debt) in both the short and long run.

_____ 20. Return on sales, return on investment, and earnings per share measure profitability.

_____ 21. Inventory turnover ratios show how efficiently a firm is using its funds.

_____ 22. International accounting is made more difficult because of fluctuating exchange rates.

MULTIPLE CHOICE

Circle the one best answer for each of the following questions.

1. Accounting information
   a. helps managers make business decisions and spot problems and opportunities.
   b. provides investors, suppliers, and creditors with the means to analyze a business.
   c. supports the government's efforts to collect taxes and regulate business.
   d. All of the above.

2. Which of the following statements is true?
   a. Bookkeeping is the record-keeping, clerical phase of accounting.
   b. The controller is a person who manages all of a firm's accounting activities.
   c. Financial accounting is the field of accounting concerned with external users of a company's financial information.
   d. All of the above.

3. The area of accounting concerned with preparing data for use by managers within the organization is
   a. financial accounting.
   b. managerial accounting.
   c. public accounting.
   d. tax accounting.

4. Which of the following statements is true?
   a. An audit is a systematic examination of a company's accounting system to determine whether its financial reports fairly represent its operations.
   b. A public accountant is a salaried accountant hired by a business to carry out its day-to-day financial activities.
   c. There is little need for the accounting profession to change.
   d. All of the above.

5. In the accounting equation,
   a. assets equal liabilities plus owner's equity.
   b. assets are a claim against a firm by a creditor.
   c. liabilities are anything of value owned or leased by a company.
   d. All of the above.

6. Which of the following statements is true?
   a. Double-entry bookkeeping is a way of recording financial transactions that require two entries for every transaction so that the accounting equation is always kept in balance.
   b. A balance sheet is a financial statement detailing a firm's assets, liabilities, and owner's equity.
   c. Liquidity is the ease with which an asset can be converted into cash.
   d. All of the above.

7. Which of the following statements is *false*?
   a. Depreciation is an accounting procedure for systematically spreading the cost of an asset over its estimated useful life.
   b. A liability is anything of value owned or leased by a company.
   c. Accounts receivable is the amount due form a customer who has purchased goods on credit.
   d. Merchandise inventory is the cost of merchandise that has been acquired for sale to customers and is still on hand.

8. Which of the following statements is *false*?
    a. A fixed asset is an asset with long-term use or value, such as land, buildings, and equipment.
    b. An intangible asset is the nonphysical asset, such as a patent or trademark, that has economic value in the form of expected benefits.
    c. Current liability is debt that is not due for more than one year.
    d. Goodwill is the amount paid for an existing business above the value of its other assets.

9. Current liabilities consisting of bills owed to suppliers, plus wages and taxes due within the upcoming year, is
    a. long-term liability.
    b. accounts receivable.
    c. accounts payable.
    d. an intangible asset.

10. A statement of a firm's financial position on a particular date, also known as a statement of financial position, is
    a. a balance sheet.
    b. an income statement.
    c. a statement of cash flows.
    d. a cost of goods sold statement.

11. The balance sheet
    a. "balances" because it includes all elements in the accounting equation and shows the balance between assets on one side of the equation, and liabilities and owner's equity on the other side.
    b. shows how profitable the organization has been over a specific period of time, typically one year.
    c. unfortunately does not enable the reader to determine the size of the company nor what the major assets, liabilities or owner's equity is.
    d. All of the above.

12. Which of the following statements is *false*?
    a. Retained earnings are earnings retained by a firm for its use rather than paid as dividends.
    b. Net income is gross profit minus operating expenses and income taxes.
    c. Operating expenses are the amount of funds that flow into a business from the sale of goods and services.
    d. Gross profit is the amount remaining when the cost of goods sold is deducted from revenues; also known as gross margin.

13. Which of the following statements is *false*?
    a. A budget is the detailed statement of estimated receipts and expenditures for a period of time in the future.
    b. An income statement is a financial statement listing a firm's annual revenues and expenses so that a bottom line shows an annual profit or loss.
    c. The three segments of an income statement are assets, liabilities, and owner's equity.
    d. The statement of cash flows shows how cash was received and spent in three areas: operations, investments, and financing.

14. The financial ratios, either short- or long-term, for estimating the risk in investing in a firm, are the
    a. liquidity ratios.
    b. solvency ratios.
    c. activity ratios.
    d. profitability ratios.

222 Part 5: Managing Operations and Information

15. A financial ratio that measures a firm's ability to pay its immediate debts is the
    a. liquidity ratio.
    b. profitability ratio.
    c. activity ratio.
    d. debt-to-owners' equity ratio.

16. A financial ratio describing the extent to which a firm is financed through borrowing is the
    a. return on equity ratio.
    b. earnings per share ratio.
    c. inventory turnover ratio.
    d. debt-to-owners' equity ratio.

JEOPARDY
You have 5 seconds to complete the question to each of the following answers.

	Accountants and Accounting Concepts	Financial Statements	Financial Ratios
$100	Accountants licensed by the state and offering services to the public. What is_____?	This provides a snapshot of the business at a particular point in time. What is_____?	Financial ratio, either sort- or long-term, for estimating the risk in investing in a firm. What is_____?
$200	Assets equal Liabilities plus Owner's Equity. What is_____?	Its three main sections are assets, liabilities, and owner's equity. What is_____?	Financial ratio for measuring a firm's potential earnings. What is_____?
$300	This equals assets minus liabilities. What is_____?	This shows how profitable the organization has been over a specific period of time. What is_____?	Financial ratio for evaluating management's use of a firm's assets. What is_____?
$400	Area of accounting concerned with preparing data for use by managers within the organization. What is_____?	This shows how a company's cash was received and spent in three areas: operations, investments, and financing. What is_____?	Solvency ratio measuring a firm's ability to meet its long-term debts. What is_____?
$500	Person who manages all of a firm's accounting activities (chief accounting officer). What is_____?	Gross profit minus operating expenses and income taxes. What is_____?	Profitability ratio measuring income earned for each dollar invested. What is_____?

MATCH THE TERMS AND CONCEPTS TO THEIR DEFINITIONS

a. accounting
b. bookkeeping
c. accounting system
d. controller
e. financial accounting system
f. managerial (or management) accounting system
g. certified public accountant (CPA)
h. audit
i. generally accepted accounting principles (GAAP)
j. management advisory services
k. private accountant
l. certified management accountant (CMA)
m. journal
n. ledger
o. fiscal year
p. asset
q. liability
r. owners' equity
s. double-entry accounting system
t. financial statement
u. balance sheet

v. current asset
w. liquidity
x. accounts receivable
y. merchandise inventory
z. LIFO (last-in-first-out) method
aa. FIFO (first-in-first-out) method
bb. prepaid expense
cc. fixed asset
dd. depreciation
ee. intangible asset
ff. goodwill
gg. current liability
hh. accounts payable
ii. long-term liability
jj. paid-in capital
kk. retained earnings
ll. income statement (or profit-and-loss statement)
mm. revenues
nn. cost of goods sold
oo. gross profit (or gross margin)
pp. operating expenses
qq. operating income

rr. net income (or net profit or net earnings)
ss. statement of cash flows
tt. budget
uu. solvency ratio
vv. profitability ratio
ww. activity ratio
xx. liquidity ratio
yy. current ratio
zz. working capital
aaa. quick (or acid-test) ratio
bbb. quick asset
ccc. debt ratio
ddd. debt-to-owners' equity ratio (or debt-to-equity ratio)
eee. debt
fff. leverage
ggg. net profit margin (or return on sales)
hhh. return on equity
iii. earnings per share
jjj. inventory turnover ratio
kkk. foreign currency exchange rate

_____ 1. Profitability ratio indicating the percentage of its income that is a firm's profit.

_____ 2. Record, divided into accounts and usually compiled on a monthly basis, containing summaries of all journal transactions.

_____ 3. Amount due from a customer who has purchased goods on credit.

_____ 4. Financial statement listing a firm's annual revenues and expenses so that a bottom line shows annual profit or loss.

_____ 5. Recording of accounting transactions.

_____ 6. Process of distributing the cost of an asset over its life.

_____ 7. Activity ratio measuring the average number of times that inventory is sold and restocked during the year.

_____ 8. Difference between a firm's current assets and current liabilities.

_____ 9. Systematic examination of a company's accounting system to determine whether its financial reports fairly represent its operations.

_____ 10. Detailed statement of estimated receipts and expenditures for a period of time in the future.

_____ 11. Debt that must be paid within the year.

_____ 12. Debt owed by a firm to an outside organization or individual.

_____ 13. Method of valuing inventories that assumes that older inventories (first in) are sold first.

_____ 14. Person who manages all of a firm's accounting activities (chief accounting officer).

_____ 15. Solvency ratio describing the extent to which a firm is financed through borrowing.

_____ 16. Solvency ratio measuring a firm's ability to pay its immediate debts.

_____ 17. Financial statement detailing a firm's assets, liabilities, and owners' equity.

_____ 18. Salaried accountant hired by a business to carry out its day-to-day financial activities.

_____ 19. Field of accounting that serves internal users of a company's financial information.

_____ 20. Costs, other than the cost of goods sold, incurred in producing a good or service.

_____ 21. Debt that is not due for more than 1 year.

_____ 22. Profitability ratio measuring income earned for each dollar invested.

_____ 23. Bookkeeping system that balances the accounting equation by recording the dual effects of every financial transaction.

_____ 24. Certified accountant specializing in management accounting.

_____ 25. Cash plus assets one step removed from cash (marketable securities and accounts receivable).

_____ 26. Accepted rules and procedures governing the content and form of financial reports.

_____ 27. Financial ratio for evaluating management's use of a firm's assets.

_____ 28. Expense, such as prepaid rent, that is paid before the upcoming period in which it is due.

_____ 29. Any of several types of reports summarizing a company's financial status to aid in managerial decision making.

_____ 30. A firm's total liabilities.

_____ 31. Twelve-month period designated for annual financial reporting purposes.

_____ 32. Method of valuing inventories that assumes that those received most recently (last in) are sold first.

_____ 33. Amount paid for an existing business above the value of its other assets.

_____ 34. Organized means by which financial information is identified, measured, recorded, and retained for use in accounting statements and management reports.

_____ 35. Total cost of obtaining materials for making the products sold by a firm during the year.

_____ 36. Value of a nation's currency as determined by market forces.

_____ 37. Comprehensive system for collecting, analyzing, and communicating financial information.

_____ 38. Asset that can or will be converted into cash within the following year.

_____ 39. Solvency ratio for determining a firm's ability to meet emergency demands for cash.

_____ 40. Earnings retained by a firm for its use rather than paid as dividends.

_____ 41. Gross profit minus operating expenses and income taxes.

_____ 42. Financial ratio for measuring a firm's potential earnings.

_____ 43. Field of accounting concerned with external users of a company's financial information.

_____ 44. Amount of money that owners would receive if they sold all of a firm's assets and paid all of its liabilities.

_____ 45. Ability to finance an investment through borrowed funds.

_____ 46. Asset with long-term use or value, such as land, buildings, and equipment.

_____ 47. Current liabilities consisting of bills owed to suppliers, plus wages and taxes due within the upcoming year.

_____ 48. Profitability ratio measuring the size of the dividend that a firm can pay shareholders.

_____ 49. Accountant licensed by the state and offering services to the public.

_____ 50. Solvency ratio that determines a firm's credit worthiness by measuring its ability to pay current liabilities.

_____ 51. Specialized accounting services to help managers resolve a variety of business problems.

_____ 52. Any economic resource expected to benefit a firm or an individual who owns it.

_____ 53. Nonphysical asset, such as a patent or trademark, that has economic value in the form of expected benefit.

_____ 54. Solvency ratio measuring a firm's ability to meet its long-term debts.

_____ 55. Chronological record of a firm's financial transactions, including a brief description of each.

_____ 56. Financial ratio, either short- or long-term, for estimating the risk in investing in a firm.

_____ 57. Cost of merchandise that has been acquired for sale to customers and is still on hand.

_____ 58. Revenues obtained from goods sold minus cost of goods sold.

_____ 59. Ease with which an asset can be converted into cash.

_____ 60. Additional money, above proceeds from stock sale, paid directly to a firm by its owners.

_____ 61. Gross profit minus operating expenses.

_____ 62. Funds that flow into a business from the sale of goods or services.

_____ 63. Financial statement describing a firm's yearly cash receipts and cash payments.

WORD SCRAMBLE

1. _____ _____   2. _____   3. _____
   betd   iorat   tessa   gincactoun

LEARNING OBJECTIVES--POTENTIAL SHORT ANSWER OR ESSAY QUESTIONS

Learning Objective #1: "Explain the role of accountants and distinguish between the kinds of work done by *public* and *private accountants*."

Learning Objective #2: "Discuss the *CPA Vision Project* and explain how the CPA profession is changing."

Learning Objective #3: "Explain how the following three concepts are used in *recordkeeping*: the *accounting equation* and *double-entry accounting*."

Learning Objective #4: "Describe the three basic *financial statements* and show how they reflect the activity and financial condition of a business."

Learning Objective #5: "Explain how computing *key financial ratios* can help in analyzing the financial strengths of a business."

Learning Objective #6: "Explain some of the special issues facing accountants at firms that do international business."

CRITICAL THINKING QUESTIONS

1. Use the accounts below to answer the following questions.

Net sales	Accounts receivable	Advertising expense
Common stock	Equipment	Marketable securities
Salaries	Retained earnings	Long-term notes payable
Cash	Inventory	Rent

   a. Which of these would be considered a current asset? Why?

   b. Which of these would be considered a fixed asset? Why?

   c. Which of these would be considered a current liability? Why?

   d. Which of these would be considered a long-term liability? Why?

   e. Which of these would be considered owner's equity?

   f. Which of these would be considered revenue?

   g. Which of these would be considered an expense?

2. Indicate the ratio that would provide information on:

   a. A firm's ability to pay current debts on short notice.

   b. A firm's overall financial performance.

   c. The amount of profits earned for each share of common stock outstanding.

   d. The number of times merchandise moves through the business.

   e. The extent to which the firm relies on debt (borrowed) financing.

   f. The size of the dividend that a firm can pay shareholders.

BRAIN TEASER

1. At the end of the year, Jan Nord, Inc. showed the following balances on accounts. Prepare a balance sheet for Jan Nord, Inc.

Land...........................	$70,000
Buildings........................	320,000
Inventory........................	110,000
Cash.............................	20,000
Accounts payable................	120,000
Marketable securities...........	42,000
Retained earnings...............	392,000
Common shares.................	80,000
(40,000 share @ $2)	
Notes payable...................	120,000
Equipment......................	60,000

ANSWERS

True-False—*Answers*

1. True
2. False: Bookkeeping, *which is sometimes confused with accounting, is just one phase of* accounting—*the recording of accounting transactions.*
3. False: *Financial* accounting is the area of accounting concerned with preparing financial information for users outside the organization.
4. True
5. True
6. False: The *controller* is the highest ranking accountant in a company.
7. False: *Public* accountants are independent of the businesses, organizations, and individuals they serve.
8. True
9. False: Assets equal Liabilities *plus* Owner's Equity is the basic accounting equation.
10. False: *An asset* is any economic resource expected to benefit a firm or an individual who owns it.
11. True
12. True
13. True
14. False: The *balance sheet* provides a snapshot of the business at a particular time, whereas the *income statement* reflects the results of operations over a period of time.
15. True
16. True
17. True
18. True
19. True
20. True
21. True
22. True

Multiple Choice--*Answers*

1. d	5. a	9. c	13. c
2. d	6. d	10. a	14. b
3. b	7. b	11. a	15. a
4. a	8. c	12. c	16. d

Jeopardy---*Answers*

	Accountants and Accounting Concepts	Financial Statements	Financial Ratios
$100	certified public accountants (CPAs)	a balance sheet	a solvency ratio
$200	the accounting equation	a balance sheet	a profitability ratio
$300	owner's equity	an income statement	an activity ratio
$400	managerial accounting	a statement of cash flows	a debt ratio
$500	a controller	net income (or net profit, or net earnings)	return on equity

Match the Terms and Concepts to Their Definitions--*Answers*

1. ggg	8. zz	15. ddd	22. hhh	29. t	36. kkk	43. e	50. yy	57. y
2. n	9. h	16. xx	23. s	30. eee	37. a	44. r	51. j	58. oo
3. x	10. tt	17. u	24. l	31. o	38. v	45. fff	52. p	59. w
4. ll	11. gg	18. k	25. bbb	32. z	39. aaa	46. cc	53. ee	60. jj
5. b	12. q	19. f	26. i	33. ff	40. kk	47. hh	54. ccc	61. qq
6. dd	13. aa	20. pp	27. ww	34. c	41. rr	48. iii	55. m	62. mm
7. jjj	14. d	21. ii	28. bb	35. nn	42. vv	49. g	56. uu	63. ss

Word Scramble--*Answers*

1. debt ratio   2. asset   3. accounting

Learning Objectives--Potential Short Answer or Essay Questions--*Answers*

Learning Objective #1:

By collecting, analyzing, and communicating financial information, accountants provide business managers and investors with an accurate picture of the firm's financial health. *Certified public accountants (CPAs)* are licensed professionals who provide auditing, tax, and management advisory services for other firms and individuals. *Public accountants* who have not yet been certified perform similar tasks. *Private accountants* provide diverse specialized services for the specific firms that employ them.

Learning Objective #2:

The Vision Project is a professionwide assessment to see what the future of the accounting profession will be like. It was initiated because of the declining number of students entering the accounting profession and because of rapid changes in the business world. Practicing CPAs and other industry leaders have participated in identifying key forces that are affecting the profession. Then they developed recommendations for change, including a set of *core services* that the profession should offer clients, and a set of *core competencies* that CPAs should possess. Overall, the new vision reflects changes in the CPA's culture and professional lifestyle.

Learning Objective #3:

The *accounting equation* (assets equal liabilities plus owners' equity) is used to balance the data in both journals and ledgers. *Double-entry accounting* acknowledges the dual effects of financial transactions and ensures that the accounting equation always balances. These tools enable accountants not only to enter, but to track, transactions. They also serve as double checks for accounting errors.

Learning Objective #4:

The *balance sheet* summarizes a company's assets, liabilities, and owners' equity at a given point in time. The *income statement* details revenues and expenses for a given period of time and identifies any profit or loss. The *statement of cash flows* reports cash receipts and payments from operating, investing, and financing activities.

Learning Objective #5:

Drawing on data from financial statements, ratios can help creditors, investors, and managers assess a firm's finances. The *liquidity, current, quick* (or *acid-test*), and *debt-to-equity ratios* all measure *solvency* (a firm's ability to pay its debt) in both the short and the long run. *Return on sales, return on investment*, and *earnings per share* measure *profitability*. *Inventory turnover ratios* show how efficiently a firm is using its funds.

Learning Objective #6:

Accounting for foreign transactions involves some special procedures. First, accountants must consider the fact that the *exchange rates* of national currencies change. Accordingly, the value of a foreign currency at any given time, its foreign currency exchange rate, is what buyers are willing to pay for it.

Exchange rates affect the amount of money that a firm pays for foreign purchases and the amount that it gains from foreign sales. U.S. accountants, therefore, must always translate foreign currencies into the value of the U.S. dollar. Then, in recording a firm's transactions—international purchases, sales on credit in other countries, and accounting for foreign subsidiaries—they must make adjustments to reflect shifting exchange rates over time. Shifting rates may result in either foreign currency transaction gains (a debt, for example, may be paid with fewer dollars) or foreign currency transaction losses.

Critical Thinking Questions--*Answers*

1. a. Cash, accounts receivable, inventory, and marketable securities would all be considered current assets.
    b. Equipment is the only fixed asset on this list.
    c. Salaries, advertising expenses, and rent accrued are the current liabilities.
    d. Long-term notes payable are the only long-term liability on this list.
    e. Common stock and retained earnings are the owner's equity.
    f. Net sales and interest from marketable securities (and retained earnings if it is earning interest) constitutes the revenue.
    g. The expenses include: salaries, advertising expenses, interest on long-term notes payable, and rent (as well as depreciation on the equipment).

2. a. One of the liquidity ratios (current ratio).
    b. One of the profitability ratios (earnings per share, and return on equity).
    c. The earnings per share ratio (one of the profitability ratios).
    d. The inventory turnover ratio (one of the activity ratios).
    e. The debt-to-equity ratio (one of the debt ratios).
    f. The earnings per share (one of the profitability ratios).

Brain Teaser—*Answer*

1. Note that Assets equal Liabilities plus Owner's Equity:

Jan Nord, Inc.
Balance Sheet

ASSETS

Current Assets		
Cash	$110,000	
Marketable Securities	42,000	
Inventory	110,000	
Total Current Assets	*$262,000*	
Fixed Assets		
Land	$70,000	
Buildings	320,000	
Equipment	60,000	
Total Fixed Assets	*$450,000*	
Total Assets		**$712,000**

LIABILITIES AND OWNER'S EQUITY

Current Liabilities		
Accounts Payable	$120,000	
Total Current Liabilities	*$120,000*	
Long-Term Liabilities		
Notes Payable	$120,000	
Total Long-Term Liabilities	*$120,000*	
Total Liabilities		*$240,000*
Owner's Equity		
Common Shares	$80,000	
(40,000 shares @ $2)		
Retained Earnings	$392,000	
Total Owner's Equity		*$472,000*
Total Liabilities and Owner's Equity		**$712,000**

Chapter 19

Understanding Money and Banking

LEARNING OBJECTIVES
After studying this chapter, you should be able to:

1. Define *money* and identify the different forms that it takes in the nation's money supply.
2. Describe the different kinds of *financial institutions* that comprise the U.S. financial system and explain the services they offer.
3. Explain how banks create money and describe the means by which they are regulated.
4. Discuss the functions of the *Federal Reserve System* and describe the tools that it uses to control the money supply.
5. Identify three important ways in which the financial industry is changing.
6. Understand some of the key activities in *international banking and finance.*

TRUE-FALSE
Indicate whether the statement is generally true or false by placing a "T" or "F" in the space provided. If it is a false statement, correct it so that it becomes a true statement.

_____ 1. Anything that is going to be money must be portable, divisible, durable, and stable.

_____ 2. Money serves three functions: it acts as a medium of exchange, store of value, and unit of account.

_____ 3. M-2 is a measure of the money supply that includes only the most liquid (spendable) forms of money.

_____ 4. The major components of M-2 are M-1, time deposits, money market mutual funds, and savings deposits.

_____ 5. A demand deposit is a fund of short-term, low-risk, financial securities purchased with the assets of investor-owners pooled by a nonbank institution.

_____ 6. Some of the major types of financial institutions that accept deposits from the general public include commercial banks, savings and loan associations, mutual savings banks, and credit unions.

_____ 7. The prime rate is the interest rate available to a bank's most creditworthy customers.

_____ 8. The Federal Reserve System (or the Fed) is the nation's central bank.

_____ 9. Banks create money (add to the money supply) whenever loans are repaid.

_____ 10. The Comptroller of the Currency and the Federal Deposit Insurance Corporation (FDIC) are the primary agencies responsible for ensuring a sound, competitive, financial system.

_____ 11. The Fed's most important function is to control the nation's money supply.

_____ 12. To change the money supply and interest rates, the Fed can change reserve requirements, the discount rate, and utilize open market operations.

_____ 13. To increase the money supply, the Fed should increase the discount rate.

_____ 14. To increase the money supply, the Fed should increase the reserve requirement.

_____ 15. When the Federal Reserve sets margin requirements for consumer stock purchases, or sets credit rules for other consumer purchases, it is exercising selective credit controls.

_____ 16. Deregulation of the banking business and interest rates, as well as the rise of intestate banking, has increased competition in the banking business.

_____ 17. A smart card is a plastic card that allows an individual to transfer money between accounts.

_____ 18. E-cash is money that can be moved among consumers and businesses via digital electronic transmission.

_____ 19. Each nation tries to influence its currency exchange rates to gain advantage in international trade.

_____ 20. A higher exchange rate usually results in a nation experiencing a greater trade surplus.

MULTIPLE CHOICE
Circle the one best answer for each of the following questions.

1. Money functions as a
   a. medium of exchange.
   b. unit of value.
   c. store of value.
   d. All of the above.

2. Money must be
    a. divisible.
    b. portable.
    c. durable and stable.
    d. All of the above.

3. Which of the following statements is true?
    a. M-2 counts only the most liquid, or spendable, forms of money: currency, demand deposits, or low-interest-bearing forms of money.
    b. The major components of M-2 are M-1, time deposits, money market mutual funds, and savings deposits.
    c. Time deposits are bank account funds that may be withdrawn at any time by simply writing a check.
    d. All of the above.

4. Which of the following statements is true about credit cards?
    a. Credit cards are extremely profitable for issuing companies.
    b. Merchants who accept credit cards pay fees to card issuers.
    c. All credit cards charge interest on unpaid balances; some charge an annual fee to card holders.
    d. All of the above.

5. Which of the following is a nondeposit financial institution?
    a. Commercial banks.
    b. Savings and Loan Associations.
    c. Insurance Companies.
    d. Credit Unions.

6. A financial institution that accepts deposits from, and makes loans to, only its members, usually employees of a particular organization, is a
    a. Credit Union.
    b. Commercial Bank.
    c. Savings and Loan Association.
    d. Mutual Savings Bank.

7. A nondeposit financial institution that specializes in making loans to businesses and consumers is
    a. an insurance company.
    b. a finance company.
    c. a securities investment dealer.
    d. a pension fund.

8. A nondeposit financial institution that pools funds managed to provide retirement income for its members is
    a. an insurance company.
    b. a securities investment dealer.
    c. a pension fund.
    d. a finance company.

9. A tax-deferred pension fund with which wage earners supplement other retirement funds is
    a. a trust service.
    b. a letter of credit.
    c. an individual retirement account (IRA).
    d. a banker's acceptance.

10. Which of the following statements is true?
    a. When banks make loans the money supply increases.
    b. The Federal Deposit Insurance Corporation (FDIC) is a federal agency that guarantees the safety of all deposits up to $100,000 in the financial institutions that it insures.
    c. Because commercial banks are critical to the creation of money, the government regulates them to ensure a sound and competitive financial system.
    d. All of the above.

11. The Federal Reserve System (Fed)
    a. acts as the government's bank.
    b. can lend money to member commercial banks.
    c. controls the nation's money supply.
    d. All of the above.

12. Which of the following statements is *false*?
    a. The Fed, as the bankers' bank, lends money (at interest) to member banks, stores required reserve funds for banks, and clears checks for them.
    b. The Fed does not have the power to audit banks.
    c. The Fed lends money to the government whenever it buys bonds issued by the Treasury Department.
    d. The Fed controls monetary policy—the management of the nation's money supply and interest rates.

13. Which of the following statements is *false* about the Federal Reserve's monetary policy tools?
    a. The discount rate is the interest rate that a bank charges its most credit-worthy customers for consumer loans.
    b. Open market operations is the Fed's sales and purchases of government securities in the open market.
    c. The reserve requirement is the percentage of banks' deposits that must be held in cash or on deposit with the Federal Reserve.
    d. The Federal Reserve can use selective credit controls to set margin requirements governing the credit granted to buyers of securities.

14. To increase the money supply the Fed could
    a. reduce the discount rate.
    b. reduce reserve requirements.
    c. buy U.S. Treasury notes and bonds on the open market.
    d. All of the above.

15. Which of the following is true?
    a. A smart card is a plastic card that allows an individual to transfer money between bank accounts.
    b. A debit card is a credit-card-size computer programmed with electronic money.
    c. A point-of-sale (POS) terminal is an electronic device that allows customers to pay for retail purchases with debit cards.
    d. All of the above.

16. If the value of the U.S. dollar in international exchange markets increases (the dollar appreciates, it gets stronger) this will likely cause
    a. the relative price of American products to become more expensive and the U.S will export less.
    b. the relative price of foreign products to become less expensive and the U.S will import more.
    c. a trade deficit in the United States.
    d. All of the above.

17. Which of the following statements is true?
    a. The law of one price states that identical products should sell for the same price in all countries.
    b. Devalued currencies make it more expensive for other countries to buy the home country's products.
    c. The World Bank is primarily concerned with promoting the stability of exchange rates and providing short-term loans to member countries.
    d. All of the above.

18. The International Monetary Fund attempts to
    a. promote stable exchange rates.
    b. provide temporary, short-term loans to member countries.
    c. encourage members to cooperate on international monetary issues.
    d. All of the above.

JEOPARDY

You have 5 seconds to complete the question to each of the following answers.

	Money	**Financial Institutions**	**The Federal Reserve**
$100	The three functions of money. What is_____ _____?	Federal or state-chartered financial institution accepting deposits that it uses to make loans and earn profits. What is_____ _____?	The major function of the Fed. What is_____ _____?
$200	The four characteristics of money if it is to be an effective medium of exchange. What is_____ _____?	Financial institution accepting deposits and making loans primarily for home mortgages. What is_____ _____?	The percentage of a bank's deposits that must be held as cash or on reserve at the Federal Reserve. What is_____ _____?
$300	Money in a checking account that can be used by the customer at any time. What is_____ _____?	Financial institution that accepts deposits and makes loans to only its members, usually employees of a particular organization. What is_____ _____?	Activity of the Fed in buying and selling government bonds on the open market. What is_____ _____?
$400	Bank accounts that pay interest and require advance notice before money can be withdrawn. What is_____ _____?	Nondeposit institution that invests funds collected as premiums charged for insurance coverage. What is_____ _____?	Federal Reserve's power to set credit terms on various types of loans. What is_____ _____?
$500	That portion of the money supply consisting of currency and demand deposits. What is_____ _____?	Nondeposit institution that buys and sells stocks and bonds both for investors and for its own accounts. What is_____ _____?	What the Fed should do to increase the money supply. What is_____ _____?

MATCH THE TERMS AND CONCEPTS TO THEIR DEFINITIONS

a. money
b. M-1
c. currency
d. check
e. M-2
f. time deposit
g. money market mutual fund
h. commercial bank
i. state bank
j national bank
k. prime rate
l. savings and loan association (S&L)
m. mutual savings bank
n. credit union

o. pension fund
p. insurance company
q. finance company
r. securities investment dealer (broker)
s. individual retirement account (IRA)
t. Keogh plan
u. trust services
v. letter of credit
w. banker's acceptance
x. automated teller machine (ATM)
y. electronic funds transfer (EFT)

z. Federal Deposit Insurance Corporation (FDIC)
aa. Federal Reserve System (the Fed)
bb. float
cc. monetary policy
dd. reserve requirement
ee. discount rate
ff. open-market operations
gg. selective credit controls
hh. debit card
ii. point-of-sale (POS) terminal
jj. smart card
kk. E-cash

_____ 1. Demand deposit order instructing a bank to pay a given sum to a specified payee demand deposit Bank account funds that may be withdrawn at any time.

_____ 2. Financial institution accepting deposits and making loans primarily for home mortgages.

_____ 3. Interest rate at which member banks can borrow money from the Federal Reserve.

_____ 4. Communication of fund-transfer information over wire, cable, or microwave.

_____ 5. Federal- or state-chartered financial institution accepting deposits that it uses to make loans and earn profits.

_____ 6. Credit-card-size computer programmed with electronic money.

_____ 7. Nondeposit institution that buys and sells stocks and bonds both for investors and for its own accounts.

_____ 8. Bank promise, issued for a buyer, to pay a designated firm a certain amount of money if specified conditions are met.

_____ 9. Financial institution that accepts deposits from, and makes loans to, only its members, usually employees of a particular organization.

_____ 10. Plastic card that allows an individual to transfer money between accounts.

_____ 11. Central bank of the United States, which acts as the government's bank, serves member commercial banks, and controls the nation's money supply.

_____ 12. Bank funds that cannot be withdrawn without notice or transferred by check.

_____ 13. Nondeposit institution that invests funds collected as premiums charged for insurance coverage.

_____ 14. Any object that is portable, divisible, durable, and stable and serves as a medium of exchange, a store of value, and a unit of account.

_____ 15. Commercial bank chartered by an individual state.

_____ 16. Policies by which the Federal Reserve manages the nation's money supply and interest rates.

_____ 17. Bank promise, issued for a buyer, to pay a designated firm a specified amount at a future date.

_____ 18. Government-issued paper money and metal coins.

_____ 19. Nondeposit pool of funds managed to provide retirement income for its members.

_____ 20. Federal Reserve authority to set both margin requirements for consumer stock purchases and credit rules for other consumer purchases.

_____ 21. Federal agency that guarantees the safety of all deposits up to $100,000 in the financial institutions that it insures.

_____ 22. Tax-deferred pension plan for the self-employed.

_____ 23. Measure of the money supply that includes all the components of M-1 plus the forms of money that can be easily converted into spendable form.

_____ 24. Interest rate available to a bank's most creditworthy customers.

_____ 25. Total amount of checks written, but not yet cleared, through the Federal Reserve.

_____ 26. Fund of short-term, low-risk financial securities purchased with the assets of investor-owners pooled by a nonbank institution.

_____ 27. Electronic device that allows customers to pay for retail purchases with debit cards.

_____ 28. Electronic machine that allows customers to conduct account-related activities 24 hours a day, 7 days a week.

_____ 29. Electronic money that moves among consumers and businesses via digital electronic transmissions.

_____ 30. Financial institution whose depositors are owners sharing in its profits.

_____ 31. Tax-deferred pension fund with which wage earners supplement other retirement funds.

_____ 32. Nondeposit institution that specializes in making loans to businesses and consumers.

_____ 33. Measure of the money supply that includes only the most liquid (spendable) forms of money.

_____ 34. Percentage of its deposits that a bank must hold in cash or on deposit with the Federal Reserve.

_____ 35. Commercial bank chartered by the federal government.

_____ 36. Bank management of an individual's investments, payments, or estate.

_____ 37. The Federal Reserve's sales and purchases of securities in the open market.

WORD SCRAMBLE

1. _____   2. _____   _____   3. _____
      cryrcuen   premi   erat   nyome

LEARNING OBJECTIVES--POTENTIAL SHORT ANSWER OR ESSAY QUESTIONS

Learning Objective #1: "**Define** *money* **and identify the different forms it takes in the nation's money supply.**"

Learning Objective #2: "**Describe the different kinds of** *financial institutions* **that make up the U.S. financial system and explain the services they offer.**"

Learning Objective #3: "**Explain how banks create money and describe the means by which they are regulated.**"

Learning Objective #4: **"Discuss the functions of the *Federal Reserve System* and describe the tools it uses to control the money supply."**

Learning Objective #5: **"Identify five important ways in which the financial industry is changing."**

Learning Objective #6: **"Understand some of the key activities in *international banking and finance*."**

CRITICAL THINKING QUESTIONS

1. What are the three main international services offered by a bank?

2. How can the Federal Reserve decrease the money?

BRAIN TEASER

1. How can an increase in the money supply stimulate the economy?

ANSWERS

True-False--*Answers*

1. True
2. True
3. False: *M-1* is a measure of the money supply that includes only the most liquid (spendable) forms of money.
4. True
5. False: A *money market mutual fund* is a fund of short-term, low-risk financial securities purchased with the assets of investor-owners pooled by a nonbank institution.
6   True
7. True
8. True
9. False: Banks create money (add to the money supply) whenever loans are *made (or granted)*.
10. True
11. True
12. True
13. False: To increase the money supply the Fed should *decrease* the discount rate.
14. False: To increase the money supply the Fed should *decrease* the reserve requirement.
15. True
16. True
17. False: A *debit* card is a plastic card that allows an individual to transfer money between accounts.
18. True
19. True
20. False: A higher exchange rate usually results in a nation experiencing a greater trade *deficit*.

Multiple Choice--*Answers*

1. d	5. c	9. c	13. a	17. a
2. d	6. a	10. d	14. d	18. d
3. b	7. b	11. d	15. c	
4. d	8. c	12. b	16. d	

Jeopardy—*Answers*

	Money	**Financial Institutions**	**The Federal Reserve**
$100	it must be generally acceptable as a medium of exchange, a unit of account, and a store of value	commercial banks	to control the money supply
$200	divisible, portable, durable, and stable	savings and loan associations	a reserve requirement
$300	demand deposits	credit unions	open market operations
$400	time deposits	an insurance company	selective credit controls
$500	M-1	a securities investment dealer (broker)	decrease the discount rate, decrease reserve requirements, buy bonds on the open market, and loosen up on credit controls

Match the Terms and Concepts to Their Definitions--*Answers*

1. d	6. jj	11. aa	16. cc	21. z	26. g	31. s	36. u
2. l	7. r	12. f	17. w	22. t	27. ii	32. q	37. ff
3. ee	8. v	13. p	18. c	23. e	28. x	33. b	
4. y	9. n	14. a	19. o	24. k	29. kk	34. dd	
5. h	10. hh	15. i	20. gg	25. bb	30. m	35. j	

Word Scramble--*Answers*

1. currency   2. prime rate   3. money

Learning Objectives--Potential Short Answer or Essay Questions--*Answers*

Learning Objective #1:

Any item that is portable, divisible, durable, and stable satisfies the four basic characteristics of *money*. Money also serves three functions: It is a medium of exchange, a store of value, and a unit of account. The nation's money supply is often determined by two measures: *M-1* includes liquid (or spendable) forms of money, currency (bills and coins), demand deposits, and other checkable deposits (such as ATM account balances and NOW accounts). *M-2* includes M-1 plus items that cannot be directly spent but can be converted easily to spendable forms: time deposits, money market funds, and savings deposits. *Credit* must also be considered as a factor in the money supply.

Learning Objective #2:

The U.S. financial system includes federal- and state-chartered *commercial banks, savings and loan associations, mutual savings banks, credit unions*, and *nondeposit institutions* such as pension funds and insurance companies. These institutions offer a variety of services, including pension, trust, and international services, financial advice and brokerage services, and electronic funds transfer (EFT), including automated teller machines.

Learning Objective #3:

By taking in deposits and making loans, banks create money or, more accurately, *expand the money supply*. The overall supply of money is governed by several federal agencies. The Comptroller of the Currency and the Federal Deposit Insurance Corporation (FDIC) are the primary agencies responsible for ensuring a sound, competitive, financial system.

Learning Objective #4:

The *Federal Reserve System* (or *the Fed*) is the nation's central bank. As the government's bank, the Fed produces currency and lends money to the government. As the bankers' bank, it lends money (at interest) to member banks, stores required *reserve funds* for banks, and clears checks for them. The Fed is empowered to audit member banks and sets U.S. *monetary policy* by controlling the country's money supply. To control the money supply, the Fed specifies *reserve requirements* (the percentage of its deposits that a bank must hold with the Fed). It sets the *discount rate* at which it lends money to banks and conducts *open-market operations* to buy and sell securities. It also exerts influence through *selective credit controls* (such as margin requirements governing the credit granted to buyers by securities brokers).

Learning Objective #5:

Many changes have affected the financial system in recent years. *Deregulation*, especially of interest rates, and the rise of interstate banking, have increased competition. *Electronic technologies* offer a variety of new financial conveniences to customers. *Debit* cards are plastic cards that permit users to transfer money between bank accounts. *Smart cards* are credit-card-sized computers that can be loaded with electronic money at ATMs or over special telephone hookups. *E-cash* is money that can be moved among consumers and businesses via digital electronic transmissions. Another change is the increase in foreign banks now maintaining a significant presence in the United States to aid international trade.

Learning Objective #6:

Electronic technologies now permit speedy global financial transactions to support the growing importance of international finance. Country-to-country transactions are conducted according to an *international payment process* that moves money among buyers and sellers in different nations. Each nation tries to influence its *currency exchange* rates to gain advantage in international trade. For example, if its currency is *overvalued*, a higher exchange rate usually results in a *trade deficit*. Conversely, *undervalued* currencies can attract buyers and create *trade surpluses*. Governments may act to influence exchange rates by *devaluing* or *revaluing* their national currencies (that is, by decreasing or increasing them). Devalued currencies make it less expensive for other countries to buy the home country's products.

Critical Thinking Questions--*Answers*

1. The three main international services offered by banks are currency exchange, letters of credit, and banker's acceptances.

2. The Fed could decrease the money supply by increasing the discount rate, increasing reserve requirements, selling government bonds, or tightening up on select credit controls.

Brain Teaser--*Answer*

1. An increase in the money supply will decrease interest rates which will stimulate borrowing and, therefore, spending. An increase in spending means more sales. More sales will stimulate production, which will increase employment and national income. A portion of the additional income earned will be spent, creating a further expansion in national employment, income, and production (GDP). The Fed should increase the money supply to fight a recession (and decrease the money supply to fight inflation during a rapidly expanding economy).

Chapter 20
Understanding Securities and Investments

LEARNING OBJECTIVES
After studying this chapter, you should be able to:

1. Explain the difference between *primary* and *secondary securities markets*.
2. Discuss the value to shareholders of *common* and *preferred stock*, and describe the secondary market for each type of security.
3. Distinguish among various types of *bonds* in terms of their issuers, safety, and retirement.
4. Describe the investment opportunities offered by *mutual funds* and *commodities*.
5. Explain the process by which securities are bought and sold.
6. Explain how securities markets are regulated.

TRUE-FALSE
Indicate whether the statement is generally true or false by placing a "T" or "F" in the space provided. If it is a false statement, correct it so that it becomes a true statement.

_____ 1. The secondary securities markets involve the buying and selling of new securities, either in public offering or through private placements (sales to single buyers or small groups of buyers).

_____ 2. The primary securities market involves the trading of stocks and bonds through such familiar bodies as the New York and American Stock Exchanges.

_____ 3. Shareholders of common stock must be paid dividends before shareholders of preferred stock.

_____ 4. Stock values are expressed in three different ways—as par, market, and book value.

_____ 5. Blue-chip stock is common stock issued by a well-established company with a sound financial history and a stable pattern of dividend payouts.

_____ 6. The book value of common stock is the current price of a share of stock in the stock market.

_____ 7. Cumulative preferred stock is preferred stock on which dividends not paid in the past must be paid to stockholders before dividends can be paid to common stockholders.

_____ 8. A stockbroker is an individual or organization who receives and executes buy-and-sell orders on behalf of other people in return for commissions.

_____ 9. A bond is an IOU—a promise by the issuer to pay the buyer a certain amount of money by a specified future date, usually with interest paid at regular intervals.

_____ 10. A municipal bond is a bond issued by the federal government.

_____ 11. Corporate bondholders get a fixed return and do not vote on company policy nor do they share in company profits or losses.

_____ 12. Investors should consider the income, growth, safety, liquidity, and tax consequences of alternative security investments.

_____ 13. Bonds that can be exchanged at the owner's discretion into common stock of the issuing company are called secured bonds.

_____ 14. Moody's and Standard and Poor's rate the safety of bonds issued by various borrowers.

_____ 15. Bonds may be secured (backed by pledges of the issuer's assets) or unsecured, and offer varying degrees of safety.

_____ 16. Like stocks and bonds, mutual funds—companies that pool investments to purchase portfolios of financial instruments—offer investors different levels of risk and growth potential.

_____ 17. Load funds do not charge commissions when investors buy in or out of mutual funds.

_____ 18. Futures contracts—agreements to buy specific amounts of commodities at given prices on preset dates—are traded in the commodities markets.

_____ 19. A price-earnings ratio (p/e ratio) is a stock's current market price divided by the company's current annual earnings per share.

_____ 20. A bull market is a period of falling stock prices.

_____ 21. The Dow Jones Industrial Average (DJIA) tracks the prices of 30 blue-chip stocks and is a barometer, not a predictor, of performance.

_____ 22. The Standard and Poor's Composite Index is a market index based on the performance of 500 large and small companies, which are selected to represent the performance of all U.S. corporations.

_____   23. Even though almost every state has its own laws governing securities trading, the federal government has the leading role in investment regulation.

MULTIPLE CHOICE

Circle the one best answer for each of the following questions.

1. Which of the following statements is *false*?
   a. The primary securities markets are where newly issued securities are bought and sold; the secondary market is where previously issued securities are traded.
   b. Bonds imply ownership rights to a company, whereas stocks represent strictly financial claims for money owed to holders by a company.
   c. The Securities and Exchange Commission (SEC) is a federal agency that administers U.S. securities laws to protect the investing public and maintain smoothly functioning markets.
   d. An investment bank is a financial institution engaged in issuing and reselling new securities.

2. Investment banks provide which of the following services?
   a. They advise companies on the timing and financial terms of newly issued securities.
   b. By underwriting—that is, buying—new securities, they bear some of the risks of issuing them.
   c. They create the distribution networks for moving new securities through groups of other banks and brokers into the hands of individual investors.
   d. All of the above.

3. Which of the following statements is true about stocks?
   a. A stock's real value is its market value—the current price of a share in the stock market.
   b. The par value of a share of stock is its value expressed as total shareholder's equity divided by the number of shares of stock.
   c. The book value is the face value of a share of stock, set by the issuing company's board of directors.
   d. All of the above.

4. Which of the following statements is true about stocks?
   a. Common stock affords investors the prospect of capital gains and/or dividend income.
   b. The market value of a share of stock is the most important measure of the value of stock to an investor.
   c. Preferred stock is less risky than common stock.
   d. All of the above.

5. Which of the following statements is true about preferred stock?
   a. Cumulative preferred stock entitles holders to missed dividends as soon as the company is financially capable of paying.
   b. Cumulative preferred stock offers the prospect of steadier income compared to other stock.
   c. Shareholders of preferred stock must be paid dividends before shareholders of common stock.
   d. All of the above.

6. Which of the following statements is true about stock trading?
   a. The American Stock Exchange (AMEX) is the largest floor-based U.S. stock exchange.
   b. The New York Stock Exchange (NYSE) is the second largest floor-based U.S. stock exchange accounting for approximately 3 percent of all shares traded in the U.S.
   c. The over-the-counter (OTC) market is an organization of securities dealers formed to trade stock outside the formal institutional setting of the organized stock exchanges.
   d. All of the above.

7. NASDAQ
   a. is an acronym for the National Association of Securities Dealers Automated Quotation System.
   b. is an organization of over-the-counter dealers who own, buy, and sell their own securities over a network of electronic communications.
   c. is the fastest-growing U.S. stock market.
   d. All of the above.

8. A bond issued by a company is called a
   a. municipal bond.
   b. corporate bond.
   c. secured bond.
   d. callable bond.

9. An unsecured bond for which no specific property is pledged as security is a
   a. debenture.
   b. serial bond.
   c. convertible bond.
   d. bearer bond.

10. A method for retiring bonds whereby the issuer puts enough money into a banking account to redeem the bonds at maturity
    a. are callable bond.
    b. are serial bonds.
    c. is a sinking fund provision.
    d. are convertible bonds.

11. Which of the following is *false?*
    a. Mutual funds are companies that pool investments from individuals and organizations to purchase a portfolio of stocks, bonds, and short-term securities.
    b. A no-load mutual fund is a mutual fund in which investors are charged sales commissions when they buy in or sell out.
    c. A futures contract is an agreement to purchase specified amounts of a commodity at a given price on a set future date.
    d. Commodities market is a market in which futures contracts are traded.

12. Which of the following statements is *false*?
    a. A margin is the percentage of the total sales price that a buyer must pat up to place an order for stock or futures contracts.
    b. The price-earnings ratio is the current price of a stock divided by the firm's current annual earnings per share.
    c. A bear market is a period of rising stock prices.
    d. The NASDAQ Composite Index is a value-weighted market index that includes all NASDAQ-listed companies, both domestic and foreign.

13. An order authorizing the purchase of a stock only if its price is equal to or less than a specific amount is a
    a. limit order.
    b. stop order.
    c. round lot order.
    d. short sale.

14. Which of the following statements is true?
    a. Program trading is the large purchase or sale of a group of stocks, often triggered by computerized trading programs that can be launched without human supervision or control.
    b. Insider trading is the legal practice of using special knowledge about a firm for profit or gain.
    c. Laws requiring securities dealers to be licensed and registered with the states in which they do business are called pie-in-the-sky laws.
    d. All of the above.

JEOPARDY

You have 5 seconds to complete the question to each of the following answers.

	Stocks	Bonds	Mutual Funds and Commodities
$100	Common stock issued by a well-established company with a sound financial history and a stable pattern of dividend payouts. What is_____?	A bond issued by a state of local government. What is_____?	A company that pools investments from individuals and organizations to purchase a portfolio of stocks, bonds, and short-term securities. What is_____?
$200	Current price of a share of stock in the stock market. What is_____?	A bond issued by a company as a source of long-term funding. What is_____?	An agreement to purchase specified amounts of a commodity at a given price on a set future date. What is_____?
$300	The value of a share of stock expressed as total shareholders' equity divided by the number of shares of stock. What is_____?	A bond backed by pledges of assets to the bondholders. What is_____?	A market in which futures contracts are traded. What is_____?
$400	Preferred stock on which dividends not paid in the past must be paid to stockholders before dividends can be paid to common stockholders. What is_____?	A bond that can be retired by converting it to common stock. What is_____?	A mutual fund in which investors pay no sales commissions when they buy in or sell out of mutual funds. What is_____?
$500	An organization of individuals formed to provide an institutional setting in which stock can be traded. What is_____?	A bond that is retired when the issuer redeems portions of the issue at different preset dates. What is_____?	The percentage of the total sales price that a buyer must put up to place an order for stock or futures contracts. What is_____?

MATCH THE TERMS AND CONCEPTS TO THEIR DEFINITIONS

a. securities
b. primary securities market
c. Securities and Exchange Commission (SEC)
d. investment bank
e. secondary securities market
f. par value
g. market value
h. capital gain
i. book value
j. blue-chip stock
k. cumulative preferred stock
l. stock exchange
m. broker
n. over-the-counter (OTC) market
o. National Association of Securities Dealers Automated Quotation (NASDAQ) system

p. bond
q. government bond
r. municipal bond
s. corporate bond
t. registered bond
u. bearer (or coupon) bond
v. secured bond
w. debenture
x. mutual fund
y. no-load fund
z. load fund
aa. futures contract
bb. commodities market
cc. margin
dd. bid price
ee. asked price
ff. market index
gg. bull market
hh. bear market

ii. Dow Jones Industrial Average
jj. Standard & Poor's Composite Index
kk. market order
ll. limit order
mm. stop order
nn. round lot
oo. odd lot
pp. short sale
qq. program trading
rr. prospectus
ss. insider trading
tt. blue-sky laws

_____ 1. Bond issued by a state or local government.

_____ 2. Market in which futures contracts are traded.

_____ 3. Market index based on the performance of 400 industrial firms, 40 utilities, 40 financial institutions, and 20 transportation companies.

_____ 4. Common stock issued by a well-established company with a sound financial history and a stable pattern of dividend payouts.

_____ 5. Registration statement filed with the SEC before the issuance of a new security.

_____ 6. Federal agency that administers U.S. securities laws to protect the investing public and maintain smoothly functioning markets.

_____ 7. Organization of securities dealers formed to trade stock outside the formal institutional setting of the organized stock exchanges.

_____ 8. Company that pools investments from individuals and organizations to purchase a portfolio of stocks, bonds, and short-term securities.

_____ 9. Order authorizing the sale of a stock if its price falls to or below a specified level.

_____ 10. Stock sale in which an investor borrows securities from a broker to be sold and then replaced at a specified future date.

_____ 11. Face value of a share of stock, set by the issuing company's board of directors.

_____ 12. Security through which an issuer promises to pay the buyer a certain amount of money by a specified future date.

_____ 13. Financial institution engaged in issuing and reselling new securities.

_____ 14. Price that an OTC broker pays for a share of stock.

_____ 15. Bond requiring the holder to clip and submit a coupon to receive an interest payment.

_____ 16. Organization of individuals formed to provide an institutional setting in which stock can be traded.

_____ 17. Purchase or sale of stock in fractions of round lots.

_____ 18. Laws requiring securities dealers to be licensed and registered with the states in which they do business.

_____ 19. Unsecured bond for which no specific property is pledged as security.

_____ 20. Individual or organization who receives and executes buy-and-sell orders on behalf of other people in return for commissions.

_____ 21. Profit earned by selling a share of stock for more than it cost.

_____ 22. Order to buy or sell a security at the market price prevailing at the time the order is placed.

_____ 23. Stocks and bonds representing secured, or asset-based, claims by investors against issuers.

_____ 24. Period of rising stock prices.

_____ 25. Mutual fund in which investors are charged sales commissions when they buy in or sell out.

_____ 26. Organization of over-the-counter dealers who own, buy, and sell their own securities over a network of electronic communications.

_____ 27. Value of a common stock expressed as total shareholders' equity divided by the number of shares of stock.

_____ 28. Summary of price trends in a specific industry and/or the stock market as a whole.

_____ 29. Illegal practice of using special knowledge about a firm for profit or gain.

_____ 30. Market in which stocks and bonds are traded.

_____ 31. Bond backed by pledges of assets to the bondholders.

_____ 32. Market index based on the prices of 30 of the largest industrial firms listed on the NYSE.

_____ 33. Market in which new stocks and bonds are bought and sold.

_____ 34. Percentage of the total sales price that a buyer must put up to place an order for stock or futures contracts.

_____ 35. Bond issued by the federal government.

_____ 36. Large purchase or sale of a group of stocks, often triggered by computerized trading programs that can be launched without human supervision or control.

_____ 37. Current price of a share of stock in the stock market.

_____ 38. Mutual fund in which investors pay no sales commissions when they buy in or sell out.

_____ 39. Preferred stock on which dividends not paid in the past must be paid to stockholders before dividends can be paid to common stockholders.

_____ 40. Order authorizing the purchase of a stock only if its price is equal to or less than a specified amount.

_____ 41. Agreement to purchase specified amounts of a commodity at a given price on a set future date.

_____ 42. Bond issued by a company as a source of long-term funding.

_____ 43. Price that an OTC broker charges for a share of stock.

_____ 44. Purchase or sale of stock in units of 100 shares.

_____ 45. Period of falling stock prices.

_____ 46. Bond bearing the name of the holder and registered with the issuing company.

WORD SCRAMBLE

1. _____   2. _____   3. _____
   rokerb   donb   gramin

LEARNING OBJECTIVES--POTENTIAL SHORT ANSWER OR ESSAY QUESTIONS

Learning Objective #1: "Explain the difference between *primary* and *secondary securities markets*."

Learning Objective #2: "Discuss the value to shareholders of *common* and *preferred stock*, and describe the secondary market for each type of security."

Learning Objective #3: "Distinguish among various types of *bonds* in terms of their issuers, safety, and retirement."

Learning Objective #4: "Describe the investment opportunities offered by *mutual funds* and *commodities*."

Learning Objective #5: "Explain the process by which securities are bought and sold."

Learning Objective #6: "Explain how securities markets are regulated."

CRITICAL THINKING QUESTIONS

1. What is the tradeoff for investors between the yield, risk, and liquidity?

2. Why might it be better for an investor to buy stock in a company that does not pay dividends as opposed to a company that does pay dividends?

BRAIN TEASER

1. What is the relationship between a bond's price and its yield?

ANSWERS

True-False--*Answers*
1. False: The *primary* securities markets involve the buying and selling of new securities, either in public offerings or through private placements (sales to single buyers or small groups of buyers).
2. False: The *secondary* securities market involves the trading of stocks and bonds through such familiar bodies as the New York and American Stock Exchanges.
3. False: Shareholders of *preferred* stock must be paid dividends before shareholders of *common* stock.
4. True
5. True
6. False: The *market* value of common stock is the current price of a share of stock in the stock market.
7. True
8. True
9. True
10. False: A municipal bond is a bond issued by *a state or local* government.
11. True
12. True
13. False: Bonds that can be exchanged at the owner's discretion into common stock of the issuing company are called *convertible* bonds.
14. True
15. True
16. True

17. False: *No-load* funds do not charge commissions when investors buy in or out of mutual funds.
18. True
19 True
20. False: A bull market is a period of *rising* stock prices.
21. True
22. True
23. True

Multiple Choice--*Answers*

1. b	5. d	9. a	13. a
2. d	6. c	10. c	14. a
3. a	7. d	11. b	
4. d	8. b	12. c	

Jeopardy—*Answers*

	Stocks	Bonds	Mutual Funds and Commodities
$100	blue-chip stock	a municipal bond	a mutual fund
$200	the market value of a share of stock	a corporate bond	a futures contract
$300	the book value of a share of stock	a secured bond	a commodities market
$400	cumulative preferred stock	a convertible bond	a no-load fund
$500	a stock exchange	a serial bond	a margin

Match the Terms and Concepts to Their Definitions--*Answers*

1. r	7. n	13. d	19. w	25. z	31. v	37. g	43. ee
2. bb	8. x	14. dd	20. m	26. o	32. ii	38. y	44. nn
3. jj	9. mm	15. u	21. h	27. i	33. b	39. k	45. hh
4. j	10. pp	16. l	22. kk	28. ff	34. cc	40. ll	46. t
5. rr	11. f	17. oo	23. a	29. ss	35. q	41. aa	
6. c	12. p	18. tt	24. gg	30. e	36. qq	42. s	

Word Scramble---*Answers*

1. broker   2. bond   3. margin

Learning Objectives--Potential Short Answer or Essay Questions--*Answers*

Learning Objective #1:
   Primary securities markets involve the buying and selling of new securities, either in public offerings or through private placements (sales to single buyers or small groups of buyers). *Investment bankers* specialize in issuing securities in primary markets. *Secondary markets* involve the trading of stocks and bonds through such familiar bodies as the New York and American Stock Exchanges.

Learning Objective #2:

Common stock affords investors the prospect of capital gains and/or dividend income. Common stock values are expressed in three ways: as *par value* (the face value of a share when it is issued), *market value* (the current market price of a share), and *book value* (the value of shareholders' equity divided by the number of shares). Market value is most important to investors. *Preferred stock* is less risky. Cumulative preferred stock entitles holders to missed dividends as soon as the company is financially capable of paying. It also offers the prospect of steadier income. Shareholders of preferred stock must be paid dividends before shareholders of common stock.

Both common and preferred stock are traded on *stock exchanges* (institutions formed to conduct the trading of existing securities) including floor-based exchanges, electronic markets, and in *over-the-counter (OTC) markets* (dealer organizations formed to trade securities outside stock exchange settings). "Members" who hold seats on exchanges act as brokers—agents who execute buy-and-sell orders—for nonmembers. Floor-based exchanges include the New York, American, and regional and foreign exchanges. NASDAQ is a leading electronic market.

Learning Objective #3:

The issuer of a *bond* promises to pay the buyer a certain amount of money by a specified future date, usually with interest paid at regular intervals. U.S. *government bonds* are backed by government institutions and agencies such as the Treasury Department or the Federal Housing Administration. *Municipal bonds*, which are offered by state and local governments to finance a variety of projects, are also usually safe, and the interest is ordinarily tax exempt. *Corporate bonds* are issued by companies to gain long-term funding. They may be secured (backed by pledges of the issuer's assets) or unsecured, and offer varying degrees of safety. The safety of bonds issued by various borrowers is rated by Moody's and Standard & Poor's.

Learning Objective #4:

Like stocks and bonds, *mutual funds*—companies that pool investments to purchase portfolios of financial instruments—offer investors different levels of risk and growth potential. *Load funds* require investors to pay commissions of 2 to 8 percent. *No-load funds* do not charge commissions when investors buy in or out. *Futures contracts*—agreements to buy specified amounts of commodities at given prices on preset dates—are traded in the *commodities market*. Commodities traders often buy on *margins*—percentages of total sales prices that must be put up to order futures contracts.

Learning Objective #5:

Investors generally use such *financial information services* as newspaper and online stock, bond, and OTC quotations to learn about possible investments. *Market indexes* such as the Dow Jones Industrial Average, the Standard & Poor's Composite Index, and the NASDAQ Composite provide useful summaries of trends, both in specific industries, and in the market as a whole. Investors can then place different types of orders. *Market orders* are orders to buy or sell at current prevailing prices. Because investors do not know exactly what prices will be when market orders are executed, they may issue *limit* or *stop orders* that are to be executed only if prices rise to or fall below specified levels. *Round lots* are purchased in multiples of 100 shares. *Odd lots* are purchased in fractions of round lots. Securities can be bought on margin or as part of *short sales*—sales in which investors sell securities that are borrowed from brokers and returned at a later date.

Learning Objective #6:

To protect investors, the *Securities and Exchange Commission (SEC)* regulates the public offering of new securities and enforces laws against such practices as *insider trading* (using special knowledge about a firm for profit or gain). To guard against fraudulent stock issues, the SEC lays down guidelines for *prospectuses*—statements of information about stocks and their issuers. Many state governments also prosecute the sale of fraudulent securities as well as enforce *blue-sky laws*, which require dealers to be licensed and registered where they conduct business. The securities industry also regulates itself through the National Association of Securities Dealers (NASD), which sets standards for membership and oversees enforcement of NASD rules.

Critical Thinking Questions--*Answers*

1. Typically, the greater the liquidity (the ability to turn into cash), the lower the risk and the lower the yield (rate of return measured as a percentage). Likewise, the less liquid an investment, the riskier it is and the greater the yield. Note that the riskier an investment becomes, the greater the yield must be to compensate an investor for that risk.

2. If you buy stock in a company that does not pay dividends, then that company will have more undistributed profits to re-invest in the company. That investment in new plant and equipment will likely enhance the company's competitive position. If the company is more competitive, then its profits will likely rise. As the profits rise, the company's stock prices will rise. It is very possible that, as an investor, the higher price for your stock (realizing a capital gain) could be greater than any dividends that could have otherwise been earned.

Brain Teaser--*Answer*

1. There is an inverse relationship between a bond's price and its yield. That is, whatever happens to the price of the bond, its yield will do the opposite. Suppose a $1,000 bond pays an interest rate of 10% or $100 annually. If you paid $1,000 for the bond, the yield would be 10% ($100/$1,000). Now suppose the market price increases to $1,100 (possibly because the current market interest rate went down and the 10% guaranteed annual payment associated with this bond now looks very attractive). You sell the bond to someone else. This person will now realize that the yield has gone down to 9.09% ($100/$1,100). So, as the price of a bond goes up, its yield goes down, and vice versa.

Chapter 21
Understanding Financial and Risk Management

LEARNING OBJECTIVES
After studying this chapter, you should be able to:

1. Describe the responsibilities of a financial manager.
2. Identify four sources of *short-term financing* for businesses.
3. Distinguish among the various sources of *long-term financing* and explain the risks entailed by each type.
4. Explain how *risk* affects business operations and identify the five steps in the *risk management process*.
5. Explain the distinction between *insurable* and *uninsurable risks*.
6. Distinguish among the different *types of insurance* purchased by businesses.

TRUE-FALSE
Indicate whether the statement is generally true or false by placing a "T" or "F" in the space provided. If it is a false statement, correct it so that it becomes a true statement.

_T_ 1. The job of the financial manager is to increase the firm's value by planning and controlling the acquisition and dispersal of its financial assets.

_T_ 2. The financial manager's three key responsibilities include cash-flow management, financial control, and financial planning.

_F_ 3. Checking actual performance against plans to ensure desired financial results occur is known as financial planning.

_T_ 4. In planning for funding requirements, financial managers must distinguish between two different kinds of expenditures: short-term (operating) and long-term (capital) expenditures.

_T_ 5. Working capital is a liquid asset out of which current debts can be paid.

_F_ 6. Sources of long-term financing include trade credit, secured and unsecured loans, and factoring accounts receivable.

_T_ 7. Trade credit is effectively a short-term loan from one firm to another.

_F_ 8. Sources of long-term financing include the use of trade credit and loans.

_____ 9. All-debt financing is the most conservative, least risky, and most expensive strategy of long-term financing.

_____ 10. A firm's capital structure is its relative mix of debt and equity financing.

_____ 11. Generally speaking, safer investments tend to offer higher returns, riskier investments lower returns.

_____ 12. Venture capital is outside equity financing provided in return for part ownership of the borrowing firm.

_____ 13. Businesses constantly face two basic types of risk: speculative risk and pure risk.

_____ 14. Speculative risk is risk involving only the possibility of loss or no loss.

_____ 15. Firms manage their risk by following some form of a five-step process: identifying risks, measuring possible losses, evaluating alternative techniques, implementing chosen techniques, and monitoring programs on an ongoing basis.

_____ 16. Four general methods for dealing with risk are risk avoidance, risk control, risk retention, and risk transfer.

_____ 17. Insurance companies issue policies only for uninsurable risk.

_____ 18. An insurable risk must be predictable in a statistical sense, the potential loss must be accidental, random and independent of other losses, and the loss must be verifiable.

_____ 19. Liability insurance is insurance covering losses resulting from medical and hospital expenses, as well as income lost from injury or disease.

_____ 20. Property insurance is insurance paying benefits to the policyholder's survivors.

_____ 21. A preferred provider organization (PPO) is an organized health care system providing comprehensive care in return for a fixed membership fee.

_____ 22. A point-of-service (POS) plan is a healthcare plan allowing members to select primary-care doctors who may provide services or refer patients to other plan providers.

MULTIPLE CHOICE

Circle the one best answer for each of the following questions.

1. The business activity known as finance (or corporate finance) typically entails
   a. determining a firm's long-term investments and obtaining funds to pay for these investments.
   b. conducting the firm's everyday financial activities.
   c. helping the firm manage the risks that it takes.
   d. All of the above.

2. Making sure the firm has enough available money to purchase the materials it needs to produce goods and services is part of the financial manager's job known as
   a. financial planning.
   b. financial control.
   c. cash-flow management.
   d. establishing trade credit.

3. To manage short-term expenditures, financial managers must pay special attention to
   a. accounts payable.
   b. accounts receivable.
   c. inventories.
   d. All of the above.

4. Long-term (capital) expenditures differ from short-term outlays in that long-term expenditures
   a. are not normally sold or converted into cash.
   b. require a very large investment.
   c. represent a binding commitment of company funds that continues long into the future.
   d. All of the above.

5. Trade credit can take the form of
   a. open-book credit.
   b. secured loans.
   c. unsecured loans.
   d. All of the above.

6. Which of the following is true concerning short-term financing for a business?
   a. To finance short-term expenditures, firms rely on debt financing, equity financing, and the use of preferred stock.
   b. Smaller firms may choose to factor accounts receivable (that is, sell them to financial institutions).
   c. Secured loans may be in the form of lines of credit or revolving credit agreements.
   d. Unsecured loans require collateral (legal interest in assets that may include inventories or accounts receivable).

7. Which of the following is true concerning long-term financing for a business?
   a. Long-term sources of funds include debt financing, equity financing, and the use of preferred stock.
   b. Debt financing uses long-term loans and corporate bonds (promises to pay holders specified amounts by certain dates), both of which obligate the firm to pay regular interest.
   c. Equity financing involves the use of owner's capital, either from the sale of common stock or from retained earnings.
   d. All of the above.

8. Which of the following is true concerning risk?
   a. Risk management is the process of avoiding risk altogether.
   b. Speculative risks involve the prospect of gain or loss.
   c. All risk is insurable.
   d. All of the above.

9. The practice of avoiding risk by declining or ceasing to participate in an activity is
   a. risk retention.
   b. risk transfer.
   c. risk avoidance.
   d. risk control.

10. The practice of covering a firm's losses with its own funds is
    a. risk retention.
    b. risk transfer.
    c. risk avoidance.
    d. risk control.

11. Which of the following criteria must be met in order for risk to be insurable?
    a. Predictability.
    b. Causality and unconnectedness.
    c. Verifiability.
    d. All of the above.

12. When an insurance company must be able to use statistical tools to forecast the likelihood of a loss then this insurance company is concerning itself with
    a. the predictability of a potential loss.
    b. the causality and unconnectedness of a potential loss.
    c. the verifiability of a potential loss.
    d. All of the above.

13. Coverage provided by a firm to employees for medical expenses, loss of wages, and rehabilitation costs resulting from job-related injuries or disease is
    a. business interruption insurance.
    b. workers' compensation coverage.
    c. group life insurance.
    d. key-person insurance.

14. Insurance covering losses resulting from medical and hospital expenses as well as income lost from injury or disease is
    a. liability insurance.
    b. workers' compensation insurance.
    c. health insurance.
    d. disability income insurance.

15. A healthcare insurance plan where selected professional providers offer services at reduced rates and permit thorough review of their service recommendations is a
    a. health maintenance organization (HMO).
    b. point-of-service organization (POS).
    c. preferred provider organization (PPO).
    d. workers' compensation organization (WCO).

JEOPARDY

You have 5 seconds to complete the question to each of the following answers.

	Short-Term and Long-Term Financing	**Risk**	**Insurance**
$100	A type of short-term financing where one firm grants credit to another. What is_____ _____?	Risk involving the possibility of gain or loss. What is_____ _____?	Insurance covering losses resulting from damage to people or property when the insured is judged responsible. What is_____ _____?
$200	A loan in which the borrower must provide collateral. What is_____ _____?	The practice of minimizing the frequency or severity of losses from risky activities. What is_____ _____?	Insurance covering losses resulting from physical damage to or loss of the insured's property. What is_____ _____?
$300	Long-term financing that uses long-term loans and corporate bonds to raise funds. What is_____ _____?	The practice of transferring a firm's risk to another firm. What is_____ _____?	Insurance paying benefits to the policyholder's survivors. What is_____ _____?
$400	Long-term financing that involves the use of owners' capital, either from the sale of common stock or from retained earnings. What is_____ _____?	Practice of avoiding risk be declining or ceasing to participate in an activity. What is_____ _____?	Insurance covering losses resulting from medical expenses as well as income lost from injury or disease. What is_____ _____?
$500	The most conservative, least risky, and most expensive long-term financing strategy. What is_____ _____?	The four criteria that an insurance company considers when issuing policies. What is_____ _____?	Coverage provided by a firm to employees for medical expenses, loss of wages, and rehabilitation costs resulting from job-related injuries or disease. What is_____ _____?

MATCH THE TERMS AND CONCEPTS TO THEIR DEFINITIONS

a. financial manager
b. cash-flow management
c. financial plan
d. inventory
e. working capital
f. trade credit
g. open-book credit
h. secured loan
i. collateral
j   pledging accounts receivable
k. unsecured loan
l. line of credit
m. revolving credit agreement
n. commercial paper

o. debt financing
p. equity financing
q. capital structure
r. risk-return relationship
s. venture capital
t. risk
u. speculative risk
v. pure risk
w. risk management
x. risk avoidance
y. risk control
z. risk retention
aa. risk transfer
bb. premium

cc. liability insurance
dd. workers' compensation coverage
ee. property insurance
ff. business interruption insurance
gg. life insurance
hh. group life insurance
ii. health insurance
jj. disability income insurance
kk. health maintenance organization (HMO)
ll. preferred provider organization (PPO)
mm. business continuation agreement

_____ 1. Loan for which the borrower must provide collateral.

_____ 2. Long-term borrowing from sources outside a company.

_____ 3. Insurance covering losses resulting from damage to people or property when the insured is judged responsible.

_____ 4. Risk involving only the possibility of loss or no loss.

_____ 5. Organized health care system providing comprehensive care in return for fixed membership fees.

_____ 6. Insurance paying benefits to the policyholder's survivors.

_____ 7. Materials and goods which are held by a company but which will be sold within the year.

_____ 8. Manager responsible for planning and controlling the acquisition and dispersal of a firm's financial resources.

_____ 9. Principle that, whereas safer investments tend to offer lower returns, riskier investments tend to offer higher returns.

_____ 10. Insurance covering losses resulting from physical damage to or loss of the insured's real estate or personal property.

_____ 11. Practice of minimizing the frequency or severity of losses from risky activities.

_____ 12. Outside equity financing provided in return for part ownership of the borrowing firm.

_____ 13. Form of trade credit in which sellers ship merchandise on faith that payment will be forthcoming.

_____ 14. Arrangement in which a lender agrees to make funds available on demand and on a continuing basis.

_____ 15. Insurance covering losses resulting from medical and hospital expenses as well as income lost from injury or disease.

_____ 16. Practice of transferring a firm's risk to another firm.

_____ 17. Insurance providing continuous income when disability keeps the insured from gainful employment.

_____ 18. Loan for which collateral is not required.

_____ 19. Management of cash inflows and outflows to ensure adequate funds for purchases and the productive use of excess funds.

_____ 20. Special form of business insurance whereby owners arrange to buy the interests of deceased associates from their heirs.

_____ 21. Process of conserving the firm's earning power and assets by reducing the threat of losses due to uncontrollable events.

_____ 22. Coverage provided by a firm to employees for medical expenses, loss of wages, and rehabilitation costs resulting from job-related injuries or disease.

_____ 23. Borrower-pledged legal asset that may be seized by lenders in case of nonpayment.

_____ 24. Use of common stock and/or retained earnings to raise long-term funding.

_____ 25. Arrangement whereby selected professional providers offer services at reduced rates and permit thorough review of their service recommendations.

_____ 26. Using accounts receivable as loan collateral.

_____ 27. Practice of avoiding risk by declining or ceasing to participate in an activity.

_____ 28. Insurance covering income lost during times when a company is unable to conduct business.

_____ 29. A firm's strategies for reaching some future financial position.

_____ 30. Standing arrangement in which a lender agrees to make available a specified amount of funds upon the borrower's request.

_____ 31. Insurance underwritten for a group as a whole rather than for each individual in it.

_____ 32. Uncertainty about future events.

_____ 33. Liquid current assets out of which a firm can pay current debts.

_____ 34. Short-term securities, or notes, containing a borrower's promise to pay.

_____ 35. Granting of credit by one firm to another.

_____ 36. Fee paid by a policyholder for insurance coverage.

_____ 37. Relative mix of a firm's debt and equity financing.

_____ 38. Practice of covering a firm's losses with its own funds.

_____ 39. Risk involving the possibility of gain or loss.

WORD SCRAMBLE

1. _____   2. _____   3. _____
   sirk   mumprei   latercolla

LEARNING OBJECTIVES--POTENTIAL SHORT ANSWER OR ESSAY QUESTIONS

Learning Objective #1: "Describe the responsibilities of a financial manager."

Learning Objective #2: "Identify four sources of *short-term financing* for businesses."

Learning Objective #3: "Distinguish among the various sources of *long-term financing* and explain the risks entailed by each type."

Learning Objective #4: "Explain how risk affects business operations and identify the five steps in the *risk management process*."

Learning Objective #5: "Explain the distinction between *insurable* and *uninsurable risks*."

Learning Objective #6: "Distinguish among the different *types of insurance* purchased by businesses."

CRITICAL THINKING QUESTIONS

1. What is the potential problem with debt-financing (sometimes called leveraging your company)?

2. What are the steps involved in the risk-management process?

BRAIN TEASER

1. Debt financing is more risky than equity financing. But, equity financing is more expensive. What might be an appropriate middle ground between debt and equity financing?

ANSWERS

True-False--*Answers*

1. True
2. True
3. False: Checking actual performance against plans to ensure desired financial results occur is known as financial *control*.
4. True
5. True
6. False: Sources of *short-term* financing include trade credit, secured and unsecured loans, and factoring accounts receivable.
7. True
8. False: Sources of *short-term* financing include the use of trade credit and loans.
9. False: All-*equity* financing is the most conservative, least risky, and most expensive strategy of long-term financing.
10. True
11. False: Generally speaking, safer investments tend to offer *lower* returns, riskier investments *higher* returns.
12. True
13. True
14. False: *Pure* risk is risk involving only the possibility of loss or no loss.
15. True
16. True
17. False: Insurance companies issue policies only for *insurable* risk.
18. True
19. False: *Health* insurance is insurance covering losses resulting from medical and hospital expenses as well as income lost from injury or disease.
20. False: *Life* insurance is insurance paying benefits to the policyholder's survivors.
21. False: A *health maintenance organization (HMO)* is an organized health care system providing comprehensive care in return for a fixed membership fee.
22. True

Multiple Choice--*Answers*

1. d	5. a	9. c	13. b
2. c	6. b	10. a	14. c
3. d	7. d	11. d	15. c
4. d	8. b	12. a	

Jeopardy--*Answers*

	Short-Term and Long-Term Financing	**Risk**	**Insurance**
$100	trade credit	speculative risk	liability insurance
$200	a secured loan	risk control	property insurance
$300	debt financing	risk transfer	life insurance
$400	equity financing	risk avoidance	health insurance
$500	equity financing	predictability, casualty, unconnectedness, and verifiability	workers' compensation coverage

Match the Terms and Concepts to Their Definitions--*Answers*

1. h	6. gg	11. y	16. aa	21. w	26. j	31. hh	36. bb
2. o	7. d	12. s	17. jj	22. dd	27. x	32. t	37. q
3. cc	8. a	13. g	18. k	23. i	28. ff	33. e	38. z
4. v	9. r	14. m	19. b	24. p	29. c	34. n	39. u
5. kk	10. ee	15. ii	20. mm	25. ll	30. l	35. f	

Word Scramble--*Answers*

1. risk   2. premium   3. collateral

Learning Objectives--Potential Short Answer or Essay Questions--*Answers*

Learning Objective #1:

The job of the *financial manager* is to increase the firm's value by planning and controlling the acquisition and dispersal of its financial assets. This task involves three key responsibilities:*cash flow management* (making sure the firm has enough available money to purchase the materials it needs to produce goods and services), *financial control* (checking actual performance against plans to ensure that desired financial results occur), and *financial planning* (devising strategies for reaching future financial goals).

Learning Objective #2:

To finance short-term expenditures, firms rely on *trade credit* (credit extended by suppliers) and loans. *Secured loans* require *collateral* (legal interest in assets that may include inventories or accounts receivable). *Unsecured loans* may be in the form of *lines of credit* or *revolving credit agreements*. Smaller firms may choose to *factor accounts receivable* (that is, sell them to financial institutions).

Learning Objective #3:

Long-term sources of funds include *debt financing, equity financing*, and the use of preferred stock. Debt financing uses *long-term loans* and *corporate bonds* (promises to pay holders specified amounts by certain dates), both of which obligate the firm to pay regular interest. Equity financing involves the use of owners' capital, either from the sale of common stock or from retained earnings. Preferred stock is a hybrid source of funding that has some of the features of both common stock and corporate bonds. Financial planners must choose the proper mix of long-term funding. All-equity financing is the most conservative, least risky, and most expensive strategy. All-debt financing is the most speculative option.

Learning Objective #4:

Businesses operate in an environment pervaded by risk. *Speculative risks* involve the prospect of gain or loss. *Pure risks* involve only the prospect of loss or no loss. Firms manage their risks by following some form of a five-step process: identifying risks, measuring possible losses, evaluating alternative techniques, implementing chosen techniques, and monitoring programs on an ongoing basis. Four general methods for dealing with risk are *risk avoidance, control, retention,* and *transfer*.

Learning Objective #5:

Insurance companies issue policies only for insurable risks—those that meet four criteria: First, the risk must be *predictable* in a statistical sense; the insurer must be able to use statistical tools to forecast the likelihood of a loss. A loss must also pass the test of *casualty*, which indicates the loss is accidental rather than intentional. Potential losses must also display *unconnectedness*—they must be random and occur independently of other losses. Finally, losses must be *verifiable* in terms of cause, time, place, and amount.

Learning Objective #6:

> *Liability insurance* covers losses resulting from damage to the persons or property of other people or firms. *Property insurance* covers losses to a firm's own buildings, equipment, and financial assets. *Life insurance* pays benefits to the survivors of a policyholder and has a cash value that can be claimed before the policyholder's death. *Health insurance* covers losses resulting from medical and hospital expenses.

Critical Thinking Questions--*Answers*

1. It may burden your company with debt it might find impossible to repay.

2. Firms manage their risk by following some form of a five-step process: identifying risks, measuring possible losses, evaluating alternative techniques, implementing chosen techniques, and monitoring programs on an ongoing basis.

Brain Teaser--*Answer*

1. A middle ground between debt and equity financing is the use of preferred stock because it has some of the features of both corporate bonds and common stocks. A major advantage to the company is the flexibility of preferred stock. Because preferred stockholders have no voting rights, the stock secures funds for the firm without jeopardizing corporate control of its management. Furthermore, corporations are not obliged to repay the principal and can withhold payment out of dividends in lean times.

Appendix 1
Understanding the Legal Context of Business

TRUE-FALSE
Indicate whether the statement is generally true or false by placing a "T" or "F" in the space provided. If it is a false statement, correct it so that it becomes a true statement.

_____ 1. Common law is law created by constitutions or by federal, state, or local legislative acts.

_____ 2. Although government regulation has benefited U.S. business in many ways, it is not without its drawbacks.

_____ 3. Trial court is a court that reviews case records of trials whose findings have been appealed.

_____ 4. Capacity refers to the competence required of individuals entering into a binding contact.

_____ 5. A tort is a civil—that is, noncriminal—injury to people, property, or reputation for which compensation must be paid.

_____ 6. In cases of product liability, a company may be held responsible for injuries caused by its products.

_____ 7. Books, articles, songs, paintings, screenplays, and computer software are all examples of tangible real property.

_____ 8. Property rights are always absolute.

_____ 9. A principal is an individual or organization authorizing an agent to act on its behalf.

_____ 10. The Uniform Commercial Code (UCC) is a body of standardized laws governing the rights of buyers and sellers in transactions.

_____ 11. Voluntary bankruptcy is bankruptcy proceedings initiated by the creditors of an indebted individual or organization.

_____ 12. The General Agreement on Tariffs and Trade (GATT) is an international trade agreement to encourage the multilateral reduction or elimination of trade barriers.

MULTIPLE CHOICE

Circle the one best answer for each of the following questions.

1. Law made by the authority of administrative agencies is
   a. common law.
   b. statutory law.
   c. regulatory (or administrative) law.
   d. natural law.

2. Which of the following are conditions of a contract?
   a. Agreement and consent.
   b. Capacity and consideration.
   c. Legality and proper form.
   d. All of the above.

3. Which of the following statements is true?
   a. Compensatory damages are monetary payments intended to redress injury actually suffered because of a tort.
   b. Punitive damages are fines over and above any actual losses suffered by a plaintiff.
   c. Intellectual property is property created through a person's creative activities.
   d. All of the above.

4. Which of the following statements is true?
   a. The U.S. Constitution grants protection to intellectual property by means of copyrights, trademarks, and patents.
   b. Intangible personal property is any movable item that can be owned, bought, sold, or leased.
   c. A copyright is the exclusive legal right to use a brand name.
   d. All of the above.

5. The exclusive right to use and license a manufactured item or substance, manufacturing process, or object design is
   a. a copyright.
   b. a patent.
   c. a trademark.
   d. intellectual property.

6. An agent's authority, derived from written agreement, to bind a principal to a certain course of action is
   a. express authority.
   b. implied authority.
   c. apparent authority.
   d. illegal.

7. Which of the following statements is true?
   a. An implied warranty is a warranty whose terms are specifically stated by the seller.
   b. The Uniform Commercial Code (UCC) describes the rights of buyers but not sellers in transactions.
   c. Bankruptcy has been rising over the last few decades.
   d. All of the above.

8. A business bankruptcy may be resolved
   a. under a liquidation plan.
   b. under a repayment plan.
   c. by reorganization.
   d. All of the above.

9. The agreement to gradually eliminate tariffs and trade barriers between the United States, Canada, and Mexico is the
   a. General Agreement on Tariffs and Trade (GATT).
   b. North American Free Trade Agreement (NAFTA).
   c. European Union (EU).
   d. World Trade Organization (WTO).

MATCH THE TERMS AND CONCEPTS TO THEIR DEFINITIONS

a. common law
b. statutory law
c. regulatory (or administrative) law
d. trial court
e. capacity
f. tort
g. intentional tort
h. compensatory damages
i. punitive damages
j. negligence
k. product liability tort
l. strict product liability
m. property
n. tangible real property
o. tangible personal property
p. intangible personal property
q. intellectual property
r. copyright
s. trademark

t. patent
u. agent
v. principal
w. express authority
x. implied authority
y. apparent authority
z. Uniform Commercial Code (UCC)
aa. warranty
bb. express warranty
cc. implied warranty
dd. bankruptcy
ee. involuntary bankruptcy
ff. voluntary bankruptcy
gg. international law
hh. General Agreement on Tariffs and Trade (GATT)
ii. North American Free Trade Agreement (NAFTA)
jj. European Union (EU)
kk. appellate court

_____ 1. Civil injury to people, property, or reputation for which compensation must be paid.

_____ 2. Tort resulting from the deliberate actions of a party.

_____ 3. Monetary payments intended to redress injury actually suffered because of a tort.

_____ 4. Tort in which a company is responsible for injuries caused by its products.

_____ 5. Fines imposed over and above any actual losses suffered by a plaintiff.

_____ 6. Conduct falling below legal standards for protecting others against unreasonable risk.

_____ 7. Anything of value to which a person or business has sole right of ownership.

_____ 8. Land and anything attached to it.

_____ 9. Any movable item that can be owned, bought, sold, or leased.

_____ 10. Principle that liability can result not from a producer's negligence but from a defect in the product itself.

_____ 11. Body of decisions handed down by courts ruling on individual cases.

_____ 12. Law created by constitutions or by federal, state, or local legislative acts.

_____ 13. Law made by the authority of administrative agencies.

_____ 14. General court that hears cases not specifically assigned to another court appellate court.

_____ 15. Competence required of individuals entering into binding contract considerations. Any item of value exchanged between parties to create a valid contract.

_____ 16. Property that cannot be seen but that exists by virtue of written documentation.

_____ 17. Property created through a person's creative activities.

_____ 18. Agent's authority, derived from written agreement, to bind a principal to a certain course of action.

_____ 19. Agent's authority, derived from business custom, to bind a principal to a certain course of action.

_____ 20. Agent's authority, based on the principal's compliance, to bind a principal to a certain course of action.

_____ 21. Exclusive ownership right belonging to the creator of a book, article, design, illustration, photo, film, or musical work.

_____ 22. Exclusive legal right to use a brand name or symbol.

_____ 23. Exclusive legal right to use and license a manufactured item or substance, manufacturing process, or object design.

_____ 24. Individual or organization acting for, and in the name of, another party.

_____ 25. Individual or organization authorizing an agent to act on its behalf.

_____ 26. Seller's promise to stand by its products or services if a problem occurs after the sale.

_____ 27. Body of standardized laws governing the rights of buyers and sellers in transactions.

_____ 28. Warranty whose terms are specifically stated by the seller.

_____ 29. Warranty, dictated by law, based on the principle that products should fulfill advertised promises and serve the purposes for which they are manufactured and sold.

_____ 30. Permission granted by the courts to individuals and organizations not to pay some or all of their debts.

_____ 31. Agreement among major Western European nations to eliminate or make uniform most trade barriers affecting group members.

_____ 32. Agreement to gradually eliminate tariffs and other trade barriers between the United States, Canada, and Mexico.

_____ 33. Bankruptcy proceedings initiated by the creditors of an indebted individual or organization.

_____ 34. Bankruptcy proceedings initiated by an indebted individual or organization.

_____ 35. International trade agreement to encourage the multilateral reduction or elimination of trade barriers.

_____ 36. Set of cooperative agreements and guidelines established by countries to govern actions of individuals, businesses, and nations.

_____ 37. Court that reviews case records of trials whose findings have been appealed.

ANSWERS

True-False--*Answers*

1. False: *Statutory* law is law created by constitutions or by federal, state, or local legislative acts.
2. True
3. False: *An appellate* court is a court that reviews case records of trials whose findings have been appealed.
4. True
5. True
6. True
7. False: Books, articles, songs, paintings, screenplays, and computer software are all examples of *intellectual* property.
8. False: Property rights are *not* always absolute.
9. True
10. True
11. False: *Involuntary* bankruptcy is bankruptcy proceedings initiated by the creditors of an indebted individual or organization.
12. True

Multiple Choice--*Answers*

1. c	6. a	
2. d	7 c	
3. d	8 d	
4. a	9 b	
5. b		

Match the Terms and Concepts to Their Definitions--*Answers*

1. f	6. j	11. a	16. p	21. r	26. aa	31. jj	36. gg
2. g	7. m	12. b	17. q	22. s	27. z	32. ii	37. kk
3. h	8. n	13. c	18. w	23. t	28. bb	33. ee	
4. k	9. o	14. d	19. x	24. u	29. cc	34. ff	
5. i	10. l	15. e	20. y	25. v	30. dd	35. hh	